AGRICULTURAL DOMESTIC SUPPORT UNDER THE WTO

The WTO Agreement on Agriculture subjects different groups of developed and developing countries to different limits on domestic support and allows various exemptions from these limits. Offering a comprehensive assessment of the Agreement's rules and implementation, this book develops guidance toward socially desirable support policies. Although dispute settlement has clarified interpretation of the Agriculture and SCM Agreements, gaps remain between the legal disciplines and the economic effects of support. Considering the Agriculture Agreement also in the context of today's priorities of sustainability and climate change mitigation, Lars Brink and David Orden build a strategy that aligns the rules and members' commitments with the economic impacts of agricultural support measures. While providing in-depth analysis of the existing rules, their shortcomings and the limited scope of ongoing negotiations, the authors take a long-term view, where policies directed toward evolving priorities in agriculture are compatible with strengthened rules that reduce trade and production distortions.

LARS BRINK is independent advisor on agricultural support policies and Fellow and former President of the Canadian Agricultural Economics Society. He has held positions with Agriculture and Agri-Food Canada and was a representative in WTO and OECD meetings for many years. Governments, international organizations, academics and interest groups seek his advice.

DAVID ORDEN is Professor of Agricultural and Applied Economics at Virginia Polytechnic Institute and State University and a former Senior Fellow at the International Food Policy Research Institute. He is an author/editor of five books including *Policy Reform in American Agriculture* (1999) and *WTO Disciplines on Agricultural Support* (2011).

CAMBRIDGE INTERNATIONAL TRADE AND ECONOMIC LAW

Series editors
Professor Lorand Bartels,
University of Cambridge
Professor Thomas Cottier,
University of Berne
Professor Tomer Broude,
Hebrew University of Jerusalem
Professor Andrea K. Bjorklund,
McGill University, Montréal

Processes of economic regionalisation and globalisation have intensified over the last decades, accompanied by increases in the regulation of international trade and economics at the levels of international, regional and national laws. At the same time, significant challenges have arisen with respect to economic liberalization, rule-based systems of trade and investment, and their political and social impacts. The subject matter of this series is international economic law, in this contemporary context. Its core is the regulation of international trade, investment, finance and cognate areas such as intellectual property and competition policy. The series publishes books on related regulatory areas, in particular human rights, labour, environment and culture, as well as sustainable development. These areas are horizontally interconnected and vertically linked at the international, regional and national levels. The series also includes works on governance, dealing with the structure and operation of international organisations related to the field of international economic law, and the way they interact with other subjects of international and national law. The series aims to include excellent legal doctrinal treatises, as well as cutting-edge interdisciplinary works that engage law and the social sciences and humanities.

Books in the series

Capital Controls and International Economic Law
Bryan Mercurio

The Law and Practice of Global ICT Standardization
Olia Kanevskaia Whitaker

Between Market Economy and State Capitalism:
China's State-Owned Enterprises and the World Trading System
Henry S. Gao and Weihuan Zhou

New Asian Regionalism in International Economic Law
Pasha L. Hsieh

AGRICULTURAL DOMESTIC SUPPORT UNDER THE WTO

Experience and Prospects

LARS BRINK

Agriculture, Trade and Policy Advisor

DAVID ORDEN

Virginia Polytechnic Institute and State University

CAMBRIDGE
UNIVERSITY PRESS

Shaftesbury Road, Cambridge CB2 8EA, United Kingdom

One Liberty Plaza, 20th Floor, New York, NY 10006, USA

477 Williamstown Road, Port Melbourne, VIC 3207, Australia

314–321, 3rd Floor, Plot 3, Splendor Forum, Jasola District Centre, New Delhi – 110025, India

103 Penang Road, #05-06/07, Visioncrest Commercial, Singapore 238467

Cambridge University Press is part of Cambridge University Press & Assessment, a department of the University of Cambridge.

We share the University's mission to contribute to society through the pursuit of education, learning and research at the highest international levels of excellence.

www.cambridge.org
Information on this title: www.cambridge.org/9781316514054

DOI: 10.1017/9781009082440

First published 2023

A catalogue record for this publication is available from the British Library.

A Cataloging-in-Publication data record for this book is available from the Library of Congress

ISBN 978-1-316-51405-4 Hardback

Lars Brink dedicates this book to Satya, beloved wife
and partner.

David Orden dedicates this book to Denise for many reasons
and to the memories of Charles R. Henderson, J. Paxton
Marshall, G. Edward Schuh and Timothy E. Josling.

CONTENTS

FIGURES

xiii

TABLES

FOREWORD

I consider it a great honor to be invited to contribute a foreword to this volume on WTO domestic support disciplines in agriculture written by two of the leading scholars in the field. The introduction of disciplines on agricultural domestic support alongside disciplines on border measures was one of the real novelties in the Agreement on Agriculture resulting from the Uruguay Round negotiations. But the nature of those disciplines, and their uneven impact across WTO members, has been a source of continuing controversy.

For this reason, this volume is both important and timely. It provides a clear account of the current rules on agricultural domestic support, how they apply to different members and the policy space they allow. It describes the changing landscape of domestic support both among members and between different types of support measures. It shows how disputes between members under the Agriculture and SCM Agreements have helped to clarify some key concepts in measuring domestic support and evaluating whether measures are deemed to be trade-distorting or not.

The volume includes a careful analysis of the extent to which the legal categories of domestic support are consistent with an economic interpretation of trade-distorting support, with a particular focus on the exemption from limit of direct payments on green box grounds and on the way market price support is measured. The authors describe the very meagre outcomes to date in terms of revising the rules under the negotiating process mandated under Article 20 of the Agreement. They discuss some of the issues around agricultural domestic support – entitlements to provide support, acquisition at administered prices of public stocks for food security purposes, cotton, and transparency – that were on the agenda for Ministerial negotiations in 2022, though without an outcome on that occasion.

With these analytical chapters as the foundation, the authors conclude with two more normative chapters. One examines whether the rules on agricultural domestic support are sufficiently flexible and well-defined to allow members to address twenty-first-century priorities – including productivity growth, biosecurity, water management, protection of bio-diversity and mitigation of climate change – and, if not, how they might be amended so as not to constrain governments from implementing appropriate policies.

The final chapter contains the authors' observations and recommendations as to how the domestic support provisions of the Agreement might be improved to strengthen its contribution to establishing a fair and market-oriented agricultural trading system. The authors are clear they wish to see further reductions in trade-distorting support on a systematic, rules-based and multilateral basis, while leaving room for contributions to climate change mitigation and achievement of other welfare-enhancing non-trade objectives. They identify numerous problematic elements confronting the achievement of this result.

The authors then ask how these problematic elements might be addressed. They reject the option that agricultural support policies could be disciplined under other WTO agreements, arguing instead that there are greater benefits in retaining and reforming the Agriculture Agreement. Their suggestions for reform revolve around four issues: balancing and reducing the amount of Article 6 support, improving the measurement of market price support, managing domestic support following the dramatic increase in several countries during the Covid-19 period and enhancing policy space to address sustainability and mitigation of climate change.

The domestic support disciplines in the Agriculture Agreement are both its least understood and most controversial elements. This volume will undoubtedly become the definitive work on agricultural domestic support for years to come. Lars Brink and David Orden have provided an inestimable service by drawing on their collective expertise and understanding of this complex topic to prepare this volume. It provides a very thorough guide to those seeking to come to grips with the issues around domestic support for the first time, whether as students or newly-appointed trade officials. It will also be an invaluable resource for seasoned trade officials, negotiators and academics as they seek to map a way forward for the reform of domestic support disciplines for agriculture in the WTO.

Alan Matthews
Professor Emeritus of European Agricultural Policy
Trinity College, University of Dublin
July 2022

ACKNOWLEDGMENTS

This book represents our cumulative effort to study and analyze the domestic support provisions of the WTO Agreement on Agriculture and related disciplines from their beginning some three decades ago. It builds upon the paper *Taking Stock and Looking Forward on Domestic Support under the WTO Agreement on Agriculture*, commissioned by the International Agricultural Trade Research Consortium (IATRC), which we completed in April 2020. It is also a sequel to the 2011 Cambridge volume *WTO Disciplines on Agricultural Support: Seeking a Fair Basis for Trade* for which David Orden was lead editor and Lars Brink a senior contributor.

We offer a comprehensive assessment of the experience over time and the prospects for future guidance through the WTO toward socially desirable domestic support policies and constraints on those that distort trade in agriculture. The analysis ranges from a description of the rules and members' commitments of the Agriculture Agreement, to discussion of the sometimes difficult interface between legal assessments and economic analysis, to the trends and patterns of support among members and across policies, to transparency and ongoing negotiations and to the policy space for members to address salient twenty-first-century priorities within their domestic support obligations. We review and assess the disputes adjudicated about domestic support under the Agriculture Agreement and the Agreement on Subsidies and Countervailing Measures.

In the decade spanned by the two publications mentioned, our study across the topic of domestic support has benefited from interchanges, queries, insights and advice from many colleagues working in similar and related areas. We have been particularly inspired by the books they have authored and edited. Without implicating any of the following persons in our analysis, arguments or conclusions, we thank, among others, Dukgeun Ahn, Kym Anderson, Scott Andersen, Ken Ash, Rick Barichello, John Beghin, David Blandford, Jim Bohland, Chad Bown, Antoine Bouët, Chris Carson, Carmel Cahill, Guoqiang Cheng, May Chow, Howard Conley, Pam Cooper, Caesar Cororaton, Harry de

Gorter, Eugenio Díaz-Bonilla, Diwakar Dixit, Guillaume Duff, Tom Edgar, Ling Yu Edgar, Anne Effland, Shenggen Fan, J. R. Deep Ford, Fred Gale, Adriana García Vargas, Mike Gifford, Joe Glauber, Anabel González, Jason Grant, Ashok Gulati, Christian Häberli, Jerry Hagstrom, Douglas D. Hedley, Jonathan Hepburn, Joanna Hewitt, Anwarul Hoda, Gary Hufbauer, Lee Ann Jackson, (the late) Tim Josling, Ulla Kask, Edwini Kessie, Sergey Kiselev, Iryna Kobuta, Ekaterina Krivonos, Anne Krueger, Christian Lau, Christina Lindström, Greg Macdonald, Mary Marchant, Will Martin, Alan Matthews, George Mina, Fabian Nilsson, George Norton, Kristina Olofsson, Robert Paarlberg, Yuliang Pang, Cédric Pene, Everett Peterson, Karen Roberto, Donna Roberts, Terry Roe, Eduardo Romano, Joachim Schleich, Randy Schnepf, Sachin K. Sharma, Alan Swinbank, Johan Swinnen, Sharon Sydow, Mui-heng Tan, Stefan Tangermann, Bob Thompson, Maximo Torero, Suzanne Thornsbury, Ann Tutwiler, Steve Verheul, Raahool Watchmaker, Xiangchen Zhang, Funing Zhong, Jing Zhu and Carl Zulauf. We also thank series editor Andrea K. Bjorklund and the book proposal reviewers for their constructive comments and positive assessments.

Preparation of this book also has benefited from opportunities we have had to present and discuss its themes at professional events. Those opportunities during the recent years included the 2019 WTO Public Forum, the 2019 Inter-Conference Symposium of the International Association of Agricultural Economists and Nanjing Agricultural University, annual meetings of the IATRC in 2019–22, and the 2020 conference of the WTO Case Law Project hosted by the European University Institute. Lars Brink's interest was stimulated by interactions with participants in meetings of the WTO Committee on Agriculture and other groups and events, for example, the 2021 Global Dialogue on Trade, and with colleagues in Geneva, in national capitals and elsewhere, including staff of the WTO Secretariat and the OECD Secretariat and contributors during 2021–22 to the New Pathways group for progress in the multilateral trade negotiations in agriculture.

We express our appreciation to Ms. Finola O'Sullivan, senior law editor at Cambridge University Press through mid-2021. Her careful guidance marshalled the 2011 book from acquisition through publication, and she was instrumental, along with Marianne Nield, in orchestrating the publication of this volume.

Finally, we thank Virginia Polytechnic Institute and State University for its support, including through the interest of and questions by students in the spring 2022 senior-level food and agricultural policy course of the Department of Agricultural and Applied Economics.

TABLE OF CASES

ABBREVIATIONS

AAP	applied administered price
ACP	African, Caribbean and Pacific
Ag-IMS	Agriculture Information Management System (WTO)
AGST	data tables referenced in members' schedules
AMIS	Agricultural Market Information System
AMS	Aggregate Measurement of Support
ARC	Agriculture Risk Coverage (US)
BPS	Basic Payment Scheme (EU)
BTAMS	Bound Total AMS
CAP	Common Agricultural Policy (EU)
CCP	Countercyclical Payments (US)
CFAP	Coronavirus Food Assistance Program (US)
CNY	Chinese yuan
COFCO	China National Cereals, Oils and Foodstuffs Import and Export Corporation
CRP	Conservation Reserve Program (US)
CTAMS	Current Total AMS
CVD	countervailing duty
DSU	Dispute Settlement Understanding
EBA	Everything But Arms (EU)
EC	European Communities
EMS	Equivalent Measurement of Support
EPA	Economic Partnership Agreement (EU)
EU	European Union
EUR	Euro
FAO	Food and Agriculture Organization of the United Nations
FERP	fixed external reference price
FRP	Fair and Remunerative Price (India)
GATT	General Agreement on Tariffs and Trade
GHG	greenhouse gas
GSM	General Sales Manager (US)
GSSE	General Services Support Estimate (OECD)

GTAP	Global Trade Analysis Project
IATRC	International Agricultural Trade Research Consortium
IDB	Inter-American Development Bank
IFPRI	International Food Policy Research Institute
INR	Indian rupee
LDC	least developed country
LRP	lagged reference price
MFP	Market Facilitation Program (US)
MLA	Market Loss Assistance (US)
MPS	market price support
%MPS	market price support as percent of value of production
NAFTA	North American Free Trade Agreement
NPS	non-product-specific
OECD	Organization for Economic Cooperation and Development
PFC	Production Flexibility Contract (US)
PLC	Price Loss Coverage (US)
PODS	Producer-Oriented Domestic Support
PS	product-specific
PSE	Producer Support Estimate (earlier Producer Subsidy Equivalent) (OECD)
SAP	State Advised Price (India)
SAPS	Single Area Payment Scheme (EU)
SCM	subsidies and countervailing measures
SCGP	Supply Credit Guarantee Program (US)
SFP	Single Farm Payment (EU)
SIM	Specific Implementation Matter
STAX	Stacked Income Protection Plan (US)
TRQ	tariff-rate quota
USD	US dollar
USDA	United States Department of Agriculture
USMCA	United States–Mexico–Canada Agreement
VoP	value of production
WTO	World Trade Organization

1

Introduction

Domestic support in favor of agricultural producers is one of three major policy areas subject to the rules and commitments of the Agreement on Agriculture of the World Trade Organization. While the other two areas addressed by the Agreement concern policy measures applying at the border, namely market access and export competition, domestic support concerns the types and amounts of support provided through policy measures applying inside the border. Resulting from the Uruguay Round of trade negotiations from 1986 to 1994, the Agreement imposes limits on some domestic support without applying a test of adverse effects. The inclusion of such provisions in a trade agreement was novel.

The Agreement's Preamble recalls that the long-term objective "is to establish a fair and market-oriented agricultural trading system" and that a process of reform should be initiated "through the negotiation of commitments on support and protection and through the establishment of strengthened and more operationally effective GATT rules and disciplines" (Agreement on Agriculture).[1] The objective, the Preamble continues, "is to provide for substantial progressive reductions in agricultural support and protection sustained over an agreed period of time, resulting in correcting and preventing restrictions and distortions in world agricultural markets." The rules on domestic support measures and commitments on limited amounts of certain support are important in regard to the objective and intent of the Agreement because internal measures can

---

[1] The Agreement on Agriculture, to which this book refers also as the Agriculture Agreement or the Agreement, is one of the agreements annexed to the Marrakesh Agreement Establishing the World Trade Organization, signed on 15 April 1994, also called the WTO Agreement. Among other agreements annexed to the WTO Agreement are the General Agreement on Tariffs and Trade 1994, also called GATT 1994, the Agreement on Subsidies and Countervailing Measures, also called the SCM Agreement, and the Understanding on Rules and Procedures Governing the Settlement of Disputes, also called the Dispute Settlement Understanding or the DSU. Unless otherwise indicated, references in this book to articles and annexes are to the Agreement on Agriculture.

have market-distorting effects. Without constraints on domestic support, it was hard to envision progress in multilateral negotiations to increase market access or limit export subsidies, as some members support their agricultural producers primarily through domestic measures, while others rely more heavily on border measures.

In pursuing their trade-related objectives, members are to have regard to what the Agreement terms non-trade concerns, including food security and the need to protect the environment. Many members use domestic support to address these and other non-trade concerns, which raises the importance of the rules applying to this policy area. The Agreement notes that special and differential treatment for developing countries was an integral part of the negotiations.

While the rules and commitments of the Agriculture Agreement continue to define the obligations of WTO members, the global landscape of applied domestic support to which these apply has changed dramatically in the nearly 30 years since the negotiations were completed. The WTO has gained additional members and different rules apply in different ways to different groups of members.[2] World agricultural markets have experienced sustained periods of relatively low and high prices, affecting the timely policy concerns and the support some members provide. Many members, both large and small, have undertaken structural change in the nature and size of their domestic support. Members have changed how they notify support to the Committee on Agriculture and some disciplines on domestic support have been clarified through dispute settlement. Non-trade policy priorities have gained prominence in recent years, including most notably sustainability in the context of the United Nations development goals and the mitigation of and adaptation to climate change.

---

[2] While the WTO refers to its members, this book interchangeably mentions members as countries. The WTO had 164 members in April 2022, one of which is the European Union (EU). Until 1 December 2009, the EU was known as the European Communities (EC) in the WTO. In this book, the EU means the EU with the number of member states, up to 28 (EU28), in the year being referenced prior to the completion of the withdrawal of the United Kingdom (UK) at the end of the transition period on 31 December 2020. The EU member states are members of the WTO in their own right but the EU applies a single schedule of commitments in place of their schedules. Members Switzerland and Liechtenstein apply one common schedule of commitments. The number of schedules of commitments was 135 until rising to 136 on 1 January 2021.

The changing landscape of applied domestic support in combination with the nuances and exceptions in the multilateral disciplines contribute to the hurdles faced in reinvigorating the negotiating process. It also contributes to poor public understanding, even in specialized media and academia, of the points of pressure for and resistance to WTO-related reforms of agricultural policies.

A broader crisis of engagement engulfs the rules-based multilateral trade system where the Doha Round negotiations, launched in 2001, failed to secure a comprehensive new legal framework to govern global trade. One manifestation was the aggressive initiation of unilateral trade-restrictive measures by the United States starting in 2017. It triggered retaliation but members otherwise largely avoided emulating these measures. The Appellate Body has ceased to function for lack of appointment of new judges and demands have increased for reform of the WTO. From 2020, the global Covid-19 pandemic brought high levels of illness, mortality and economic disruption, leading to questions about the structure and governance of the world economy in its aftermath. War in Ukraine then disrupted global food, fertilizer and energy markets, sending prices to record levels.

Throughout these changing and challenging circumstances, domestic support for agricultural producers has remained at amounts summing to hundreds of billions of US dollars (USD) each year. On average for 2016–18, the most recent years for which notifications of support under the Agriculture Agreement were reasonably complete at time of writing, the notified support in all categories summed to USD 594 billion. The Organization for Economic Cooperation and Development (OECD), measuring support somewhat differently, reported an average amount of USD 642 billion for 2018–20 for 54 countries (OECD 2021a). These substantial amounts consist of budgetary outlays and transfers from consumers to producers. Thus, it remains a global governance issue to assess what types of support WTO members provide through various measures, how the multilateral rules and members' commitments influence this support and what options might be pursued to further the long-term objective of the Agreement on Agriculture.

1.1 Domestic Support Rules

The rules in the Agriculture Agreement articulated in Art. 6, titled Domestic Support Commitments, divide support measures in favor of agricultural producers into three distinct categories and a residual category.[3] The categorization resulted from the need to accommodate the interests of influential countries in the Uruguay Round of negotiations under the GATT (General Agreement on Tariffs and Trade) in combination with economic considerations in relation to the objective and intent of the Agreement.[4]

The Agreement exempts three categories of measures from limits on support. First, measures meeting a fundamental requirement of having "no, or at most minimal, trade-distorting effects or effects on production" are exempt from limit by Annex 2, titled Domestic Support: The Basis for Exemption from Reduction Commitments and commonly denoted as the green box. Exemption also requires that a measure meet basic criteria of being publicly funded and not having the effect of providing price support. Twelve paragraphs of Annex 2 set policy-specific criteria and conditions for measures under which government expenditures are exemptible from support limits, including expenditures on providing general services to agriculture or the rural community and direct payments to producers under nine headings. Leaving levels of support in these categories without limit encourages the adoption of policies that fit within the green box.

No other exempted measures are required to have at most minimal trade-distorting effects or effects on production. Measures can therefore be exempt from limit even if they distort trade more than minimally. One such category of exempt measures consists of developing countries' investment subsidies generally available to agriculture, input subsidies generally available to low-income or resource-poor producers and support to encourage diversification from growing illicit narcotic crops (Art. 6.2). Developed countries' support through trade-distorting measures of this type is subject to limit, so Art. 6.2 is one form of special and differential treatment. A third category of exempt measures consists of payments under production-limiting programs, subject to criteria relating to the fixity of area and yields or livestock numbers or the share of base production on which payments are made (Art. 6.5, commonly denoted the blue box). The exemption is available to both developed and developing countries.

---

[3] The Agreement generally refers to policy measures providing domestic support as measures, but also refers to policies. We follow this convention, often referring to a measure but also to a policy or a program of support. Policy can also have a broader interpretation: a policy might include several individual measures or programs.

[4] Barton et al. (2006) offers one comprehensive assessment of the political, legal and economic considerations that have driven evolution of the multilateral trade regime from GATT to the WTO. See also, *inter alia*, Hoekman and Kostecki (2009), Martin and Mattoo (2011) and, for agriculture, Josling et al. (1996).

The remaining domestic support measures fall into a residual category under which support is subject to a limit or limits operating in different ways. This category is often loosely called the amber box, a term that is applied with various meanings. The non-exempt support is measured through an Aggregate Measurement of Support (AMS) for each product (product-specific AMS) and a separate sum of support that is not specific by product (non-product-specific AMS). As specified in Art. 1 (Definition of Terms), Art. 6 and Annex 3 (Domestic Support: Calculation of Aggregate Measurement of Support), each AMS includes those direct payments and other subsidies that are not exempted under the green box or, in practice, under Art. 6.2 or the blue box. A product's AMS includes any market price support (MPS) calculated under Annex 3 of the Agreement, which differs from economic market price support.

The Current Total Aggregate Measurement of Support (Current Total AMS or CTAMS) is the annual sum of all AMSs except any AMS that is no larger than its *de minimis* level and exclusive of any Art. 6.2 or Art. 6.5 support. The *de minimis* level is a nominal value of production multiplied by a *de minimis* percentage, which is 5, 8.5 or 10% depending on a member's group identification. Specification of the two higher *de minimis* percentages is another form of special and differential treatment for developing countries.

The CTAMS of 33 members is subject to a positive ceiling specified in their WTO schedules of commitments under the heading Total AMS Commitments. This book refers to the final commitment level after any reductions as the Bound Total AMS (BTAMS). The schedules of most members show a blank, that is, no BTAMS, or a nil or zero BTAMS.[5] A member with no or a nil BTAMS must keep each AMS within its annual *de minimis* level. A positive BTAMS offers support flexibility by allowing one or more AMSs to exceed the *de minimis* level. The BTAMS of original members derives from the amounts of certain support measured during a base period of 1986–88 (later years for accession members).[6] The flexibility therefore largely benefits those developed members with the historically largest support.

---

[5] This book uses nil BTAMS and zero BTAMS interchangeably.

[6] The contracting parties of the GATT who participated in the 1994 conclusion of the Uruguay Round negotiations are original members of the WTO. The 36 additional members who had by April 2022 acceded to the WTO under Art. XII of the WTO Agreement are often called Art. XII members or, as in this book, accession members. Accession negotiations for 24 countries were underway as of April 2022.

1.2 Scope of the Book

This book provides an integrated overview of agricultural domestic support of WTO members in relation to the rules and commitments under the Agreement on Agriculture informed by assessments from an economic perspective. It examines the experience of implementation, negotiations and dispute resolution under the Agriculture Agreement and other WTO disciplines affecting agricultural domestic support during the past three decades and draws on this experience to evaluate the prospects for effective future multilateral disciplines.

Chapter 2 articulates the domestic support rules of the Agriculture Agreement and evaluates the policy space it affords different groups of members, including accession members like China, the Russian Federation (Russia), Ukraine and Viet Nam that are major agricultural producers. The different but overlapping disciplines on agricultural domestic support under the SCM Agreement (Agreement on Subsidies and Countervailing Measures) are also discussed.

Chapter 3 surveys key evidence on the relationship between the Agriculture Agreement as a legal entity and the economic impacts of policies in its various categories. The analysis focuses on two issues – income support and measurement of market price support – that have been relevant to dispute settlement concerning domestic support.

Chapter 4 studies the changing patterns of domestic support in agriculture revealed in members' notifications. This involves assessing changes in the notified amounts of different categories of support in aggregate and by selected members providing the largest amounts of support. The evaluation highlight two main developments. First, there has been a substantial global shift since 1995 toward support that members exempt as having at most minimal trade-distorting effects or effects on production (green box support) in contrast to support in categories that do not meet this requirement. This was envisioned as a desirable outcome at the inception of the WTO, but the consequences of leaving green box support exempt from limit were unknown. Second, support is concentrated among a small group of members that now includes China and India as well as the European Union (EU), the United States (US) and Japan. Contrasting the place of China and India among large-support members in later years against their smaller roles when the Agreement was negotiated highlights the need for fresh assessment of the contributions required from various members to achieve balanced and effective constraints on distorting domestic support policies.

Subsequent chapters of the book build on the structural and support analysis to assess the efficacy of the existing rules and commitments. They draw on experience under the Agriculture Agreement to take the long view of how progress can be made in correcting and preventing restrictions and distortions in world markets while having regard to non-trade concerns and special and differential treatment.

Chapter 5 reviews the role of the Committee on Agriculture in providing transparency about domestic support measures and levels. The rules on agricultural domestic support are effective only if compliance is monitored and enforced, but they can also be interpreted differently. The Committee is mandated to review progress in the implementation of commitments based on notifications submitted by members. Timing and formats for notifications were adopted in 1995, requiring members to indicate how they classify their policy measures within the categories of the Agreement and report amounts of support under these measures. Discussion in the Committee has helped to clarify some issues.

Chapter 6 appraises the limited negotiations continuing within the Committee on Agriculture in Special Session (the negotiating forum). Although the Doha Round negotiations faltered, members remain committed to negotiations on continuation of the reform process under Art. 20 of the Agriculture Agreement. Some issues on which negotiations continue relate to agricultural domestic support.[7] The priority many members give to these issues in the negotiations is linked to the importance of agriculture for many members and to the growing interest in the incidence and impacts of subsidies more generally. Members' support policies, their commitments and their negotiating interests diverge and the domestic support rules and their interpretation remain in play.

Alleged violations of the rules and commitments under the Agriculture Agreement can be pursued through WTO dispute settlement. Disputes involving particularly the measurement of MPS have been raised for adjudication toward Korea on beef, China on wheat, rice and corn and India on sugarcane. Dispute settlement has clarified certain points of interpretation of the Agreement. Chapter 7 reviews the legal findings in these disputes and highlights the contrasting circumstances of measuring

---

[7] Domestic support in this book encompasses at various points some or all of the support under a member's "domestic support measures in favour of agricultural producers" (Art. 6.1), i.e., Art. 6 support and Annex 2 support, separately or together. This extends wider than the elements discussed in the domestic support area in ongoing WTO negotiations on agriculture.

MPS for China and India. Even as the calculation of MPS under the Agreement is clarified, the rules remain problematic in terms of effecting reduced economic distortions. An alternative measurement is proposed to address this shortcoming.

Agricultural domestic support was also a concern in the long-running dispute under the SCM Agreement that involved significant price suppression resulting from cotton policies in the United States and in disputes under the Agriculture and SCM Agreements concerning export subsidies arising from the domestic price support regime for dairy in Canada and sugar in the European Communities (EC). In the cotton dispute, payments under certain domestic support measures were found to cause serious prejudice to the interests of Brazil. In the Canada and EC disputes, the finding was that the price support regime created export subsidies that exceeded the member's scheduled limit under the Agriculture Agreement. Review of these disputes is part of the assessment of the experience of disciplining agricultural domestic support under the WTO.

Many of the priorities governments have pursued in agriculture in recent years differ from those when the Agreement on Agriculture was negotiated. Chapter 8 evaluates the policy space that the Agreement allows for domestic support in five selected areas of increased salience: productivity growth, biosecurity in agriculture, water management, sustaining and enhancing biodiversity and mitigation of climate change. Much support addressing these evolving priorities can be accommodated under green box criteria for general services or under environmental programs and other measures making exemptible payments to producers. Some policy measures on the horizon to address twenty-first-century priorities may use innovative designs while being exempted within the green box. For others additional green box provisions would be constructive and compatible with achieving reductions in trade-distorting domestic support.

Chapter 9 brings together the structural, descriptive and analytical assessments. It draws conclusions concerning ways to refresh the Agriculture Agreement with respect to domestic support to be a more effective instrument to achieve a fair and market-oriented agricultural trading system while leaving ample space to address other policy priorities. The assessment is structured around discussion of what has proven through the many years of experience to be the problematic aspects of the Agreement and what has turned out to be less problematic than may have been expected. These insights suggest where trade-offs and improvements might be found that would strengthen the Agriculture

Agreement as a framework for members' commitments and the rules they follow in providing support in favor of agricultural producers.

1.3 Key Questions in the Analysis

The assessment of nearly 30 years of experience concerning domestic support under the Agriculture Agreement addresses eight important questions:

(1) What are the rules of the Agriculture Agreement on the limits on certain support and how do they apply to different groups of members to determine their policy space for domestic support?
(2) What types and levels of support have been notified and how has this changed over time?
(3) Do the notifications provide accurate and meaningful measurement of the support governments provide in favor of agricultural producers?
(4) Has dialogue about the notifications contributed to international transparency on agricultural domestic policies and the support they provide to producers?
(5) What issues are on the table in negotiations on domestic support at the WTO?
(6) Has dispute settlement reinforced constraints on trade-distorting domestic support?
(7) Are the rules of the Agriculture Agreement sufficiently conducive to addressing evolving policy priorities related to sustainability and climate change?
(8) How might the rules and commitments be updated to better achieve the long-term objective of the Agriculture Agreement considering that the global landscape of applied domestic support has changed since the Agreement was negotiated?

1.3.1 Rules of the Agriculture Agreement

The rules and implications of the domestic support provisions of the Agriculture Agreement on support subject to limit have proven to be easily misunderstood. This is often rooted in overlooking the significance of key distinctions, such as distinctions between measures and support, among measures that are classified in different categories, between applied support and a limit on support and between applied support that counts and does not count towards the limit.

Disentangling these distinctions requires differentiating among several groups of members depending on whether they have a positive BTAMS or not, are eligible for the developing-country Art. 6.2 exemption or not and the applicable *de minimis* percentage. The variety of rules that apply in different ways to different members is a source of tension among members. The Agriculture Agreement's commitments give members that had the largest base-period support the flexibility to maintain AMS support above *de minimis* levels. This negotiated bifurcation has been problematic, especially by allowing some members to offer high levels of support for certain individual products. Conversely, as *de minimis* levels are proportional to nominal values of production, they generally increase over time. Members with larger agriculture sectors can accommodate larger amounts of AMS support within their *de minimis* levels and any positive BTAMS. Thus, China and India, without a positive BTAMS but with large values of production in agriculture, have more room for AMS support than the EU and the United States, respectively, each with a positive BTAMS but with a lower *de minimis* percentage and lower production value.

1.3.2   Types and Amounts of Support

While in strict terms an AMS accounts for all support other than green box support, in practice members also exempt from AMSs the support they report under Art. 6.2 and Art. 6.5. The analysis in this book generally follows the convention of this practice. Unless otherwise noted, AMS support refers to the residual support other than Art. 6.2 support, blue box support and green box support. Art. 6 support – sometimes called trade-distorting or non-green-box support – refers to the sum of AMS support whether *de minimis* or larger, Art. 6.2 support and Art. 6.5 support. The distinction between *de minimis* AMSs and AMSs exceeding their *de minimis* levels is often a critical consideration in the analysis.

As few as 10 members account for more than 90% of notified Art. 6 support. In the early years of the WTO, the largest amounts were reported by the EU, Japan and the United States. In later years, China and India have reported the largest amounts. The responsibility of only a small number of members for so much of the Art. 6 support, and the shifting composition of that group, has implications for possible new or updated rules and commitments on domestic support.

AMS support over the period 1995 through 2016–18 followed a downward trend for many years after the Agriculture Agreement took effect and then began to increase. Members generally have ample room to introduce or raise AMS support, for many members within AMS *de minimis* limits and for others also beyond those levels within their BTAMS. Although most members notify that they have stayed within their respective limits, some members have used more of their room for AMS support than others, particularly for certain products. The CTAMS of the United States was close to its BTAMS in 2019, highlighting the importance of distinguishing between applied support and limits on support and the relevance of the limits. Art. 6.2 support has increased and India's share of it greatly exceeds the total share of other developing country members. Blue box support has declined from the early years.

Despite the ample room to increase trade-distorting domestic support, a noteworthy development is that trade-distorting Art. 6 support has fallen globally, and green box support has risen nominally and as a percentage of the agricultural value of production. While much attention has focused on China's rising Art. 6 support, China makes an even larger contribution to the amount of green box support. Green box support, which many members report as their only form of support, has increased continuously from 2001 and dominates the notified support in later years. This includes the direct payments to producers exempted under Annex 2, which have come to account for nearly 40% of all green box support. One main form of these direct payments to producers is decoupled income support, the amount of which cannot depend on prices, production undertaken or factors of production employed in any year after a defined and fixed base period. Payments under headings such as structural adjustment and environmental programs are among other forms of Annex 2 exemptions.

1.3.3 Meaningful Measurement

Members have made significant changes in domestic agricultural policies since 1995, often discernible in subsequent notified support. The EU's notifications track the gradual replacement of MPS by blue box then Annex 2 exempted direct payments over an extended period of time. From 1996, the United States eliminated payments made when market prices fell below targeted levels and introduced fixed payments largely not dependent on current prices and production, followed by new assistance payments in 1999 in response to lower market prices. Each of these policy changes is seen in US support notifications, as are the elimination of the fixed payments and introduction of a new countercyclical revenue program in 2014, increased crop insurance premium subsidies and additional support measures starting in 2018. In China, a regime of discrimination against agriculture through price and tax policies gave way to positive net support. This has included direct payments to grain producers and sharply higher support prices for some crops after world market prices increased in the late 2000s. The higher domestic prices led to increased economic support when world prices declined in the mid-2010s. China's notified support reflects the change in policy as higher support prices increased its MPS. In contrast to China, the support prices of India, which exempts support under Art. 6.2, have mostly been maintained below corresponding world prices. Sugarcane is an exception, where support prices have exceeded corresponding world price levels without India notifying any MPS for sugarcane since 1995. In short, members have in general reported new policies and changing levels of support. However, many issues of interpretation arise concerning the ways in which they report both policies and support.

Measures meeting the criteria for *Direct payments to producers* and *Decoupled income support* (para. 5 and para. 6, Annex 2) are among those under which support is exempted from limit. Payments thus exempted by the EU averaged, for example, EUR 37.4 billion (USD 42.5 billion) in 2016–18. Whether such payments are at most minimally trade or production distorting remains an issue of inquiry. While not a settled matter, many studies suggest these payments have at most relatively small production effects. The panel and Appellate Body in *US – Upland Cotton* excluded similar US payments from those found to cause significant price suppression in the world market.

The contrast between MPS under the Agriculture Agreement and an economic evaluation can raise doubt about the extent to which notifications show meaningful measurements of domestic support. Economic price support is measured using the difference between the domestic price of a product and its corresponding border price from international markets observed for the same time period and level in the value chain. Multiplying this price gap by total national production gives a policy support measurement that accounts for the combined effects of domestic price regulations and a variety of border measures that may restrict or subsidize imports or exports. This type of measurement enters the Producer Support Estimates (PSEs) of the OECD (2021a), the World Bank assessment of levels and trends in agricultural support from the mid-1950s onwards (Anderson 2009) and other economic studies.

In contrast, the negotiated MPS measurement in the Agriculture Agreement uses a different price gap and often a different quantity. It compares an applied administered price (AAP), which is a policy-determined domestic support price, to a fixed external reference price (FERP), which does not vary with world market conditions or exchange rates. The resulting price gap is multiplied by a "quantity of production eligible to receive the applied administered price," commonly called eligible production, which also is a policy-defined variable.

The two MPS measurements align only in limited circumstances, particularly because the FERP is for original members still based on 1986–88 world prices. The notified MPS has therefore, despite its name, not been a good indicator of economic support. This economic interpretation problem extends to any product-specific AMS and the CTAMS when they include MPS. Thirty years of experience allows evaluation of the magnitude of the differences and the limited usefulness of the Agreement's MPS measurement in economic terms. The difficulty in interpreting notified MPS economically has implications for assessing how tightly, from very restrictively to not at all, the Agreement constrains price support that distorts trade. The disputes about MPS in China and India are important context for such assessments.

1.3.4 International Transparency

Notification of members' domestic support is intended to make available, in a standardized format, a systematic and informative categorization of policy measures and to quantify the amount of support they provide. This is designed to create the transparency needed for the Committee on Agriculture to carry out its mandate of reviewing the implementation of commitments under the Agriculture Agreement. However, many members have been lax in submitting timely domestic support notifications. Even the largest agricultural producing and trading members are often several years behind in their submissions. Delays in notification hinder the Committee's review of implementation and also impair timely public transparency.

Members interpret not only the Agreement's rules but also the notification requirements and formats differently. A member's categorization of policy measures and measurements of support can be questioned by other members, which in some cases improves transparency, but the Committee cannot require members to follow specific practices. The Committee is mandated to give consideration to the influence of excessive inflation on members' ability to meet their commitments, while in practice some members make their own inflation adjustments.

Within these constraints, the Committee on Agriculture is a forum for discussing the implementation of members' commitments. The largest number of questions raised in the Committee on individual notifications and related Specific Implementation Matters (SIMs) concern domestic support. Members posed 4,051 such questions in the 98 meetings of the Committee on Agriculture during 1995 to mid-2021, mainly on AMS support, green box support and transparency. While the five members with the most support, that is, the EU, the United States, Japan and in later years China and India, received nearly 40% of the questions, scrutiny extended to the support measures of a large number of other members. Questions tend to seek more specific information than shown in notifications or information about policies in recent years where notifications were still outstanding. Although many answers are limited in depth, the extent to which they give any additional information contributes to a better understanding of members' changing policies and support. Policy concerns are inherently about the future not the past. Yet the annual WTO notifications are backward-looking and thus cannot provide the explicit projection information on which to base forward-oriented assessments. This also limits achieving transparency.

1.3.5   Issues on the Table

The disciplines on domestic support were an important part of the agricultural component of the Doha Round negotiations from 2001 through 2008. The draft modalities on the table (WTO 2008a) went much further than the Agriculture Agreement in constraining certain trade-distorting support. The proponents of tighter constraints on agricultural support hoped to embed those new obligations within a broad trade deal, but the negotiations failed, in part over continuing disagreements on agriculture.

Domestic support has remained a high-profile issue in subsequent negotiations in the context of the inconclusive Doha Round. Members' proposals have addressed whether and how to further limit support in CTAMS and *de minimis* AMSs, limit Art. 6.2 and Art. 6.5 support and reduce support for cotton. Progress has been scant and the potential outcomes resulting from members' proposals are unclear as the negotiations continue to lack momentum. The continued negotiations have prepared input for ministerial conferences but only a few decisions concerning domestic support have resulted.[8] One decision in 2013 made expenditures related to land reform and rural livelihood security in developing countries exemptible under the green box.

The Agriculture Agreement allows developing countries to exempt from AMS the expenditures for accumulating public stocks for food security purposes even when using administered prices instead of market prices for the acquisition, but this requires accounting for a price gap in the AMS. Ministers decided in 2013 on an interim mechanism, reaffirmed in 2014, on developing country acquisition for public stocks for food security purposes. If the acquisition generates an MPS large enough to make an AMS or CTAMS exceed its limit, the mechanism shelters the member from challenge under the WTO dispute settlement rules, contingent on the member meeting a number of conditions and requirements. Finding a permanent solution remains a contentious issue.

At the 2015 conference, ministers decided to eliminate agricultural export subsidy entitlements within given time frames and set rules on export financing support (export credits, export credit guarantees or insurance programs) and on international food aid. These decisions have an important implication for operating domestic price support programs. When a government keeps prices above world levels it must, to be in compliance, manage any resulting accumulation of stocks within its domestic market rather than dispose of those stocks internationally using export subsidies, subsidized export financing or food aid outside set rules.

1.3.6 Dispute Settlement

Different but overlapping sets of legal obligations on domestic support measures in favor of agricultural producers arise under the Agriculture Agreement and the SCM Agreement. In a number of situations one or more members have initiated disputes about domestic support measures under these Agreements, demonstrating that they viewed the nullification or impairment of anticipated benefits or other adverse effects sufficiently egregious to merit legal remedy. In *Korea – Various Measures on Beef* (DS161, DS169), *China – Agricultural Producers* (DS511) and *India – Sugar and Sugarcane* (DS579, DS580, DS581), the complainants argued that MPS was provided in excess of an AMS or CTAMS limit but made

---

[8] Eleven ministerial conferences took place between 1996 and 2017, followed by the twelfth conference in June 2022. A ministerial conference is the highest authority through which WTO members take decisions on, e.g., interpreting an agreement.

no claims of adverse effects from those measures under the SCM Agreement. In *US – Upland Cotton* (DS267), Brazil argued that serious prejudice to its interest resulted from certain support policies that caused significant price suppression in the world market, but it did not claim that the United States had exceeded its BTAMS under the Agriculture Agreement. In *Canada – Dairy* (DS103, DS113) and *EC – Export Subsidies on Sugar* (DS265, DS266, DS283), the issue involving domestic support was whether a regime of production quotas for domestic utilization and high within-quota support prices cross-subsidized exports in violation of the Agriculture or SCM Agreement export subsidy disciplines. These disputes clarified the application of certain provisions of the two agreements, demonstrated ability of the agreements to discipline domestic support in the circumstances in which they arose and to different degrees contributed to members' decisions to modify support policies.

The dispute *Korea – Various Measures on Beef* ended without factual findings on MPS and AMS for beef in relation to Korea's annual reduction commitments on Total AMS. Korea terminated its beef price support program during the proceedings. The dispute *China – Agricultural Producers* was brought in the circumstance of increased economic price support during 2012–15. Whether to match the FERP to China's accession base years of 1996–98 or base it on 1986–88 as specified in the Agriculture Agreement was one issue. Deciding the 1996–98 FERP was correct, the panel concluded that China was out of compliance with its limits on AMS support for wheat and rice in each of the four years. China lowered wheat and rice support prices to bring its measures into compliance. It also used an opening the panel left for a government to manage the size of MPS by announcing caps on eligible production less than total production yet larger than purchases under the support program. Different complexities arise for India, which notifies MPS only in years when the government itself purchases the product at the AAP. Government mandates the minimum prices sugar mills pay to sugarcane producers in India but does not purchase sugarcane. In *India – Sugar and Sugarcane*, the panel established that MPS need not involve government purchases and measured MPS for sugarcane during 2014–18 under the Agriculture Agreement in amounts much larger than economic price support. If the panel ruling were to be implemented, compliance would require changes in India's sugarcane support measures. However, the dispute remains unresolved in absence of an Appellate Body able to rule on India's appeal of the panel decisions.

The dispute *US – Upland Cotton* arose in circumstances of low world commodity prices during 1999–2002 and remained in contention for nearly 20 years. The main issue concerning domestic support was alleged adverse effects on Brazil resulting from price-contingent payments the United States made to cotton producers. In both the dispute and compliance proceedings, the panel and Appellate Body concluded that price-contingent payments based both on current and past levels of cotton production contributed to significant price suppression. This is the only dispute related to agricultural domestic support in which an arbitrator eventually authorized retaliation for non-compliance. The United States revamped its cotton support measures but retained support prices (known as loan rates) for current production and after an interlude introduced new price-contingent payments on a base level of past cotton production. With improved world market conditions the subsidy amounts under these programs were lower than during the years for which significant price suppression was found and the later US programs have not been challenged. A challenge to US export subsidization in *US – Upland Cotton*, including through subsidized export financing, helped to bring about the 2015 ministerial decision to place disciplines on export credit, credit guarantees or insurance programs.

The dispute *EC – Export Subsidies on Sugar* arose in 2002 when the EC was a leading sugar exporter despite domestic sugar prices nearly three times world price levels. Adjudication found, concerning domestic support, that the domestic sugar production quotas and support prices allowed sugar beet producers to sell beets at below average total cost of production to processors of exported sugar and that the processors could use their domestic sales revenue to cross-subsidize processing for exports at below average total cost, both resulting in excessive export subsidies. The decision came at a time when the EU's Common Agricultural Policy (CAP) was shifting away from MPS toward direct payments and added impetus for sugar support policy to move in this direction, leading to substantial adjustment in the sugar sector. *Canada – Dairy* had involved similar domestic support issues and findings about sales of milk used for exported dairy products, with adjustments to its support programs not as consequential as those of the EU.

1.3.7 Evolving Priorities

Policy priorities are evolving in ways that have implications for the domestic support measures in favor of agricultural producers currently in use and the development of alternative measures, as well as the associated levels of support. Members have in their international engagement articulated the triple challenge facing food systems of ensuring food security, supporting livelihoods of producers and doing so in environmentally sustainable ways. The United Nations Sustainable Development Goals of 2015 identifies correcting and preventing trade restrictions and distortions as a step toward eliminating hunger, consistent with the Agriculture Agreement. Governments formulate policy priorities concerning climate change adaptation and mitigation while foreseeing this becoming an even greater priority. Domestic support disciplines conducive to the provision of public goods and to addressing externalities and market failures without creating more room for trade-distorting measures or support is thus a crucial twenty-first-century need. The rules of the Agriculture Agreement offer many options to accommodate policy efforts to address salient priorities, but there are also constraints and some definitional ambiguities concerning the use of such measures.

Government expenditures are not subject to limits on AMS support if the programs conform with the provisions of the green box (Annex 2). Green box expenditures on general services, such as research or extension and advisory services, can contribute to the achievement of objectives concerning sustainability and climate that have gained policy prominence in the areas of productivity growth, biosecurity in agriculture, water management, safeguarding and enhancing biodiversity, mitigation of climate change and others. In addition to general services, direct payments to producers under the green box can address these evolving priorities.

The use of green box expenditures and payments to achieve certain objectives is circumscribed by the fundamental requirement that any exempted measure have at most minimal trade-distorting effects or effects on production. While the risk of payments inducing larger production and hence trade-distorting effects motivated this requirement, its role remains to be clarified when a payment measure results in less production, as may be the case in pursuing some priorities. The time dimension of effects on production also needs to be considered. Certain green box measures, for example, investments in productivity-enhancing research or irrigation infrastructure, raise production and can, without creating distorting incentives for a given technology and resource base, shift a member's comparative advantage over time.

The amounts of payment under measures fitting into several green box paragraphs are subject to conditions related to producers' increased costs or income losses. While these conditions reduce the risk of the exempted payments becoming instruments for support that distorts production, they also constrain giving producers incentives to participate in a program. There could be a need to negotiate particular exemption provisions for larger payments in relation to some priorities while meeting the green box fundamental requirement. An example is where producer incentives would be critical for attaining objectives in regard to sustaining and enhancing biodiversity.

Measures to address mitigation of climate change are being developed rapidly as the importance of this priority continues to rise. The green box criteria for *Payments under environmental programmes* (para. 12, Annex 2) are not entirely clear whether criteria or conditions related to production methods or inputs must be included nor about the eligibility of payments for mitigation of climate change. Clarification is needed to increase certainty of interpretation for designing properly exemptible mitigation measures.

Payments to producers for the achievement of a given outcome defined in terms of biodiversity or climate change mitigation are of increasing interest compared to payments for using certain production or land use practices imperfectly correlated with such outcomes. Absence of conditions related to production methods or input use in such outcome-based programs may open an option for income support payments determined from a prior base period as an incentive for producers to participate where the assessed value of the outcome compared to the status quo is higher than costs or loss of income.

Direct payments to producers connected with evolving policy priorities do not need to be exempted under the green box. As many members' AMS support is below applicable limits, they can pursue evolving priorities to some extent by using measures under which support is subject to limit. At some point a priority may take on such urgency that it needs to be addressed through Art. 6 domestic support measures that are exempted from limit. The appropriate criteria for such exemption would weigh the trade-off between effectiveness of a measure in addressing the evolving priority, such as mitigation of climate change, and more than minimal trade or production effects.

1.3.8 Potential Updating

The final question addressed is what revisions of the rules and commitments on trade-distorting support would make the Agriculture

Agreement more effective than it has been so far in stimulating reform toward domestic support that is less trade-distorting. Domestic support discipline is rarely observed in regional trade agreements, which gives the multilateral WTO a unique negotiating role. Most members see shortcomings in the Agreement's domestic support provisions but consensus to complete the negotiation of better provisions has been lacking. Melding the Agriculture Agreement into the SCM Agreement and related provisions of GATT 1994 rather than retaining or renegotiating it separately is not foreseeable but whether this would be a constructive option can be asked. Given the continuing large amounts of agricultural domestic support, updating the Agreement is a more realistic way forward but requires fixing its problematic dimensions.

It is evident that for a long time to come the Agriculture Agreement will have to discipline in a mutually effective manner a diverse set of support policies. As a means to achieving substantial progressive reductions in support and protection, the Agreement will need to better distinguish those support measures that distort more from those that distort less or, more categorically, distorting and non-distorting measures. Basing the distinction of measures on their economic effects would allow the formulation of more meaningful obligations. Limiting support from the distorting measures more tightly would reduce distortions. Members' amounts of domestic support could nonetheless remain unchanged or increase if distorting policies were replaced by non-distorting policies, as demonstrated by the experience over the past three decades. Distorting support is concentrated among only a handful of members. The largest reduction of distortions on a global scale could thus be achieved by differentiating policy classification rules and support limits so as to target that handful.

Effective discipline on distorting support requires more economically meaningful measurement of MPS than under the Agriculture Agreement. This book suggests retaining the use of AAP but replacing the FERP with a moving average of lagged border prices and clarifying that the price gap applies to total production. A moving average of lagged border prices as the reference price allows the reference price in many situations to be closer to the current border price than using a FERP based on increasingly distant past years. A more time-sensitive and economically meaningful measurement may be the key to resolving the tension relating to the consequences of including in AMS the MPS resulting from developing country acquisition at administered prices of public food-security stocks. An MPS calculated using a moving average of lagged border prices represents more closely the economic producer support generated by such acquisition, which generally reduces the likelihood of exceeding support limits.

Support exempted on green box grounds has grown substantially since the inception of the Agriculture Agreement, which has largely not been problematic. Being able to exempt certain support would become even more important under tightened rules and commitments on trade-distorting support. Some green box support enhances productivity growth, generates public goods that improve market performance or addresses local or global environmental externalities. These are positive outcomes in terms of using resources efficiently and sustainably to improve world food security and the environment. The green box offers unlimited room for expenditures on general services and direct payments to producers through measures that meet its provisions. Updating and refining the fundamental requirement, criteria and conditions of the green box, and perhaps going beyond those in the Agreement, would clarify the characteristics that qualify support measures for exemption from limit. This would allow appropriately addressing not only climate change mitigation but also other evolving priorities.

1.4 Foundation for Progress

The different commitments applying to different groups of members, the problems related to differences in interpreting the domestic support provisions of the Agreement on Agriculture and the difficulties faced in revising the Agreement suggest a need to build a foundation for mean-ingful and feasible further reforms. This book undertakes to contribute to that foundation. The analysis enables an evaluation of the relationship between the information in members' notifications and the policy reforms envisioned for the Agreement, as well as an assessment of the economic effects of support reported under the Agreement's categories of policy measures. While the issue of compliance is a legal matter, eco-nomic reasoning sheds light on the underlying aim of conformity – the effectiveness of the Agreement in reducing trade distortions associated with agricultural domestic support policies while giving members appro-priate space to address non-trade concerns. Economic reasoning also sheds light on how disciplines of the Agreement can be improved to reach this aim. Reform prospects are narrow in the short and medium term. It is hoped nonetheless that the analysis presented in this book will inform the important debate on future policies and help to address the ongoing challenge of making agricultural domestic support less market-distorting while contributing to the mitigation of climate change and the achievement of other high-profile evolving policy objectives.

Domestic Support Disciplines of the Agriculture and SCM Agreements

The domestic support that governments can provide to agriculture attracts substantial interest for several reasons. Domestic support makes a country produce and trade differently than if fully pursuing its comparative advantages. Domestic support can also shift a country's comparative advantage over time and thus change its trade profile. The disciplines on the nature and size of the support governments at home and abroad provide or may provide consistent with their international obligations under, particularly, the Agriculture Agreement and the SCM Agreement are of interest to many parties with varying degrees of familiarity with the provisions of these agreements. Government interest in these disciplines is fueled by pressure to enact desired farm policies while meeting their international responsibilities and by the potential to strengthen the agreements through multilateral negotiations.

This chapter reviews the context for developing the WTO disciplines on domestic support in agriculture and examines the resulting limits, allowances and exemptions, including Art. 6.2, Art. 6.5 (blue box) and Annex 2 (green box). The differences in the rules as they apply to different groups of members and the consequent room for limited and exempt support among different groups of developed and developing countries are highlighted. The chapter explores the interface of the provisions on domestic support with those on export competition in the Agriculture Agreement and with the provisions of the SCM Agreement regarding actionable subsides, prohibited export subsidies and countervailing measures. Overall, the set of rules governing domestic support is complex.

2.1 Development of the Agriculture Agreement Disciplines

In the Uruguay Round negotiations of the GATT, the topic of domestic support differed from the traditional focus on measures applied at the border to impede import access or facilitate exports. Many years earlier, the Haberler Report had outlined three elements of what it called agricultural protection (GATT 1958).[1] Measures that directly discourage imports and measures that directly encourage exports were two of those elements. Measures that "directly encourage home production" were the third element. This distinction between two categories of border measures and a third category of measures not operating at the border was carried into the architecture of the 1994 Agreement on Agriculture in its three pillars of market access, export competition and domestic support.

The Haberler Report also categorized agricultural protective measures into two groups based on certain other characteristics. Measures that raise the domestic price received by producers and paid by consumers above the world market price form one group. This, the report clarified, requires the use of some form of border measure (import protection or export subsidy) to insulate the domestic market from the world market. Schemes that allow consumers to pay world market prices but raise producers' revenue "by the payment of some form of subsidy" are the other group. The eventual distinction in the Agriculture Agreement between two categories of domestic support measures is along similar lines – namely, MPS, on the one hand, and non-exempt direct payments and other subsidies on the other – and also resulted from differences among negotiating parties in their main types of support policy. While the vocabulary of the Agreement includes, for example, support, subsidies and payments without defining these terms, support as commonly used has a broader meaning than subsidies as budgetary payments or revenue forgone by government.

By the time of the Uruguay Round, accounting in one indicator for the economic support provided for a product through a wide range of policy measures had become feasible. This indicator included support deriving from domestic price policies and subsidies and from border policies that enable the domestic price to exceed the corresponding international price. Josling's work on such an indicator was pioneering (FAO 1973, 1975), followed by work at the OECD (1987) and the United States Department of Agriculture (USDA 1987). Although different in some respects, all three indicators bore the name Producer Subsidy Equivalent (PSE).

---

[1] Professor Haberler chaired a panel of experts set up by the contracting parties of the GATT to examine international trade trends and their implications, including a "widespread resort to agricultural protection."

As relevant data was being developed for PSE calculations, participants in the negotiations proposed the use of modified PSE-like indicators that accounted for smaller sets of policy measures than did the OECD PSE. The exclusions, which tended to be based on the extent to which policies were considered not to distort production and trade, foreshadowed what was later called the green box and blue box exemptions and even *de minimis* allowances. The United States proposed to bring to zero over ten years a measurement of aggregate support including both domestic and border policies "that directly or indirectly subsidize agriculture" (GATT 1987). Other methods to aggregate support for a product across many policies included the Trade Distortion Equivalent suggested by Canada and the Support Measurement Unit suggested by the EC (GATT 1988a, 1988b).[2]

The eventual Agriculture Agreement sets out separate obligations on market access, export subsidies and domestic support. The part of domestic support that is subject to limit is measured by calculating a product-specific AMS for each basic agricultural product, which includes both price support and payment support (including revenue forgone) but does not account for support provided through measures operating only at the border. The support subject to limit also includes a non-product-specific AMS. The scope of the policy aggregation in measuring support had thus been reduced to aggregating only across domestic policies but not border policies. The introduction of limits on support provided through certain policies not operating at the border was one step in the direction envisaged in the 1958 Haberler Report.

The differences between the Agreement's AMS and the OECD PSE are important for economic analysis.[3] The calculation of the MPS component of a year's AMS using the gap between that year's policy-determined domestic AAP and a FERP that is a constant based for the original members on the years 1986–88, is particularly consequential.

---

[2] See, *inter alia*, Josling et al. (1996), Barton et al. (2006), McMahon (2006) and Brink (2011) for further discussion of the origins of the Agriculture Agreement.

[3] The policy coverage of the OECD's original PSE was later separated into policies included in the General Services Support Estimate (GSSE) and the Producer Support Estimate (with the continuing acronym PSE). Effland (2011), the contributors to Orden et al. (2011), Josling and Mittenzwei (2013) and Brink (2018b), among others, compare the measurement approaches of the Agriculture Agreement and the OECD, including the differences between AMS and PSE in policy coverage and measurement of price support.

This price gap is multiplied by the quantity of production eligible to receive the administered price, which is also a policy-determined variable. The kinship of AMS and PSE implied a reference price that would vary from year to year. However, the EU (at the time, EC) insisted on fixing the external reference price in order for the amount of support subject to limit to be under government control rather than influenced by changes in world market prices and exchange rates. In contrast, the price gap that matters for economic analysis is the gap between the domestic price in a given year and a reference price representing the opportunity cost determined by the year's actual world market price and exchange rate.

An AMS is a measurement of support and not a measurement of distortions. Since it measures certain support in ways that deviate from how support is measured in a PSE and from its usual economic representation, it presents particular challenges for economic interpretation. A member's AMSs are input for determining whether it has satisfied its legal obligations on certain domestic support. The legal nature of both the Agriculture Agreement's scheduled limits and its rules, including the rules for calculating the amounts of support, effectively override the use of measurement methods that are more directly based on economics and more amenable for use in economic analysis.

2.2   Complying with Limits on Certain Support

2.2.1   Overview of the Domestic Support Rules

The Agriculture Agreement identifies the ceiling limit or limits to which certain kinds of domestic support are subject. It also lays down rules for the measures under which support is not subject to limit and for measuring the support that counts toward the applicable limit or limits. The implications of these provisions have proven to be complicated. Overlooking the significance of key distinctions can result in misunderstanding those implications. Measures (policies) are distinct from support, and measures are classified into distinct categories. Applied support is distinct from a limit on support, and applied support that counts toward the limit is distinct from applied support that does not so count. A representative schematic of the domestic support rules as applied in practice is depicted in Figure 2.1.

Each member of the WTO is legally bound by its Schedule of Concessions and Commitments, established at the conclusion of the Uruguay Round or

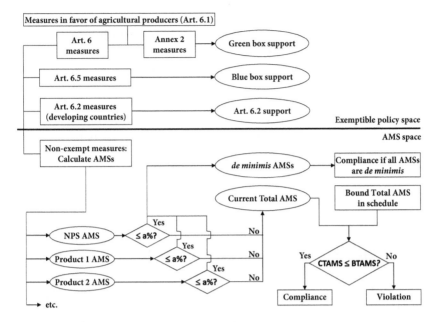

Figure 2.1 Schematic of domestic support limits and exemptions
Note: Percentages (a%) are 5, 8.5 or 10% for different groups of members.
SOURCE: Authors' interpretation of the Agriculture Agreement.

when it became a member of the WTO. In the schedule, the one-page Part IV, Section I (titled Total AMS Commitments) gives the member's "Annual and final bound commitment levels" or ceilings on certain domestic support. The final ceiling commitment level after any reductions is referred to in this book as the BTAMS or, depending on the context, the commitment level, ceiling, limit, constraint, cap or entitlement.[4]

The schedules of 16 developed members and 17 developing country members – nearly one quarter of the 136 schedules – show a positive

---

[4] The Agreement's reduction commitments refer to some members' obligation to reduce the ceiling commitment level over several years to a final level, i.e., their positive BTAMS. Original members of the WTO carried out the reduction from 1995 to 2000 (developed countries by 20%) or to 2004 (developing countries by 13%). Developing countries include least-developed countries (LDCs), which under WTO rules are the countries that the United Nations designates as such. LDCs were exempted from reduction commitments in the Uruguay Round. Seven of the thirty-six accession members scheduled reduction commitments over some years and have completed these reductions.

amount of BTAMS.[5] Many members' schedules show a nil entry. For a member with a positive or nil entry, compliance with its commitment requires its CTAMS not to exceed the BTAMS, even if nil (Art. 3.2 and Art. 6.3). Still others show a blank for the BTAMS, which indicates no BTAMS exists. For these members without a BTAMS, compliance with limits depends on the size of individual AMSs.

The Agreement's provisions on domestic support stipulate that a member's commitments shall apply to all "domestic support measures in favour of agricultural producers" except those in the categories of measures exempted under Art. 6.2, Art. 6.5 and Annex 2 (Art. 6.1). All support measures that are not exempted shall be included in calculating CTAMS (Art. 7.2(a)). AMSs that are no larger than their *de minimis* levels need not be included in calculating CTAMS (Art. 6.4). For members without a BTAMS, no AMS may exceed its *de minimis* level (Art. 7.2(b)). This is effectively the case also for members with a nil BTAMS, since any larger AMS would enter the CTAMS and make it exceed nil. For any member, the limit or limits on domestic support apply to the amounts of support that only certain measures provide. The BTAMS and CTAMS in domestic support relate to each other in a similar way as a bound tariff and the applied tariff relate to each other in market access. Likewise, in the case of no or a nil BTAMS, an AMS's *de minimis* level relates correspondingly to the AMS. However, the measured support that counts toward the limit or limits is more complicated to express than an applied tariff.

The popularly known set of colored boxes derives from the distinction between exempt and non-exempt measures. The Agreement does not identify any boxes or colors. It is nonetheless commonly understood that Art. 6.5 defines the exemptible blue box and Annex 2 defines the exemptible green box. Common usage has not given any color to the Art. 6.2 exemption, although it is sometimes called a development box. The residual and less well-defined non-exempt measures are often called amber, a term that is used with various meanings. Support under measures that meet the requirements, criteria and conditions of Art. 6.2, Art. 6.5 and Annex 2 is not subject to the support limits.

The annual level of support provided in favor of producers that is subject to limit is calculated as AMSs of two kinds (Art. 1(a) and

---

[5] The 16 developed members with a positive BTAMS include the UK following its withdrawal from the EU and, at time of writing, the anticipated splitting of the BTAMS of the EU28 into one for the EU27 and one for the UK.

Annex 3).[6] First, support provided in favor of the producers of a basic agricultural product is an AMS that the Agreement also refers to as product-specific support (Art. 6.4(a)). A "basic agricultural product" is the product as close as practicable to the point of first sale, relying on information in a member's schedule and supporting material incorporated therein (Art. 1(b)). Product-specific AMSs are thus not necessarily calculated for the products identified in Annex 1 of the Agreement with reference to Harmonized System tariff chapters, codes and headings. Annex 3 requires the calculation of a product-specific AMS "for each basic agricultural product receiving market price support, non-exempt direct payments, or any other subsidy not exempted from the reduction commitment" (para. 1, Annex 3). Second, support provided in favor of agricultural producers "in general" (Art. 1(a)) is accounted for in a single non-product-specific AMS, which is understood under the rules of Annex 3 to include non-exempt direct payments and any other subsidy not exempted from the reduction commitment.

The MPS is one of the components of a product's AMS. It is calculated using the price gap between the AAP and FERP multiplied by the quantity of eligible production (para. 8, Annex 3). The AMS does not include budgetary payments made to maintain the gap, such as buying-in or storage costs. The Agreement does not define AAP or eligible production but stipulates that the FERP be based on the years 1986–88 and generally be average f.o.b. unit values for net exporting countries and c.i.f. unit values for net importing countries, adjusted for quality differences as necessary (para. 9, Annex 3). The inclusion of the MPS in the AMS corresponds to the explicit inclusion of price support in what both GATT 1994 and the SCM Agreement mean by a subsidy without specifying a formula for its measurement. Non-exempt direct payments and the value of other non-exempt measures, such as input subsidies and marketing-cost reduction measures, enter the AMS using budgetary outlays or, in some situations, using a price gap calculation (paras. 10–13, Annex 3).

Specific agricultural levies or fees must be deducted in the AMS calculation (para. 4, Annex 3) and a negative component, such as a

---

[6] The Agriculture Agreement also defines an Equivalent Measurement of Support (EMS) in similar terms as an AMS (Art. 1(d)). An EMS is calculated where MPS exists but calculating it under the rules of Annex 3 is not practicable (Annex 4). EMSs are treated as AMSs when calculating CTAMS. Only a few members have used EMSs and only for a few products (e.g., the EU for individual fruits and vegetables). Both numbers have declined.

negative MPS resulting from a policy of setting the AAP below the FERP, can enter the AMS calculation. While levies, fees or similar negative components have generally not been large enough to make the AMSs negative, MPSs have generated negative AMSs for some members. Since a negative AMS means the opposite of an AMS being support "in favour of" producers as defined in Art. 1(a), its role under the Agreement is unclear. Members tend to treat it as nil such that it does not offset positive AMSs when AMSs are summed.

2.2.2   CTAMS and De Minimis Allowances

The CTAMS is the sum of those AMSs larger than a given level, that is, CTAMS is not necessarily the total of all AMSs (Art. 6.4).[7] A crucial distinction between AMS and CTAMS is that "Aggregate" in AMS refers to aggregating support across various policy measures, such as direct payments, input subsidies and MPS, whereas "Total" in CTAMS refers to summing certain AMSs into a single CTAMS. The level at or below which a product-specific AMS can be left out of CTAMS – the *de minimis* level – is the amount corresponding to a given percentage of the product's value of production.[8] The corresponding level for the non-product-specific AMS is the given percentage of the member's total agricultural value of production.

Three *de minimis* percentages apply: 5% for developed countries and 10% for developing countries as specified in the Agreement (Art. 6.4) and 8.5% for China and Kazakhstan as negotiated as part of their accession protocols. If an AMS is larger than its *de minimis* level, the whole AMS, not just the excess, enters the calculation of CTAMS. The rules do not apply to individual subsidies or support on a measure-by-measure basis — there is no classification of policies into *de minimis* measures and non-*de minimis* measures.

---

[7] The Agreement defines "Total Aggregate Measurement of Support" and "Total AMS" as a sum of AMSs and EMSs (Art. 1(h)). It uses the term Total AMS in several ways: (a) "Base Total AMS" for certain support in the Uruguay Round base period, (b) "Annual and Final Bound Commitment Levels" in the Total AMS section of schedules and (c) "Current Total AMS" for certain applied support. To avoid confusion, this book minimizes use of the phrase Total AMS by using more specific expressions to distinguish among various support totals.

[8] Value of production in the context of domestic support in the Agriculture Agreement is usually calculated at domestic prices, including price support. Value of production is an economically less meaningful measurement of the size of a sector than its value-added.

The *de minimis* level of an AMS determines what this book calls a *de minimis* allowance. The *de minimis* allowances for the AMSs of members without BTAMS or with a nil BTAMS operate as upper limits. For members with a positive BTAMS, they operate as thresholds: an AMS may exceed its *de minimis* level and is then added in its entirety into the CTAMS. Whether operating as a limit or a threshold, the *de minimis* allowance recognizes that AMS support in relatively low amounts as a percentage of value of production may be of less concern than larger amounts of AMS support in the context of reducing support and protection.

All limits and measurements of domestic support in the Agriculture Agreement are expressed as nominal amounts, such as millions of currency units, not as percentages or other rates of support.[9] It is sometimes convenient, however, to express them as percentages in order to facilitate a comparison against the *de minimis* percentages. This contrasts against quantitative economic analysis, where percentage rate expressions are the norm.

2.2.3 Exemptions Based on Policy Criteria: Article 6.2, Article 6.5 and Annex 2

Measures claimed to meet the criteria for exemption, whether under Art. 6.2, Art. 6.5 (blue box) or Annex 2 (green box), account for the largest number of notified support policies. Some members exempt or have exempted very large amounts under the provisions of each of these categories of support. The magnitude of the exempted amounts has fueled discussions in the WTO and elsewhere about the legitimacy of the exemptions in two respects: should certain categories of support be exemptible; and in categories agreed to be exemptible, do members' exempted measures meet the applicable rules?

Article 6.2

Developing countries may exempt from CTAMS the support under certain measures that economic analysis indicates distort production and trade and that developed countries must include in CTAMS. Special and differential treatment for developing countries was an integral element of

---

[9] Art. 1(a) defines an AMS in monetary terms. A CTAMS is therefore also expressed in monetary terms. Members with a BTAMS in their schedules express this commitment level as a number of currency units.

the Uruguay Round negotiations, as noted in the Preamble of the Agriculture Agreement.[10] It was agreed that "government measures of assistance, whether direct or indirect, to encourage agricultural and rural development are an integral part of the development programmes of developing countries" (Art. 6.2). Three types of support are therefore exemptible from a developing country's CTAMS: investment subsidies generally available to agriculture, input subsidies generally available to low-income or resource-poor producers and support to encourage diversification from growing illicit narcotic crops. As negotiated in their accessions, China and Kazakhstan are not eligible for the Art. 6.2 exemption.

Art. 6.2 specifically allows the exemption of these kinds of support from the calculation of CTAMS. Members' practice of exempting the support from the calculation of individual AMSs makes an AMS smaller and less likely to exceed its *de minimis* level than if the exemption applied only to the CTAMS calculation. It also makes the non-exempt support in an AMS less likely to enter the CTAMS of a developing country with a BTAMS. Alternative readings of Art. 6.2 in terms of this practice potentially eroding the discipline on AMSs have not been tested in WTO dispute settlement.

The Agriculture Agreement uses different wording in Art. 6.2 regarding the general availability of investment subsidies and of input subsidies. The implications are not clear. Both subsidies need to be generally available in some sense to qualify for exemption: generally available to agriculture or generally available to low-income or resource-poor producers, respectively. A subsidy that is generally available to agriculture is also generally available to low-income or resource-poor producers. The contrasting and narrower stipulation of availability of input subsidies to low-income or resource-poor producers might require more specific targeting of input subsidies than of investment subsidies in the member's legal instrument that authorizes the subsidies. The stipulation might, alternatively, require that input subsidies be generally available at least to low-income or resource-poor producers. Neither meaning has been examined from a legal perspective through dispute settlement.

Article 6.5 (Blue Box)

The Art. 6.5 exclusion of "direct payments under production-limiting programmes" from CTAMS originated with the role of the EU and the

---

[10] The Agreement's Art. 15, titled Special and Differential Treatment, applies generally for developing countries to the provisions of the Agreement and to their commitments.

United States as two of the major parties negotiating the Agreement.[11] The EU was in the process of shifting much of its farm support from price support to direct crop payments based on fixed area and yields and to livestock payments (such as beef cattle and sheep) based on a fixed number of head. Some crop payments involved a set-aside of arable land on which crop production was not permitted. The United States made crop payments on no more than 85% of a farm's administratively established base acres and fixed past yields and also required land set-asides determined annually, sometimes at zero. The EU and the United States agreed that support under their respective payment programs of this kind would be excluded from the CTAMS. The general provisions to this effect (Art. 6.5) were subsequently accepted by the other parties in the negotiations.

Under Art. 6.5, direct payments to producers under production-limiting programs must, if they meet certain criteria, be excluded from the CTAMS. It remains unclear what constitutes a production-limiting program and in what way, if at all, that label relates to the specified criteria. The EU and US land set-aside provisions, while operating differently, would by themselves have limited or even reduced production at the time. The criteria for exclusion require the payments to be based on fixed area and yields, or to be made on 85% or less of the base level of production or, for livestock payments, to be made on a fixed number of head. In practice, the handful of members using the blue box exclusion (some with, some without a positive BTAMS) do not exclude the support from the CTAMS but from individual AMSs. As under Art. 6.2, this practice may erode the discipline that otherwise would govern AMS support.

Annex 2 (Green Box)

The Uruguay Round negotiators recognized that agricultural support provided through some types of policies has only small, if any, effects on production and trade and exempted it from commitment. Art. 1(a) and Art. 6.1 exempt Annex 2 measures from the domestic support measures that are subject to commitment, that is, green box support is exempted from any AMS and therefore also from limit. The measures providing the exempted support need to meet the fundamental

---

[11] Art. 6.5 refers to the exemption of certain payments from reduction commitments and their exclusion from CTAMS. This book in many instances refers to both as an exemption.

requirement "that they have no, or at most minimal, trade-distorting effects or effects on production" and accordingly conform to given criteria and conditions (para. 1, Annex 2).

The fundamental requirement of no, or at most minimal, trade-distorting effects or effects on production distinguishes the green box from Art. 6.2 and the blue box, which do not require the exempted support to have at most minimal such effects. Art. 6.2 support and Art. 6.5 support is sometimes said to be exempt from limit because the support does not distort production or trade. However, such support is exempt from limit even when it distorts production or trade in the sense of increasing production more than minimally, albeit sometimes by less than other support.

A green box exempt measure must meet the basic criteria of providing support through a publicly funded program not involving transfers from consumers and not having the effect of providing price support to producers (para. 1, Annex 2). Moreover, the measure must meet one of twelve sets of policy-specific criteria and conditions. These stipulations are introduced with the word "Accordingly" in para. 1 of Annex 2. One interpretation of the use of this word is that, while the fundamental requirement to have "at most minimal" effects is a freestanding obligation, it motivates the need to meet also the basic and policy-specific criteria and conditions. Another interpretation is that meeting the basic and policy-specific criteria satisfies in legal terms the fundamental requirement. Although either of the alternative readings could be crucial in determining whether a measure provides support that can be exempted from AMSs, the wording has not been clarified through WTO dispute settlement.[12]

The green box distinguishes among three types of policy measures under which support is exemptible: (1) expenditures on general services, (2) expenditures under the headings of public stockholding for food security purposes and domestic food aid and (3) direct payments to producers.

The *General services* category (para. 2, Annex 2) involves government expenditures (or revenue forgone) for services to agriculture or the rural community. This category excludes direct payments to producers or processors. The general services programs for which the green box

---

[12] In *US – Upland Cotton*, the parties viewed the relation between the policy-specific criteria and the fundamental requirement differently but the panel did not decide whether the fundamental requirement is a freestanding obligation or not.

specifies conditions include research, pest and disease control, training services, extension and advisory services, inspection services, marketing and promotion services and infrastructural services. The list of exemptible general services is open-ended, such that other general services that meet the general criteria of para. 1 can also be exempted.[13]

While its fundamental requirement is that measures have no, or at most minimal, trade-distorting effects or effects on production, the green box nevertheless accommodates and exempts from limit various public expenditures under *General services* that raise agricultural productivity and thus have positive effects on production. The implied rationale is that these expenditures do not distort individual producer incentives, which may be the case for a given resource base and technology. Shifts in productivity and hence in comparative advantage and trade inherently arise over time from such expenditures, and productivity growth is essential for global food security. Similar reasoning applies to infrastructure investments, termed infrastructural services.

Under the heading *Public stockholding for food security purposes* (para. 3, Annex 2), the green box exempts expenditures for the accumulation and holding of stocks from AMS under certain conditions. Purchases and sales must be made at market prices and financial transparency is required. A developing country has the option to exempt the acquisition expenditure even if the stock is acquired and released at administered prices, provided that the difference between the acquisition price and the external reference price is accounted for in the AMS (para. 3, footnote 5, Annex 2). Expenditures on *Domestic food aid* (para. 4, Annex 2) to sections of the population in need are exemptible under similar conditions as public stockholding, except that government purchases must be made at market prices.[14]

An open-ended paragraph with the heading *Direct payments to producers* (para. 5, Annex 2) and eight other paragraphs (paras. 6–13) with policy-specific headings give criteria and conditions for payments made to producers to be exemptible. The headings are: *Decoupled income support* (para. 6), *Government financial participation in income insurance and income safety-net programmes* (para. 7), *Payments (made either*

---

[13] The 2013 WTO ministerial decision to exempt also expenditures under a general services category concerned with land reform is discussed in Chapter 6.

[14] Footnote 5 & 6 of Annex 2 indicates that the provision of foodstuffs at subsidized prices with the objective of meeting food requirements in developing countries shall be considered in conformity with para. 3 and para. 4.

directly or by way of government financial participation in crop insurance schemes) for relief from natural disasters (para. 8), *Structural adjustment assistance provided through producer retirement programmes* (para. 9), *Structural adjustment assistance provided through resource retirement programmes* (para. 10), *Structural adjustment assistance provided through investment aids* (para. 11), *Payments under environmental programmes* (para. 12) and *Payments under regional assistance programmes* (para. 13).

The criteria under the heading *Direct payments to producers* (para. 5) allow the exemption of certain direct payments that do not meet the criteria under the headings of paras. 6–13. However, the criteria for exempting such direct payments are identical to most of the criteria under *Decoupled income support* (para. 6). They preclude direct payments from exemption if the amounts are related to current production, domestic or international prices or factors of production in any year after a prior base period, which in the case of para. 6 must be defined and fixed. The requirement that payments not be related to current production, prices or factor use underlies the criteria also under several other headings of exemptible direct payments, which additionally in some cases require the payment program to be designed for particular objectives. Eligibility for payments under the headings related to income insurance and safety-nets or relief from natural disasters (including crop insurance schemes) is related to current production but require, respectively, an income or a production loss of more than 30% compared to levels of previous years.[15] In either case, a price decline alone does not trigger eligibility for payment. Income insurance payments can amount only to less than 70% of a producer's loss. Payments made directly or through crop insurance programs can cover the total cost of replacing losses but require a declaration of a natural or like disaster, which limits the situations in which losses can be compensated and the payments claimed as exempt. Payments under environmental programs may also be linked to current production or

---

[15] The heading relating to crop insurance specifies "government financial participation in crop insurance schemes." This would likely refer conceptually to the subsidy paid by government on the insurance premium at time of contract, not the indemnity paid under the insurance. Some members have notified premium subsidies, others net indemnities, which are more variable. For example, the United States, acknowledging that its crop insurance measures do not fit the green box criteria, first notified net indemnities (annual indemnities less farmer-paid premiums) as non-product-specific AMS support and then shifted in 2008 to instead reporting premium subsidies as product-specific AMS support. The United States notifies administrative and operating reimbursements and underwriting gains to insurers as general services.

factor use although the payment must not exceed the extra costs or loss of income involved in complying with the program.

While the green box refers to no more than minimal trade-distorting effects or effects on production, it is not clear whether these include the effects of policies that reduce production, or only those that increase production. The Haberler phrase "directly encourage home production" singled out the producing-more case (GATT 1958). Similarly, in the Uruguay Round, policy-induced increases in production were the distortions of concern.[16] Certain payments that may raise productivity and increase output in the medium- and long-run are exemptible, similar to certain expenditures on *General services*. They include payments under programs providing investment aids or regional assistance to facilitate the restructuring of operations in response to demonstrated structural disadvantages. Conversely, the criteria under two of the direct payment headings involving structural adjustment specify producer retirement or removing land or other resources from production, which likely reduces production. Payments claimed as exempt under environmental programs may, when conditioned on long-term land idling to reduce soil erosion, conserve wetlands or attain other environmental benefits, have production-reducing effects, possibly more than minimally. Policies to safeguard and enhance biodiversity or mitigate climate change may reduce some production more than minimally. Their development would benefit if the meaning of the green box fundamental requirement was more clear, as discussed in Chapter 8.

2.3   Differentiated Policy Space for Support

2.3.1   *Different Rules for Different Groups of Members*

The rules and commitments of the Agriculture Agreement on domestic support enable governments to provide unlimited amounts of support through certain measures and limited AMS support. The unlimited support includes support exempted under Art. 6.2, Art. 6.5 and Annex 2. The residual support that cannot be exempted is subject to a member-specific limit or limits.

---

[16] The Agreement's Preamble notes in this regard "taking into account the possible negative effects of the implementation of the reform programme on least-developed and net food-importing developing countries." Art. 16 commits developed countries to taking actions articulated in a related 1994 ministerial decision.

Table 2.1 *Diversity of domestic support provisions by groups of members in 2021*

136 schedules pertaining to 164 members	Positive BTAMS in schedule	Eligible for Art. 6.2 exemption	*De minimis* percentage
97 developing	No	Yes	10%
17 developing	Yes	Yes	10%
China and Kazakhstan	No	No	8.5%
4 developed	No	No	5%
16 developed	Yes	No	5%

Note: Developing country label (includes least-developed countries) inferred from *de minimis* percentage different from 5%; numbers may deviate slightly from self-declared status.
Source: Authors' interpretation of the Agriculture Agreement, member schedules, accession protocols, and notifications.

The combination of exemptions, limits and *de minimis* allowances in domestic support applies differently to five distinct groups of members. Table 2.1 shows the number of members as of 2021 in each of these groups, identified by combinations of having a positive BTAMS or not, being eligible or not for the Art. 6.2 exemption and the given *de minimis* percentage. Table 2.2 then identifies each member as having a positive BTAMS or not, being an original or accession member and being a developed or developing country member. The multiple specifications in the domestic support rules result in different degrees of flexibility among members. These differences need to be taken into account in generalizing about the Agreement's provisions on domestic support.

A total of 114 developing country members are eligible for the Art. 6.2 exemption and the 10% *de minimis* percentage. Among these 114 members, 97, including 15 accession members, lack a positive BTAMS, while 17, including 4 accession members, have a positive BTAMS. China and Kazakhstan have a nil BTAMS, cannot use the Art. 6.2 exemption and have a *de minimis* percentage of 8.5%. The 20 developed countries do not have access to the Art. 6.2 exemption and have the 5% *de minimis* percentage. They include 16 members with a positive BTAMS of which 6 are accession members, 1 is an accession member with a nil BTAMS, and 3 are accession members without a BTAMS.

Table 2.2 Members of the WTO in 2021 having no, a nil or a positive BTAMS

Positive BTAMS (33)				No or nil BTAMS (103)		
Original (23)		Accession (10)		Original	Accession (21)	
Developed (10)	Developing (13)	Developed (6)	Developing (4)	Developing (82)	Developed (4)	Developing (15)
Australia	Argentina	Moldova	Jordan	See sub-table to Table 2.2	Albania	Afghanistan
Canada	Brazil	Montenegro	Saudi A.		Armenia	Cabo Verde
EU27	Colombia	N. Macedonia	Tajikistan		Georgia	Cambodia
Iceland	Costa Rica	Russian Fed.	Viet Nam		Kyrgyz Rep.	Ecuador
Japan	Israel	Ch. Taipei				Lao P.D.R.
New Zealand	Korea	Ukraine			Developed country label unclear for domestic support (2)	Liberia
Norway	Mexico					Mongolia
Switz. & Liech.	Morocco					Nepal
United Kingdom	Papua New G.					Oman
United States	South Africa				China	Panama
	Thailand				Kazakhstan	Samoa
	Tunisia					Seychelles
	Venezuela B.R.					Tonga
						Vanuatu
						Yemen

Sub-table to Table 2.2 Original members with no or nil BTAMS (82; no developed members)

Angola	Chad	Gambia	Kuwait	Niger	Solomon Islands
Antigua & Barb.	Chile	Ghana	Lesotho	Nigeria	Sri Lanka
Bahrain	Congo	Grenada	Macao	Pakistan	Suriname
Bangladesh	Côte d'Ivoire	Guatemala	Madagascar	Paraguay	Tanzania
Barbados	Cuba	Guinea	Malawi	Peru	Togo
Belize	D.R. Congo	Guinea-Bissau	Malaysia	Philippines	Trinidad & Tob.
Benin	Djibouti	Guyana	Maldives	Qatar	Turkey
Bolivia, P.S. of	Dominica	Haiti	Mali	Rwanda	Uganda
Botswana	Dominican Rep.	Honduras	Mauritania	S.Kitts & Nevis	United Arab Em.
Brunei Darussal.	Egypt	Hong Kong	Mauritius	Saint Lucia	Uruguay
Burkina Faso	El Salvador	India	Mozambique	S.Vinc. & Gren.	Zambia
Burundi	Eswatini	Indonesia	Myanmar	Senegal	Zimbabwe
Cameroon	Fiji	Jamaica	Namibia	Sierra Leone	
Central Afr. Rep.	Gabon	Kenya	Nicaragua	Singapore	

Note: See Table 2.1 for note and source. Some member names are abbreviated.

2.3.2 *Policy Space for AMS Support*

Limits on individual AMSs are calculated, for members with no or a nil BTAMS, by applying the member's *de minimis* percentage to the nominal values of production of individual products and to the total agricultural value of production. The total agricultural value of production is also in principle the sum of the values of production of all individual products. Accordingly, the full amount of AMS support that could theoretically be accommodated within the *de minimis* limits is equal to the *de minimis* percentage times double the total agricultural value of production or, equivalently, the doubled percentage times the total agricultural value of production. This room for AMS support is a theoretical maximum – unreachable in practice – since it would mean managing AMS support perfectly for all individual products in a member's agriculture sector just up to the year's *de minimis* limit on each product's AMS and also on the non-product-specific AMS. It nevertheless illustrates the orders of magnitude of members' *de minimis* AMS room.

The sum of total agricultural values of production of the 103 members with no or a nil BTAMS averaged about USD 2,100 billion in 2016–18.[17] Applying the doubled *de minimis* percentages to these values yields a sum of these members' theoretical AMS room of USD 386 billion.[18] The corresponding 2016–18 average room within the *de minimis* thresholds of the 33 members with a positive BTAMS summed to USD 195 billion. The sum of these 33 members' positive annual BTAMS averaged about USD 171 billion (USD 153 billion for the 16 developed countries and a much smaller USD 18 billion for the 17 developing countries).

An AMS cannot at the same time be a *de minimis* AMS (not counted in CTAMS) and not be a *de minimis* AMS (counted in CTAMS).

---

[17] This book expresses aggregations of support and values of production in USD. Total agricultural values of production are gross production values from the Food and Agriculture Organization of the United Nations (FAO 2021). As a result of changes in currency values, a member's amounts of support and values of production may, when expressed in USD, show changes over time that deviate from the underlying changes in those amounts and values expressed in local currency. The values for 2016–18 were at time of writing not available for 23 members, all with relatively small agricultural values of production. The indicated sums for groups of members are thus slight underestimates.

[18] The calculation of maximum AMS room rests on the standard reading of Art. 1(b) that the number of products, even none, for which a member calculated AMS in the tables of supporting material incorporated by reference in Part IV of its schedule does not limit the number of products for which the member later calculates AMSs. For a member with no or a nil BTAMS, the *de minimis* AMS limits apply. The number of products for which members notify AMSs varies widely, from none to 80 or more.

A member's room for AMS support is therefore not simply the sum of all *de minimis* thresholds and its BTAMS. Properly describing the AMS room for members with a positive BTAMS needs to be member-specific, account separately for the AMS thresholds and the BTAMS and recognize the interdependence that follows from the all-or-nothing nature of the Agreement's provision on *de minimis* AMSs.[19]

Keeping these considerations in mind, the sum of all members' imputed *de minimis* allowances and 33 BTAMS levels averaged USD 752 billion in 2016–18, which, as explained, overestimates the room for AMS support. The sum of BTAMS levels accounted for 23% of this total, leaving 77% for AMS support within the *de minimis* limits and thresholds. Even with a nil BTAMS, the member with the largest room for AMS support is China, with an average of USD 181 billion in 2016–18. This derives from its large value of production in agriculture (about one-third of the world total) and its 8.5% *de minimis* percentage (doubled to 17% for this calculation). The third largest value of production in agriculture and a BTAMS of USD 82.4 billion gave the EU a sum of 10% of the value of production and BTAMS that in 2016–18 averaged USD 120 billion, that is, considerably less than the amount calculated for China. Likewise, the combination of the second largest total agricultural value of production in India and a higher *de minimis* percentage yields more room for AMS support (an average of USD 81 billion; 20% of value of production in 2016–18) than for the United States (USD 53 billion; 10% of value of production and BTAMS of USD 19.1 billion).

While instructive in terms of calculated theoretical limits, these amounts do not capture that members with positive BTAMS, such as the EU and the United States, have greater flexibility than members with no or a nil BTAMS, such as China and India, in managing AMS support. As long as the BTAMS is respected, individual AMSs can significantly exceed their *de minimis* thresholds, permitting the targeting of support to certain products. However, as the nominal values of production tend to increase over time, the corresponding *de minimis* allowances for AMS support also increase. By contrast, the BTAMS stays constant, which means its relative size compared to members' *de minimis* allowances is shrinking. The sum of just 10 major members' *de minimis* allowances could approach USD 1,000 billion in 2030 (linear trend projection based on WTO 2019a).

---

[19] Brink (2006) examines these issues in terms of the support components effectively available for use. Brink (2015a, 2018a) reviews the provisions of the Agreement that combine to determine the limits on and space for domestic support of different members.

2.4 The SCM Agreement and Export Subsidy Constraints Relating to Domestic Support

2.4.1 Relation of the Agriculture and SCM Agreements

The Agriculture Agreement identifies the categories of domestic support measures under which support is not subject to limit and establishes a member's limits on support under the residual measures. The domestic support rules and commitments arose from recognition of the benefits of reducing the amounts of trade-distorting support to agriculture in conjunction with lowering border protection and disciplining export subsidization. The Agreement addresses domestic support under the overarching presumption, stated in its Preamble, that this support needs to be constrained to achieve a fair and market-oriented agricultural trading system. No evidence of market effects is required to demonstrate that a member violates its domestic support obligations under the Agriculture Agreement.

Agricultural domestic support measures are also subject to disciplines of the SCM Agreement on prohibited and actionable subsidies, as well as related articles of GATT 1994. The Agriculture Agreement stipulates that GATT 1994 and other agreements annexed to the WTO Agreement "shall apply subject to the provisions of this Agreement" (Art. 21). Legal scholars and the Appellate Body have interpreted this to imply that GATT 1994 and other agreements apply except to the extent that the Agriculture Agreement contains specific provisions dealing specifically with the same matter, and both Agreements cannot be complied with at the same time. For export subsidies, for example, WTO consistency would first be examined under the Agriculture Agreement and examination under the SCM Agreement would follow. Notwithstanding this ordering of evaluation, arguments under the Agriculture Agreement might rely on the SCM Agreement for guidance in interpretation.

Under SCM Agreement Art. 1, titled Definition of a Subsidy, subsidies exist where a measure involves one of a variety of financial contributions (including direct transfers of funds, revenue forgone and the provision of goods and services other than general infrastructure), the financial contribution is made by a government, any public body or a private body entrusted or directed by a government, and it confers a benefit relative to what the market would provide. Subsidies also include "any form of income or price support in the sense of Article XVI of GATT 1994."

2.4.2   Actionable Subsidies

A subsidy is actionable if it is specific (SCM Art. 1.2 and Art. 2) and causes adverse effects to the interests of other members (SCM Art. 5). Adverse effects include injury to the domestic industry of another member, nullification or impairment of benefits accruing directly or indirectly to another member under GATT 1994 and serious prejudice to the interests of another member. Serious prejudice may arise in cases that include displacement of imports into the market of the subsidizing member or of exports of another member to third-country markets (SCM Art. 6.3(a) and (b)). It may also arise in case of significant price undercutting in a market, significant price suppression, price depression or lost sales (SCM Art. 6.3 (c)) or, for primary products, from an increase in the world market share of the subsidizing member (SCM Art. 6.3(d)).[20] The SCM Agreement sets out the circumstances in which certain remedies may be sought.

The Agriculture Agreement and the SCM Agreement place domestic support measures in favor of agricultural producers under different but overlapping sets of legal obligations, subject to Agriculture Agreement Art. 21.[21] Measures exempt from limit under the Agriculture Agreement

---

[20] Although the discipline in SCM Art. 6.1 expired at the end of 1999 (as per SCM Art. 31), it identified certain cases in which serious prejudice was deemed to exist, including the case of a product's *ad valorem* subsidization exceeding 5%. A similar presumption seems to underlie the Agriculture Agreement's limit on support under certain domestic support measures without test of adverse effects, and its *de minimis* exemption of an AMS from CTAMS. Likewise, SCM Art. 8 (also expired) identified non-actionable subsidies, including certain support for research, assistance to disadvantaged regions and to promote adaptation to new environmental requirements. These provisions are analogous to parts of Annex 2 of the Agriculture Agreement.

[21] Coppens (2014) and Bartels (2016) discuss the relationship between the Agriculture Agreement, the SCM Agreement and related articles of GATT 1994. Certain agricultural product subsidies were for a time not subject to the rules on adverse effects and serious prejudice of SCM Art. 5 and SCM Art. 6. This followed from Art. 13 in the Agriculture Agreement (Due Restraint), which expired at the end of 2003. It sheltered domestic support measures that conformed fully to Annex 2 of the Agriculture Agreement from certain challenges under the SCM Agreement and GATT 1994. It also gave conditional shelter for *de minimis* AMSs and a CTAMS within the BTAMS as well as measures and support under the Agriculture Agreement's Art. 6.2 and Art. 6.5 from certain other challenges under the SCM Agreement and GATT 1994 "provided that such measures do not grant support to a specific commodity in excess of that decided during the 1992 marketing year." Steinberg and Josling (2003) assessed how the SCM Agreement might be used to constrain agricultural domestic support once due restraint expired. They considered serious prejudice the most plausible legal theory and emphasized the ability of economic models to establish causality from support measures to market outcomes resulting in serious prejudice, as borne out in *US - Upland Cotton*.

can be a cause of, or contribute to, adverse effects under the SCM Agreement. While the SCM Agreement constrains the use of such measures and measures providing AMS support, the Agriculture Agreement constrains the amount of AMS support. The SCM Agreement subjects a member's subsidies, which include any form of price support, to its rules and identifies the adverse effects that can be grounds for challenge. The Agriculture Agreement's obligation is for a member to maintain the amount of support from non-exempt measures within applicable limits, which makes excessive support a ground for challenge. The support counted in an excessive AMS or CTAMS may be provided through measures that do not contravene any SCM provisions. Conversely, an AMS or the CTAMS may be within its applicable limit but support is in the form of a subsidy that contravenes a provision of the SCM Agreement. In *US – Upland Cotton* (discussed in Chapter 7) the CTAMS was within the BTAMS each year. However, under the SCM Agreement, payments included in AMSs that were made under price-contingent measures were found to cause significant price suppression, resulting in serious prejudice to the interests of Brazil.

2.4.3 Export Subsidy Disciplines Interfacing with Domestic Support Measures

Both the Agriculture Agreement and the SCM Agreement address export subsidies. Export subsidies are generally prohibited by the SCM Agreement (SCM Art. 3). Agricultural export subsidies consistent with the Agriculture Agreement benefited from an exception to that prohibition. An export subsidy that is inconsistent with the Agriculture Agreement may also be prohibited by the SCM Agreement.

The rules set out in Art. 3 and Arts. 8–11 of the Agriculture Agreement apply to export subsidies on agricultural products. Art. 9.1 specifies in detail six types of export subsidies subject to these limits including direct subsidies, sale or disposal at prices lower than comparable prices in the domestic market, payments on the export financed by virtue of governmental action, subsidies to reduce the cost of marketing exports, internal transport costs more favorable than for domestic shipments and subsidies on agricultural products contingent on their incorporation in exported products. Art. 10.1 sets out rules to prevent the circumvention of export subsidy commitments through measures not listed in Art. 9.1. Members agreed to work toward development of internationally agreed disciplines concerning export credits, export credit guarantees or insurance programs and to abide by such disciplines once agreed (Art 10.2). Additional provisions of Art. 10 address the burden of proof of absence of export subsidization and international food aid transactions.

Under the Agriculture Agreement, 25 members scheduled ceiling commitments other than nil on export subsidies on agricultural products or groups of products based on their levels of export subsidization in 1986–90. Separate limits apply to budgetary outlays and to quantities of subsidized exports and were subject to reductions (Art. 9.2).[22] Export subsidies are not permitted on any agricultural product not specified in Part IV, Section II, of a member's schedule (Art. 3.3 and Art. 8).

Export subsidies (and also subsidies conditional on use of domestic over imported goods) that are specific are prohibited under Art. 3 of the SCM Agreement. SCM Annex I provides an Illustrative List of Export Subsidies. Expedited dispute settlement procedures are specified for prohibited subsidies (SCM Art. 4) and they are to be withdrawn "without delay" compared to removal of the adverse effects or withdrawal of an actionable subsidy within six months (SCM Art. 7). For agricultural export subsidies, the prohibition applies except "as provided in the Agreement on Agriculture" (SCM Art. 3.1).[23] As a result, export subsidies provided in conformity with the Agriculture Agreement do not fall under the prohibition in the SCM Agreement.

At the 2015 WTO ministerial conference, members agreed to eliminate their remaining scheduled agricultural export subsidy entitlements and decided on disciplines on export credits, export credit guarantees or insurance programs (WTO 2015a). Members were to eliminate their entitlements within a range of time frames between immediately and 2022 by modifying their schedules under GATT 1994 Art. XXVIII. Under the decision on export credits, export credit guarantees or insurance programs, the subject of Art. 10.2, members undertook not to provide such support, called export financing support, other than in conformity with the 2015 ministerial decision.[24] The Agriculture Agreement allowed

---

[22] At the end of 2000, outlays for and quantities benefiting from export subsidies were to be, respectively, no greater than 64% and 79% of base levels for developed members and 76% and 86% for developing members.

[23] Art. 13 of the Agriculture Agreement also exempted export subsidies conforming to its Arts. 8–11 from certain challenges through 2003. SCM Art. 27 exempts certain developing country members from the prohibition of export subsidies, conditional on least-developed country designation, level of gross national product or for a specified number of years.

[24] The decision defined export financing support, set maximum repayment terms for such support and required that some support programs be self-financing and cover their long-term operating costs and losses.

developing country members to provide certain kinds of agricultural export subsidies in relation to the cost of marketing exports and internal transport through the year 2000 even without a scheduled limit (Art. 9.4). This flexibility was extended at subsequent WTO ministerial conferences and expires in 2023 for many developing countries and in 2030 for others.

The Agriculture Agreement disciplines on export subsidies and the SCM Agreement disciplines on prohibited subsidies are different but overlapping. The question arises under either agreement whether domestic support measures can result in the provision of export subsidies. The answer has been determined in the affirmative, at least under the Agriculture Agreement. In *Canada – Dairy* and *EC – Export Subsidies on Sugar*, domestic production quota and price support measures were found to have created export subsidies that exceeded the respondents' export subsidy commitments under the Agriculture Agreement.

2.4.4 Countervailing Measures

The SCM Agreement lays out the procedural and substantive conditions under which members may investigate and impose countervailing duties (CVDs) "for the purpose of offsetting any subsidy bestowed directly or indirectly upon the manufacture, production or export" of goods imported by that member, where imports of such goods cause material injury to a domestic industry (SCM Art. 10, footnote 36). The risk of facing CVD investigation and imposition of duties may deter a member from adopting support measures that it is concerned could become subject to this remedy. Assessment of this effect would rest on political economy case studies – for example, Canada has favored whole-farm support programs over product-specific support in part out of concern over potential CVD action by the United States (Hedley 2017).

If in a WTO dispute over the respondent's imposition of a CVD the adopted ruling affirms the legitimacy of the CVD, it would confirm that the complainant's subsidy has injurious effects. Fifty-four WTO dispute cases involving CVDs were initiated between 1995 and 2020. Review of the 14 among these that involved agricultural products finds no dispute with a ruling in favor of the countervailing respondent. Thus, these disputes give no evidence to shed light on the existence of injury from domestic support measures in favor of agricultural producers in relation to the SCM Agreement.

Only a few of members' CVD investigations are challenged at the WTO. For example, Hufbauer (2021) tabulates 498 CVD investigations launched between 1995 and 2018 by nine major economies. A systematic review of the evidence presented on the existence of subsidies in the investigations related to agricultural products would provide information to complement or perhaps corroborate information on members' domestic support in notifications to the Committee on Agriculture. Although this could add insights, it would be a separate inquiry and is outside the scope of this book.[25] Hufbauer (2021) asserts that while the SCM Agreement has somewhat curtailed the use of CVDs, they "are still probably the most important international restraint on subsidies." This generalization seems less evident for domestic support measures in favor of agricultural producers, given the particular disciplines of the Agriculture Agreement.

2.4.5   Disputes Involving Domestic Support Measures

The WTO disputes on domestic support measures that cite one or both of the Agriculture and SCM Agreements are shown in Table 2.3. It lists 16 numbered disputes initiated between 1995 and 2021 under 9 dispute short titles. All of these disputes cite the Agriculture Agreement concerning either domestic support or export subsidies, of which 10 also cite the SCM Agreement concerning either actionable or prohibited subsidies. Nine of the sixteen disputes have been adjudicated with panel or Appellate Body reports adopted. Outcomes are pending in *India – Sugar and Sugarcane* (DS579, DS580 and DS581), in which the panel reports are under appeal, while four disputes (DS507, DS357, DS365 and DS451) did not progress beyond consultations or a panel established but not composed.

Nine of the disputes involved alleged excessive domestic support violating a member's obligations under the Agriculture Agreement. Only one of these nine disputes also addressed issues of actionable subsidies under the SCM Agreement. In five of these nine disputes the complainants challenged both domestic support compliance and export subsidy compliance. In four of these five disputes the complainants raised export subsidy issues under both the Agriculture and SCM Agreements. The six disputes among these nine for which a panel was established involve challenges of excessive AMSs or CTAMS deriving from MPS.

---

[25] WTO trade remedies in the form of anti-dumping measures and safeguard measures are the subject of two separate agreements and the Agriculture Agreement makes provision for special safeguards (Art. 5). These measures are also outside the scope of this book.

Table 2.3 *Disputes involving domestic support measures citing the Agriculture and SCM Agreements, 1995–2021*

Short title (year consultations requested)	Dispute	Complainant	Decision	Issues raised in panel request			
				Agriculture Agreement		SCM Agreement	
				Domestic support	Export subsidies	Actionable subsidies	Prohibited subsidies
Domestic support under the Agriculture Agreement							
India – Sugar and Sugarcane (2019)	579	Brazil	Pending	X	X		
	580	Australia	Pending	X	X		X
	581	Guatemala	Pending	X	X		X
China – Agricultural Producers (2016)	511	United States	Yes	X			
Thailand – Subsidies Concerning Sugar (2016)	507	Brazil	No	X	X	X	X
US – Agriculture Subsidies (2007)	357	Canada	No	X	X		X
	365	Brazil	No	X			
Korea – Various Measures on Beef (1999)	161	United States	Yes	X			
	169	Australia	Yes	X			

Table 2.3 (cont.)

Short title (year consultations requested)	Dispute	Complainant	Decision	Issues raised in panel request			
				Agriculture Agreement		SCM Agreement	
				Domestic support	Export subsidies	Actionable subsidies	Prohibited subsidies
Domestic support under the SCM Agreement							
China – Measures Relating to the Production and Exportation of Apparel and Textile Products (2012)	451	Mexico	No		X	X	X
US – Upland Cotton (2002)	267	Brazil	Yes	X	X	X	X
Export subsidies arising from domestic support							
EC – Export Subsidies on Sugar (2002)	265	Australia	Yes		X		X
	266	Brazil	Yes		X		X
	283	Thailand	Yes		X		X
Canada – Dairy (1997)	103	United States	Yes		X		X
	113	New Zealand	Yes		X		X

Notes: Short titles were not assigned to DS507 and DS451, which only proceeded to consultations. Table refers to issues raised in consultation requests for these disputes. Domestic support issues under the Agriculture Agreement in DS267 only concerned whether conditions for the application of Art. 13 (Due Restraint) were met.
Source: Authors' tabulation of requests for consultations and decisions of the Dispute Settlement Body.

Two other of the sixteen disputes involved actionable subsidies under the SCM Agreement and also involved export subsidies under both agreements. Another five of the disputes raised the concern that domestic support measures resulted in the provision of export subsidies through cross-subsidization. The three groups of disputes are discussed further in Chapter 7, including differences in the arguments over domestic support under the two agreements.

2.5 The Complexity of Rules Governing Agricultural Domestic Support

The difficulties in agricultural trade that the Haberler group was set up to address were to some extent tackled with the inclusion of domestic support constraints in the 1994 Agreement on Agriculture. Countries' policy concerns influenced these constraints as decisively as economic rationale. As a result, a complex array of different rules and commitments apply to different groups among developed and developing members. Limits apply to some domestic support measured in a particular way, that is, to individual AMSs or AMSs summed to CTAMS. Green box (Annex 2) support is exempt from AMSs and is unlimited on the basis of having at most minimal trade-distorting effects or effects on production. Support provided under certain types of policies (Art. 6.2 and Art. 6.5) does not enter either the calculation of CTAMS or, in practice, any AMSs and is unlimited, even though it may affect production or trade more than minimally. While the exemption under Art. 6.2 is available only to developing countries, Art. 6.5 and Annex 2 compliant support is exemptible for all members.

Different percentages apply to different groups of members for their calculation of the current year's *de minimis* AMS levels. While the majority of members face *de minimis* limits on individual AMSs, the schedules of 33 members include a positive BTAMS. This gives a member greater flexibility in managing the provision of AMS support. As *de minimis* levels derive from nominal values of production, they generally increase over time. Members with larger agriculture sectors can accommodate larger amounts of AMS support within their *de minimis* levels and any BTAMS, and with more flexibility the larger the BTAMS. However, China and India, without a positive BTAMS but with large values of production in agriculture, have more room for AMS support than the EU and the United States, respectively, each with a positive BTAMS but with a lower *de minimis* percentage and lower values of production.

In addition to the constraints on domestic support under the Agriculture Agreement, the SCM Agreement provides recourse against prohibited subsides and actionable subsidies that cause adverse effects. Support counted in an AMS faces two kinds of constraints: the applicable limits on AMS support and the constraints on measures under the rules of the SCM Agreement. Measures under which support is exempt from AMS limits may nonetheless cause adverse effects. Disputes that have addressed domestic support have arisen under both agreements.

Many developing countries have been unable to provide much or any AMS support in the past, but as incomes rise some developing countries have demonstrated growing ability and willingness to offer such support. The economies of developing countries grow over time and, especially those that grow rapidly, are approaching the same levels of per-capita income where developed countries saw fit in the past to deliver significant support to their agricultural producers, often through distorting measures. Because a positive BTAMS gives greater flexibility in managing AMS support, a point of friction arises between members with no or a nil BTAMS, most of which are developing country members, and those with a positive BTAMS, which include the developed and developing country members with the most support in the past. Some developing countries have used, and others may in the future seek to use, their growing economic capacity to significantly increase various types of distorting domestic support to agriculture. This can lead to inclinations to interpret the provisions of the Agriculture Agreement generously and to resist future tightening through negotiations, as discussed in following chapters.

3

Economic Analysis of Exemptions and Administered Prices

While the Agreement on Agriculture is part of a legally binding international agreement, not an economic blueprint, the economic dimensions of how it is implemented link closely to the achievement of the Agreement's intention to provide for substantial progressive reductions in agricultural support and protection. This chapter discusses the evolving international context for analyzing domestic support and its trade-distorting potential in economic terms. It then focuses on two major areas where members' policy options in relation to the domestic support provisions of the Agreement have attracted particular analytical interest. They relate to the exemption of direct payments from AMS calculation on green box grounds, particularly by the EU and the United States, and the measurement of MPS under the Agriculture Agreement compared to economic analysis, which remains critical for China, India and some other members. Insights contributed by economic analysis on these and several other issues are highlighted and some of the questions that remain to be addressed are examined.

3.1 Economic Effects of Domestic Support

3.1.1 Evolving International Context for Measuring Support

Prior to the 1986 launch of the Uruguay Round, countries wished to explore the effects of possible outcomes of the upcoming negotiations on their agricultural sector and whole economy. This interest led to model-based economic analysis using the wedge between a product's border price and the effective domestic producer price (producer revenue per unit), which resulted from the combination of border measures, price regulations and government payments to producers. In the lead-up to the Uruguay Round, early analysis using indicators that combined measurements of agricultural price support and producer payments were reported in, for example, OECD (1987), Abbott et al. (1988) and Roningen and Dixit (1989). This work was done before the rules on measuring domestic support in the Agriculture Agreement had been finalized. The price support component was an economic measurement deriving from border measures, not the MPS measurement calculated from domestic policy settings. The interest in indicators of economic price support and payment support in many countries led to the development of data bases such as those eventually published by the OECD as its PSEs and by other international organizations and national governments.

Economic analysis of domestic support undertaken in the years following the 1995 beginning of the WTO has addressed a need to understand the potential effectiveness of members' WTO commitments in reining in the amount of domestic support or encouraging shifts toward less distorting forms of support. Carried out by national governments, academics and interest groups, the analysis draws on such sources as members' notifications to the Committee on Agriculture and the expanding data sets of the OECD and other institutions on agricultural policy support and associated monitoring and evaluation.[1] Major policy changes, in particular in the EU and the United States, have contributed to the interest in analyzing the effects of different types of domestic support. This involves mainly the EU producer payments exempted first under the blue box and later the EU and US support exempted as *Direct payments to producers*, particularly *Decoupled income support*, under the green box. The launch of the Doha Round in 2001 induced exploration of the effects of possible outcomes of those negotiations. Impetus for analysis also came from the accession to the WTO of China in 2001 and other countries with large or increasing agricultural production such as Viet Nam in 2007, Ukraine in 2008 and Russia in 2012.

Further context for analysis of domestic support in economic terms comes from the ongoing negotiations. In the absence of a comprehensive agreement from the Doha Round, the agriculture negotiations have sought to settle a few specific domestic support issues at ministerial conferences. The limits and exemptions for various types of domestic support are one area of interest. A second area of interest relates to the measurement of MPS, which has come to the fore in counter-notifications and disputes. Within this context, the consequences when

---

[1] The International Organizations Consortium for Measuring the Policy Environment for Agriculture (AgIncentives 2021) includes FAO, the Inter-American Development Bank (IDB), the International Food Policy Research Institute (IFPRI), OECD and the World Bank Group.

a developing country supports producers excessively by acquiring public stocks for food security purposes at administered prices continue to be a major negotiating concern of some members.

3.1.2 AMS Support and Other Trade-Distorting Domestic Support

AMS support and trade-distorting domestic support are not synonyms, in spite of often being so portrayed. As the review of the Agriculture Agreement in Chapter 2 makes clear, most or perhaps all AMS support is likely to distort trade and all is subject to limit. Support under Art. 6.2 and Art. 6.5 measures is exempt from limit based on compliance with the negotiated criteria in the respective articles, with no requirement that it be non-distorting. The exemption of green box support from limit rests on meeting the explicit fundamental requirement of having at most minimal trade-distorting effects or effects on production, as well as basic and policy-specific criteria and conditions. Yet some green box support clearly raises productivity or creates infrastructure and affects production and trade over time.

Moreover, a distinction between only AMS support as trade-distorting and all other support as not trade-distorting is contrary to the results of economic analysis. The OECD has long identified some of the categories of support that are included in its PSE as "potentially most distorting." That designation is based on analysis such as Dewbre et al. (2001), OECD (2001) and Martini (2011). The analysis ranks different categories of PSE support in terms of the trade distortion they generate relative to the trade distortion from the same amount of economic MPS (the distortion generated by MPS is the *numéraire*).

Economic MPS, payments based on current output and payments based on unconstrained use of variable inputs have significantly higher potential to distort agricultural production and trade than payments based on other criteria. These make up the support the OECD (2021a) reports as potentially most trade distorting. Economic MPS and payments based on output are similar in terms of distorting trade. Payments based on the unconstrained use of variable inputs are found to distort trade more than economic MPS: the ratio of the trade effects of such input subsidies to the trade effects of MPS has been estimated as roughly 1.3 to 1 (Dewbre et al. 2001).[2]

---

[2] Part of the explanation of this result is that the elasticity of supply of the subsidized inputs is assumed to be greater than the elasticity of supply of other factors of production.

While the categories of support in the referenced analysis are those of the OECD PSE measurements, they map in several ways onto the Agriculture Agreement categories of domestic support. For example, members have exempted some payments included in PSEs as area-based as meeting the blue box criteria. Output payments and MPS are usually part of members' AMSs. What is measured under the label MPS differs between PSE and AMS, but the domestic price levels in both cases result from policy choices. While some members include in their AMSs the support based on unconstrained use of variable inputs, such as fertilizer, fuel or irrigation water, others claim it as exempt under Art. 6.2. The analytical findings help to clarify that what members label as AMS support is only one part of trade-distorting domestic support.

3.2   Exempted Direct Payments

Much domestic support analysis has focused on the payments members have exempted as blue box or green box support based on their compliance with the policy-specific criteria or their effect on production and trade (e.g., Meléndez-Ortiz et al. 2009). While corresponding analysis of support exempted under Art. 6.2 is relatively scarce in view of the increasing amounts of such support by a few developing countries and potential use by others, Gulati and Narayanan (2003) and Birner et al. (2011) have analyzed India's input subsidies.

A particular area of interest for economic analysis has been the possibility that certain exempted direct payments have more than minimally distorting effects in spite of meeting the policy-specific criteria of the green box (Rude 2001). Policy measures exempted as green box *Direct payments to producers* (para. 5, Annex 2) and *Decoupled income support* (para. 6, Annex 2) have been analyzed in terms of distorting trade. The findings of this analysis can be used, when it points at minimal trade distortions, to make arguments that a member properly exempts those payments from AMS limits or the converse when it points at significant trade distortion. Analysis has also focused on whether certain direct payment measures fail to meet the policy-specific criteria under a particular heading of the green box and therefore are not exemptible. There has been analytical interest in *Payments under environmental programs* (para. 12, Annex 2), particularly from the perspective of changes in those rules that might be pursued to accommodate addressing climate change and other evolving priorities.

3.2.1 *Support Policy Evolution in the EU and the United States*

The analysis of blue box and green box payments has given particular attention to the EU and the United States, since these members have exempted large amounts of such payments. This warrants a brief outline of the evolution of their agricultural domestic support policies.[3] Prior to the launch of the Uruguay Round, MPS had been the primary policy measure in both the EU and the United States, backed up by supply controls and accumulation of stocks. From the founding of the CAP in 1962, support prices in the EU were maintained above international price levels for food crops, feed grains, fruits and vegetables, milk, sugar, beef and other livestock products and other products. Variable import levies were initially utilized at the border to maintain stable internal prices insulated from world markets.

When the EU emerged as a net exporter of grains and other products starting around 1980, export subsidies became a key policy measure. This proved costly and unsustainable, both for the early member states and in terms of EU enlargement. A series of policy reforms starting in 1992 subsequently moved the EU away from MPS. Introduction of so-called compensatory payments tied to areas of crops and heads of livestock led to EU interest in negotiating the blue box exemption. Further reforms starting in 2000 moved payments to a whole farm basis, the Single Farm Payment (SFP) Scheme, which the EU exempted under Annex 2. In terms of price and income support, the EU has moved largely in a unilateral direction toward direct payments decoupled from current prices or production. Reforms in 2013 replaced SFP with a Basic Payment Scheme (BPS) and a Single Area Payment Scheme (SAPS). Payments under these measures are determined, with successive modifications, by levels of production in the past. By 2016–18, only butter and common wheat continued to receive MPS.

The origins of the US agricultural domestic support, known as its permanent legislation, lie in the Agricultural Adjustment Act of 1938 and the Agricultural Act of 1949. The provisions of this legislation are

---

[3] The summaries in following paragraphs are exceedingly brief. Schnepf (2021), Sumner (2021) and Swinbank (2021) offer more explanatory summaries of EU and US policies. For historical perspective see, *inter alia*, Orden et al. (1999), Moyer and Josling (2002), Daugbjerg and Swinbank (2009), Knudsen (2009), Coppess (2018) and Mercier and Halbrook (2020). Annual monitoring reports by the OECD discuss policy developments among covered countries.

supplanted on intervals of about five years by recurrent legislation, known as farm bills and denoted as Farm Acts in US notifications. Domestic support in the United States historically focused on a smaller set of products than in the EU, primarily food grains, feed grains, cotton, oilseeds, milk and sugar. Through the early 1980s, there were two main support measures. First, loan rates are support prices at which producers could forfeit their crops to the government or later receive a payment if loan rates were above market prices. Each loan rate program provides a price floor to producers for all their current output. Second, an additional set of higher support prices (known as target prices) triggered deficiency payments for certain output but did not directly undergird price levels. Since deficiency payments are price contingent, that is, rising or falling inversely with market prices, they came to be characterized as counter-cyclical in the parlance of US farm policy discussion.[4] The loan and deficiency payment support measures were backed up by short-term and long-term acreage idling, the former specifically intended to raise market prices to reduce budgetary costs and the latter through several conservation programs serving this purpose but also having environmental objectives.

By the mid-1980s, the US deficiency payments had come to be determined by past base acres planted to a crop and past yields (sometimes called program or fixed yields) and to be made on no more than 85% of base acreage, while still requiring annual acreage idling. This led to the US interest in negotiating the blue box exemption. The 1996 farm bill nonetheless introduced fixed direct payments at legislated levels independent of current prices called Production Flexibility Contract (PFC) payments, then Direct Payments.[5] These payments were also determined by past base acres and program yields, but annual acreage controls were eliminated and almost complete planting flexibility was allowed regardless of what crop determined the payments on base acres.

The United States exempted the fixed direct payments as green box *Decoupled income support*, but support policy did not settle on such payments. Instead, when world market prices declined in the late 1990s, loan rate payments rose and the United States renewed a program of countercyclical deficiency payments based on past output and current

---

[4] The support of this type enacted in the 2002 and 2008 farm bills was specifically titled Countercyclical Payments, while similar programs have had other names.

[5] The US payment program named Direct Payments was authorized in the 2002 and 2008 farm bills. This specific program is not to be confused with the more general para. 5 heading *Direct payments to producers* in Annex 2.

price differences. Planting flexibility on base acres was retained, so payment did not depend on current production of a specific crop. Later the United States added another countercyclical program based on product revenue in place of prices, again making payments on base acres with planting flexibility. The fixed PFC and Direct Payments that had started in 1996 were eliminated in the 2014 farm bill. The United States reports loan rate payments as product-specific AMS support and the payments made on base acres as non-product-specific AMS support.

3.2.2   Studies of EU and US Exempted Payments

Analysis of the EU compensatory payments, whose introduction pre-dated the Agriculture Agreement, indicated relatively small effects on production (Cahill 1997). The analysis foreshadowed questions that later arose in evaluating the role of the blue box and para. 5 and para. 6 of Annex 2 as the provisions under which the EU has exempted large amounts of direct payments. The green box payments were found in early studies to provide less production incentives and be less trade distorting than the initial compensatory payments (Rude 2008), although the magnitudes of these differences were not necessarily clear (Moro and Sckokai 2013).

Matthews et al. (2017) reviewed the large literature on the production and trade effects of the payments referred to in EU regulations as decoupled, most of which the EU exempts under para. 6.[6] They studied the channels through which the exempted direct payments might influence production and hence trade, covering the impact of direct payments on labor use, land use, investment behavior and farm productivity. The conclusion is guarded, referring to "the possibility that even decoupled payments in the EU may have production and thus trade effects." The report points out that the assumptions about how to incorporate decoupled payments in analytical models are responsible for the results, and there is no empirically grounded justification for handling decoupled payments in one way rather than another.

---

[6] What EU regulations call decoupled payments are not necessarily the same as payments meeting the criteria of para. 6 of the green box. Since 2013, the EU has exempted payments through the BPS, made in 18 member states until the UK withdrawal, under para. 6 and payments through SAPS, made in 10 member states, under para. 5 as *Direct payments to producers* claimed as meeting the criteria 6(b) to 6(e) of para. 6, as required in para. 5. BPS and SAPS payments in 2018 were EUR 29.4 billion and EUR 8.1 billion (USD 34.8 billion and USD 9.6 billion), respectively.

The United States exempted about USD 5 billion per year as *Decoupled income support* from 1996 through 2014. Although the payment amounts were not as large as in the case of the EU, much analysis has focused on estimating the possible effects on production and trade of these US payments by themselves and along with other payments not claimed as exempt. For example, Goodwin and Mishra (2006) found that the distortions brought about by the exempted payments, although statistically significant in some cases, were very modest.

Abler and Blandford (2005) reviewed the literature at the time, concluding that PFC payments and also price-contingent countercyclical payments made on base acres and fixed yields with planting flexibility had some impact on production relative to a case of no such payments. Again, in general, the estimated impacts were small. In contrast, de Gorter et al. (2008) and de Gorter (2009) argued that inframarginal support made on a fixed level of past output, whether exempted under para. 6 or countercyclical to price movements hence not exemptible, caused production distortions that could in theory be greater than those of an equivalent amount of fully coupled subsidies. The production effects would, with declining average variable and total costs, result from cross-subsidization and exit deterrence, the extent of which would depend on the distribution of farm sizes and cost structures. Moreover, under four farm bills since 2002, producers have been able to update some base acre and program yield parameters determining the size of their fixed or price-contingent payments, a prospect that could add production stimulus. For corn and soybeans, Hendricks and Sumner (2014) argued any such effect would be relatively small because of the characteristics of the cropping alternatives. The literature reviewed by, for example, O'Donoghue and Whitaker (2010) reflects the diversity of findings regarding any connection between payments exempted as *Decoupled income support* and increased production.

Since the United States no longer exempts large direct payments as green box *Decoupled income support*, the urgency of gauging any production and trade effects of such payments has faded. That said, in addition to reviewing the literature in recent years, Tong et al. (2019) estimated the effects on US agricultural exports (including livestock) of producer payments from 1999 to 2011. The analysis usefully separates the payments the United States exempted under para. 6 from other green box payments, such as certain disaster payments, and from payments that are not exempted on green box grounds. They concluded that the effects on US exports of direct payments exempted under para. 6 were negligible, consistent with theoretical arguments by Chambers and Voica (2016). This would satisfy the green box fundamental requirement of at most minimal trade-distorting effects and the payments would on this basis qualify for green box classification.

Relatively much effort has gone into evaluating the effects of EU and US direct payments compared to similar analysis for other members. However, Wagener and Zenker (2021) analyzed a price insurance scheme in Thailand from 2009–11, which closely mirrored US counter-cyclical payments, and found resulting production increases. Banga (2014) found positive effects on agricultural productivity and technical efficiency associated with changes in green box support between 1995 and 2007 in some of the 26 countries studied. This support included all green box payments and also green box expenditures on *General services, Public stockholding for food security purposes* and *Domestic food aid*. The amounts some members exempt on green box grounds have increased rapidly. China and India, for example, each more than quintupled their green box exempted expenditures between 2005 and, respectively, 2016 and 2019, as discussed in Chapter 4. Analysis for later years of all support that members exempt from AMS calculations may in due course provide additional insight.

3.2.3   *Compatibility of Payments with Policy-Specific Criteria*

Apart from the question of payments claimed as *Decoupled income support* having significant trade effects or not, analysts have examined the compatibility of EU and US direct payments with the policy-specific criteria of para. 6 of Annex 2. A particular concern is whether the payment meets criterion 6(b), which requires the amount of payment not to be related to or based on the "type or volume of production" after the base period. Failing to meet this criterion would disqualify the payment from being exempted from AMS. Swinbank and Tranter (2005) suggested that the EU's SFP Scheme failed to qualify in two ways: the land on which the payment was claimed could not be used to produce fruits and vegetables and the land must be kept in good agricultural and environmental condition. EU policy changes in 2007 made land on which fruits and vegetables were produced eligible for payments, which overcame at least part of the problem (Swinbank 2009). While payments remain conditional on an agricultural activity being carried out on agricultural areas, the EU clarified that this activity does not require the production, rearing or growing of agricultural products (it can, for example, consist of removing unwanted scrub vegetation). In *US – Upland Cotton*, the Appellate Body found that the US PFC and Direct Payments did not meet the type-of-production criterion in para. 6(b) because of restrictions on what could be produced on eligible land.[7] Later US farm legislation eased these restrictions.

Payments under environmental programmes lists only a few criteria (para. 12). While they were the relevant ones at the time of negotiating the Agriculture Agreement, members' environmental programs have since changed. New types of programs are being developed and implemented in which payments are based on environmental performance instead of certain producer practices. This raises questions about the compatibility of the programs with para. 12 as a whole and with particular wording in it, such as payments being dependent on fulfilling "conditions related to production methods or inputs." Exemption of direct payments under para. 12 may in some cases relate more to an environmental objective of the measure than to the para. 12 criteria.

Analysts have considered a variety of issues regarding *Payments under environmental programmes*, including the observation that an environmental program in agriculture that is designed to meet the para. 12 criteria may reach its environmental objectives only at a high cost. Building on the pioneering analysis of Blandford and Josling (2007), Steenblik and Tsai (2009) identify the resulting low cost-effectiveness as a concern in the presence of budget constraints. Swinbank (2009) notes that the positive correlation between the site-specificity of payments and their transaction costs can make it difficult for a government to design a cost-effective scheme within the confines of the wording of para. 12. Hasund and Johansson (2016) focus on the compatibility with para. 12 of value-based or results-based payments as an alternative to traditional practice-based or cost-based payments to achieve environmental objectives. Bureau (2017) furthers the discussion beyond para. 12 to the fundamental requirement in Annex 2 about minimal trade-distorting effects or effects on production. The increasing priority on environmental measures is discussed in Chapter 8.

---

[7] Compatibility of PFC and Direct Payments with para. 6(b) mattered for a key calculation under Art. 13 (Due Restraint) of the Agriculture Agreement (see Chapter 7).

3.3   Issues Concerning Market Price Support

3.3.1   Measuring and Interpreting MPS

The following formulas show the different variables involved in the calculation of MPS under the Agriculture Agreement and in economic terms, as previously discussed:

$$Agreement\ MPS_t = [AAP_t - FERP_{fixed\ years}] \times [Eligible\ Production_t]$$

$$Economic\ MPS_t = [Domestic\ Price_t - Border\ Price_t] \times [Total\ Production_t]$$

where the variables defining the Agreement MPS are those of para. 8 and para. 9 of Annex 3, and t is the time indicator for the current year.[8] The AAP is a policy variable, while the domestic price can be an observed price or a calculated average market price, which will often track but need not equal the AAP. The FERP is constant over time, while the border price varies from year to year with international market conditions and exchange rates. In practice, the border price is adjusted with margins to correspond to the farm level domestic price. The eligible production is the quantity of production eligible to receive the AAP, while the calculation of economic MPS uses total production.

The economic MPS represents an often major part of the policy-induced economic incentive to produce. The Agriculture Agreement seeks to rein in this incentive, which makes it important to assess how a member's compliance with its domestic support obligations, which involve the Agreement MPS, affects the economic MPS. The differences among members in terms of their obligations and policies, as well as the parameters and data to use in calculating MPS under the Agreement, favor member-specific assessments. For example, the contributors to Orden et al. (2011) examine through an economic lens the MPS and other policy choices of eight developed and developing members in relation to their domestic support obligations. How domestic support

---

[8] The economic MPS as reported in the OECD PSEs and similar uses is an *ex post* measurement of support once market outcomes in year *t* are observed. For estimating the effects of a price support program or border protection, an alternative measurement to the *ex post* observed outcome is the *ex ante* effect on producers' price expectations. By truncating the lower part of the distribution of possible prices to be received a price support raises expected price and reduces price variance, which can stimulate production. The *ex ante* effect, which is difficult to measure, occurs even if the outcome results in no measured price support being provided in any given year. This book follows the convention of reporting *ex post* MPS measurements.

rules and commitments may affect domestic policy settings and resulting economic support is assessed in the context of *Korea – Various Measures on Beef, China – Agricultural Producers*, notifications and counter-notifications about India's MPS for wheat, rice and cotton, and *India – Sugar and Sugarcane* in Chapter 7.

The different components that make up domestic support under the Agriculture Agreement are difficult to represent in economic analysis. Border protection is commonly modeled as a relative price gap, or the combination of border protection and producer payments can be represented by a nominal rate of assistance (Anderson 2009). The Agreement, however, calculates MPS as required by Annex 3, and it expresses BTAMS and the measurements of applied support as nominal amounts. Modeling domestic support as measured in the Agreement or its components separately from those relating to border protection therefore requires the introduction of variables usually not seen in economic models.

In analysis that represents the economic support provided by border policies separately from budgetary transfers, accounting also for the MPS calculated under Annex 3 would add little to the analytical results in economic terms in most circumstances. The complexity in modeling Agriculture Agreement domestic support and the limit or limits applying in different ways for different members in different years to the AMS part of domestic support may also help to explain why economic analysis often accounts only for the budgetary transfer component of domestic support while accounting separately for border protection. The results of economic analysis referring to domestic support need to be interpreted with care in a WTO context, since what the analysis refers to as domestic support may include only budgetary transfers and not the Agreement's MPS.[9] The need for care is particularly relevant if the economic analysis concerns compliance with the nominal limits identified by the Agreement.

The architecture of the Agriculture Agreement is inherently redundant as far as MPS in domestic support is concerned, given the provisions on market access and export competition. Already the Haberler Report highlighted this inevitability (GATT 1958). The redundancy is behind what is sometimes expressed as a concern about double-counting of

---

[9] For example, the widely used GTAP database uses only budgetary transfers to represent domestic support (Huang 2013, Aguiar et al. 2019). Some reporting of modeling analysis clearly attributes estimated effects to the budgetary transfers part of domestic support, e.g., Anderson and Valenzuela (2021).

MPS. However, a member's domestic support commitments are distinct from its commitments on border measures, and the applied variables that are subject to the respective commitments are different. In market access, the applied tariff must not exceed the bound tariff, and in domestic support the measured amount of non-exempt support must not exceed its limit, whether an AMS *de minimis* limit or the BTAMS. The fact that market access commitments and domestic support commitments are distinct from each other requires a separate accounting of what is subject to each kind of commitment and avoids double-counting.

3.3.2 Eventual Infeasibility of Supporting Producers by Means of Administered Prices

The calculation of MPS is a contentious subject in the Committee on Agriculture, ongoing negotiations and disputes. The size of the measured MPS under Agriculture Agreement rules can make the resulting product-specific AMS exceed its limit or threshold in spite of economic MPS being small or nil. This can arise for both developed and developing countries. The incidence of the contention varies among members since it depends, for any given economic MPS, on changes in the AAP compared to the FERP, the member having no or a nil BTAMS or a positive BTAMS, its *de minimis* percentage and the fact that most values of production are rising in nominal terms while BTAMS is fixed.

A product's MPS can increase more rapidly than its *de minimis* allowance increases (Matthews 2015). Assume that the administered price applies to all production and for simplicity the quantity of eligible production remains unchanged when the administered price is raised. When the administered price is raised by *a* dollars per tonne, the price gap in the MPS calculation also increases by *a* dollars per tonne.[10] This larger gap is multiplied by the quantity of eligible production to generate a proportionately larger amount of MPS. However, although the producer price used to calculate value of production may also rise by *a* dollars per tonne, only a percentage of that additional value is added to the *de minimis* allowance (5, 8.5 or 10% as applicable).

Over time the increases in the administered price will therefore generate MPS large enough to exceed the product's *de minimis* AMS allowance

---

[10] This book uses tonne for a metric ton (1,000 kilograms), the standard unit in international trade and distinct from a short ton (2,000 pounds).

even if only keeping pace with inflation. This happens even though the allowance increases as the value of production increases. The problem is aggravated when the FERP is based on prices observed as long ago as 1986–88 as the Agriculture Agreement stipulates. The reference price from some 35 years ago usually makes the MPS larger than when using a more recent reference price. Most members that have acceded to the WTO have used data for more recent years in their accession documents. In *China – Agricultural Producers*, the panel concluded that the FERP for calculating MPS for wheat and rice should be based on the years 1996–98 used in China's accession. Since the 1996–98 FERPs are higher than if based on 1986–88, this decision implied lower MPSs, as discussed in Chapter 7.

There is little disagreement from an economic perspective that the calculation of the Agreement MPS has elements that need changing. Some Uruguay Round negotiators may have envisioned limiting the support delivered through an administered price but not making it impossible to use an administered price as a policy instrument, while others may have had eventual elimination of MPS programs in mind. Negotiators clearly had in mind a path toward revising the Agriculture Agreement a few years after 1994, as set out in Art. 20. The authority given to the Committee on Agriculture to take excess inflation into account in assessing members' ability to comply with their commitments reflects recognition of the difficulties of the MPS formula. The base years for the FERP could be updated or revised. Such proposals did not animate the negotiations in the Doha Round although members focused some attention on the issue in the continued inconclusive negotiations. An update would in many cases have led to a higher FERP, a smaller price gap and greater feasibility of supporting producers by means of an administered price.[11] The eventual impossibility of using an administered price may be a consequence of the ongoing negotiations not having set a more recent base period for the external reference price. At the same time, it is an achievement in terms of prompting greater market orientation: an administered price is not a market price.

---

[11] This would be the case for some original members (Brink 2021) and was the case for China for wheat and rice. However, among the nine other accession members that calculated MPS in their base period, a subsequent benefit from using a more up-to-date FERP to calculate a smaller MPS materialized for only a few products (Brink 2020).

3.3.3   Acquisition at Administered Prices for Public Stockholding and AMS Support

The calculation and treatment of MPS with regard to the rules under *Public stockholding for food security purposes* (para. 3, Annex 2) is a major unresolved issue in the ongoing negotiations initiated soon after implementation of the Agriculture Agreement began. The consequences of MPS making AMS support exceed its limit(s) have later entered into consideration.

The Agreement's rules allow the exemption from AMS of a government's expenditures in relation to the accumulation and holding of stocks as an integral part of a food security program. One of the conditions for the exemption is that government food purchases shall be made at current market prices. The issue for analysis has been the Agriculture Agreement's footnote 5 in para. 3, which allows developing countries to exempt the expenditures even if they acquire and release the stocks at administered prices. The exemption is conditional on the member accounting for the difference between the administered price and the external reference price in the AMS. Although footnote 5 does not mention MPS, accounting for the price difference is conventionally interpreted as calculating MPS and including it in AMS as detailed in Annex 3.

The difference between the acquisition price, as the administered price, and the FERP from 1986–88 (or later for accession members) can indicate a large price gap, even when the AAP is close to the current market price. The conditionality formulated in the Agreement's footnote 5 in effect inhibits excessive producer support measured as an AMS by means of buying at an administered price but it does not impede the acquisition of stocks for food security purposes at market prices. In the continued negotiations, some developing country members suggested several options for changing the rules relating to this conditionality, some of which would effectively eliminate or override its inhibiting role under certain conditions. Other members worried about the trade consequences of such changes.

The WTO ministerial conference in 2013 and the General Council in 2014 took decisions on this issue on an interim basis, with arrangements remaining in place until a permanent solution is agreed and adopted. They essentially enable developing countries to exceed their limits on individual AMSs or BTAMS without risking a challenge under WTO dispute settlement rules, as long as the excessive AMS support results from accounting for the price gaps as per footnote 5. The decisions apply only to programs that existed when the 2013 decision was taken and provide support for traditional staple food crops. Conditions with regard to transparency and guarding against trade distortions are attached to the shelter. General and statistical information must be provided to the Committee on Agriculture on, for example, prices, production and trade using a given template.

India was by early 2022 the only member to have claimed shelter under the interim mechanism (for rice in 2018, 2019 and 2020) and remains a leading proponent of a permanent solution similar to the interim solution shielding against a dispute challenge of domestic support compliance. India is one of the world's top exporters of foodstuffs such as rice, sugar and bovine meat. Producers and exporters in other countries are therefore wary of the role that government purchases at administered prices may play in stimulating production or in building exportable stocks. Under the conditions governing the interim mechanism, several members requested consultations with India on such matters.

Acquisition at administered prices may not be the only or the best avenue to increase food security if, for example, a country's inadequate food security is the result of segments of its population not having the disposable income to obtain sufficient nutritional intake. High administered producer prices can raise consumer prices, but the acquired stocks can be used to provide food at lower prices to targeted segments of the population. It is not clear how acquiring the necessary quantities at market prices instead of administered prices might affect the ability of stockholding programs to meet their consumer-oriented objectives, such as releasing certain quantities of food to the targeted population.

A member's shift from acquiring the needed stocks at an administered price to acquiring them at the market price would eliminate the need to calculate MPS under the Agriculture Agreement, and acquisition for public stockholding would not be constrained by AMS limits. Focusing on the market effects of stockholding policies, OECD (2018) laid out a framework for evaluating the differences between buying at market prices and buying at administered prices. Among the eight Asian countries included in that analysis of public stockholding for rice, only two make publicly available the kind of stocks data that would facilitate economic analysis of a shift to acquisition at market prices. This is part of the explanation for the dearth of analysis of the implications for food security of such a shift.

3.3.4 Alternative Rules for MPS

Analysts have considered how the rules of the Agriculture Agreement on MPS calculations might be revised through negotiations to become more economically meaningful.[12] Montemayor (2014) explored for five developing countries, with reference to wheat and rice in a selected year in the 2008–11 time span, the effects on support measurements under different scenarios representing modified rules for calculating MPS. The scenarios differed in their definitions of reference price and eligible production. The large number of combinations for a given country were used to examine how much administered prices or eligible production would need to change in order for the product's AMS to be within its limit. Applying the rules for MPS calculation under most of the scenarios resulted in the countries exceeding their *de minimis* limits for product-specific AMSs.

Recognizing the problems associated with calculating MPS in conjunction with footnote 5 in para. 3 of Annex 2, Díaz-Bonilla (2017) suggested revising the footnote such that when the AAP is set at a level no higher than the domestic price corresponding to the border price plus any wedge resulting from import or export measures, the relevant price gap is nil, and no MPS is calculated. However, MPS would be calculated when the domestic market price for some reason was lower than the AAP and food stocks were being exported. Including MPS in AMS could then lead to the member's compliance with its AMS limit being challenged.

Replacing the FERP with a moving average of lagged border prices, as elaborated in Chapter 7, would bring the Agreement MPS into closer alignment with economic MPS. This would alleviate the concerns about the rules of the Agreement restricting too severely developing countries' use of administered prices when acquiring public stocks for food security purposes. Developing country groups included this option in negotiating proposals, and a similar option was suggested by Cahill and Tangermann (2021) and by Glauber and Sinha (2021). A draft decision for the 12th ministerial conference mentioned an assessment of the external reference price, raising the visibility of this issue (WTO 2022e).

---

[12] In addition to that mentioned in the following paragraphs, such analysis includes Orden et al. (2011), Hoda and Gulati (2013), Konandreas and Mermigkas (2014), Matthews (2014, 2015), Josling (2015), Galtier (2015, 2017), ICTSD (2016), Hoda (2017), Glauber and Sinha (2021) and Nedumpara et al. (2022).

3.4   Matching Agriculture Agreement Rules and Economic Policy Consequences

Economic analysis reinforces that AMS support and trade-distorting support are not synonymous. Art. 6 support is a more comprehensive measurement of trade-distorting support. Analysis of domestic support with regard to the rules of the Agriculture Agreement has focused on certain green-box exempted direct payments potentially having trade-distorting effects or effects on production and the compliance of measures providing such support with the policy-specific exemption criteria and conditions.

The calculation of MPS under the Agriculture Agreement, which differs from economic MPS, has been contentious and has come to the fore in negotiations and disputes. Issues arise about compliance with members' domestic support obligations, the economic implications of compliance of the Agreement's MPS with AMS limits, the eventual infeasibility of providing support by means of administered prices within those limits and the legal consequences of MPS resulting from acquisition at administered prices of public stocks for food security purposes making AMS support exceed its limit. These and other dimensions of domestic support under the Agriculture Agreement rules offer scope for further analysis to underpin members' policy choices.

Trends among Different Types of Domestic Support

Members submit notifications to the Committee on Agriculture under Art. 18.2 of the Agreement on Agriculture, reporting on the implementation of their domestic support commitments each year. This chapter reviews members' support based on the notified information and outlines trends and patterns over time between 1995 and 2018 both for all notifying members together and for members providing the most support. It also draws on certain notifications available for subsequent years at time of writing to highlight later developments. Notified support is presented by the Agreement's categories. Selected members' use of the AMS policy space afforded through *de minimis* allowances and BTAMS is examined. Several summations across categories of support are presented and comparisons made with measurements of support reported by the OECD. Transparency issues, including the requirements to notify, members' compliance with the timing and contents of notifications under those requirements and the review process in the Committee on Agriculture in relation to domestic support are discussed further in Chapter 5.

4.1 Notified Domestic Support

The review accounts for AMS support and exempted Art. 6.2, blue box and green box support of different types, based on the 1,384 so-called Table DS:1 notifications circulated from 1995 to mid-2021.[1] Notifications represent each member's own interpretations of the Agriculture Agreement regarding placement of support measures in the Agreement's categories and the amount of support they provide. These interpretations vary

---

[1] A Table DS:1 notification (annual for most members and bi-annual for LDC members) comprises the summary Table DS:1 and nine supporting tables showing support in all categories. Introduction of new or modified measures claimed as exempt from reduction are notified separately in Table DS:2 notifications (see Chapter 5).

among members and over time. Some members notify support in their own currency, others in USD, EUR or with other adjustments. Of the 136 members with domestic support schedules in mid-2021, a Table DS:1 notification for at least one year since 1995 had been submitted by 108. Most members notify domestic support with a delay of one or more years, sometimes many years. Seventy members had by mid-2021 submitted a domestic support notification for at least one of the years 2016–18. The number of members that had by mid-2021 submitted such a notification for the year declined from 67 members for 2016 to 53 and 42 members, respectively, for 2017 and 2018.[2] While outstanding notifications were mostly those of low-support members, China's latest notification by mid-2021 was only from 2016. India's notifications for 2018, 2019 and 2020 were more timely than its notifications in earlier years and contain information to support its case for seeking shelter from dispute challenge over its excessive rice AMS when acquiring public stocks at administered prices.[3]

Most tables in this chapter show members' support at five-year intervals from 1995 to 2015, followed by a preliminary 2016–18 average. Figures likewise end with a 2016–18 average. The preliminary 2016–18 average allows inclusion of support data for the 63 members notifying support other than nil for at least one year during this period. Where a member's notifications had data for the three years (36 members), the average uses this full information. For two years of such data (10 members), the two-year average is extrapolated as the 2016–18 average and, likewise, for only one year of such data (17 members), that year's support is extrapolated as the 2016–18 average.[4] While 2019 and 2020

---

[2] Among the 70 members notifying for at least one year during 2016–18 as of mid-2021, seven reported nil support either during 2016–18 or in 2016 or 2017 followed by no notification. No member went from notifying positive support in 2016 to notifying nil support in 2017 or 2018 (and likewise in 2017). Of the 70 members, 3 members did not notify for 2016, 2 of which notified support other than nil for 2017 (followed by no notification) and one for 2017 and 2018.

[3] India's domestic support notifications are in the WTO series G/AG/N/IND/* (e.g., G/AG/N/IND/27, circulated 1 April 2022, for marketing year 2020/21).

[4] The 10 members with two years of notified support other than nil for 2016–18 were Australia, Botswana, Canada, Guinea, Papua New Guinea, Saudi Arabia, Seychelles, Chinese Taipei, United Arab Emirates and Viet Nam. The 17 members with only one year of notified support other than nil were Argentina, China, Egypt, Thailand, Turkey and 12 others. A 2016–18 average is not calculated for several members that are relatively large agricultural producers because their latest notifications as of mid-2021 were only for earlier years, among them Pakistan (2015), South Africa (2014) and Ukraine (2012). The final averages for 2016–18 will eventually include support from additional members for

data were very partial at time of writing, notifications available from India and the United States allow additional discussion of their increased support in a later year. The 36 accession members are represented from their first full year of membership. Support in the various currencies members use in notifications is converted to USD.[5] Support is also expressed as percentages of values of production in agriculture evaluated at domestic prices (in this chapter, value of production is often abbreviated as VoP).

The top 15 members in terms of 8 categories or sums of support in 2016–18 are shown in descending order in Table 4.1. Among these members, the five members with the largest average Art. 6 support including non-exempt and exempt support were India, China, United States, EU and Japan, followed by Russia, Indonesia, Turkey, Brazil and Canada. The 10 members in that set in somewhat different order, and with Korea replacing Indonesia, also accounted for the largest amounts of the AMS category of Art. 6 support, which is the sum for each member of all positive product-specific AMSs and the non-product-specific AMS whether *de minimis* or larger.[6] The first five members of these sets plus Korea, Mexico, Switzerland, Thailand and Russia reported the largest amounts of green box support. Some members are included in Table 4.1 only because they reported significant Art. 6.2 support, while just a few members reported any blue box support. Many other members notified no AMS support, only Art. 6.2 support or only green box support. Some developing countries consistently reported that they provided no domestic support of any kind.

---

the 2016–18 period and information additional to the one or two years of data available by mid-2021 for 27 of the 63 members. The former will raise notified support, but the latter could make the final average smaller or larger depending on how support in the additionally notified years compares to support in the one or two years used to extrapolate the preliminary average.

[5] Support is expressed in nominal terms unless otherwise indicated. Exchange rates are notified currency per USD, annual average (IMF 2021). The data corresponds well with data in a WTO data base for 2001 onwards (WTO 2021f). A given year corresponds to a calendar year, marketing year, financial year or fiscal year in the notifications. For ease of reading, only the first part of any split year used by a member is usually indicated. Thus, for example, 2018 corresponds to that calendar year or to a member's notified year expressed as 2018/19 or as hyphenated 2018–19 (in contrast, the notation 2018–19 in this book stands for the two-year period 2018 and 2019).

[6] Calculated negative AMSs are not included since Art. 1 and Art. 6.1 refer to support in favor of producers and measures in favor of producers, respectively.

Table 4.1 Member rankings by eight domestic support categories, averages 2016–18

Art. 6 support A=B+E+F			AMS support B=C+D			Product-specific AMSs C			Non-product-specific AMS D		
Rank	Member	USD mill.	Rank	Member	USD mill.	Rank	Member	USD mill.	Rank	Member	USD mill.
1	India	30,469	1	China	23,292	1	China	19,415	1	United States	7,675
2	China	29,167	2	United States	19,486	2	United States	11,811	2	China	3,877
3	United States	19,486	3	EU	9,610	3	EU	8,491	3	Russia	2,669
4	EU	14,986	4	Japan	7,998	4	Japan	6,013	4	India	2,503
5	Japan	8,424	5	India	7,273	5	India	4,770	5	Japan	1,985
6	Russia	3,395	6	Russia	3,395	6	Norway	1,300	6	Brazil	1,663
7	Indonesia	3,149	7	Canada	2,134	7	Turkey	910	7	Canada	1,493
8	Turkey	2,841	8	Turkey	2,014	8	Korea	881	8	EU	1,119
9	Brazil	2,240	9	Brazil	1,744	9	Russia	726	9	Turkey	1,103
10	Canada	2,134	10	Korea	1,442	10	Canada	641	10	Switzerland	1,012
11	Norway	1,994	11	Switzerland	1,388	11	Israel	604	11	Korea	561
12	Thailand	1,964	12	Norway	1,323	12	Viet Nam	536	12	Viet Nam	268
13	Korea	1,442	13	Viet Nam	804	13	Saudi Arabia	427	13	Australia	173
14	Switzerland	1,388	14	Israel	644	14	Mexico	403	14	Saudi Arabia	106
15	Viet Nam	1,042	15	Saudi Arabia	532	15	Switzerland	376	15	Chinese Taipei	76

Art. 6.2 support E			Blue box support F			Green box support G			All domestic support H=A+G		
Rank	Member	USD mill.	Rank	Member	USD mill.	Rank	Member	USD mill.	Rank	Member	USD mill.
1	India	23,197	1	China	5,875	1	China	197,631	1	China	226,798
2	Indonesia	2,998	2	EU	5,376	2	United States	116,085	2	United States	135,571
3	Thailand	1,833	3	Norway	671	3	EU	74,192	3	EU	89,179
4	Turkey	828	4	Japan	640	4	India	24,539	4	India	55,009
5	Mexico	630	5	Iceland	6	5	Japan	16,935	5	Japan	25,360
6	Brazil	496				6	Korea	6,510	6	Korea	7,952
7	Colombia	374				7	Mexico	4,160	7	Russia	5,456
8	Philippines	364				8	Switzerland	2,748	8	Mexico	5,202
9	Egypt	343				9	Thailand	2,426	9	Indonesia	5,070
10	Viet Nam	239				10	Russia	2,061	10	Thailand	4,389
11	Sri Lanka	221				11	Indonesia	1,921	11	Switzerland	4,136
12	Peru	91				12	Viet Nam	1,769	12	Turkey	4,080
13	Nepal	77				13	Canada	1,760	13	Brazil	3,974
14	Mali	65				14	Brazil	1,734	14	Canada	3,894
15	Tunisia	62				15	Australia	1,399	15	Norway	2,966

Notes: See text for years entering 2016–18 averages. AMSs (positive values) included whether *de minimis* or larger.
SOURCES: Member notifications with USD conversion where applicable at annual average exchange rates (IMF 2021).

Table 4.2 *Members' positive BTAMS levels*

Developed members	BTAMS USD mill.	% of value of production	Developing members	BTAMS USD mill.	% of value of production
Original					
EU28	82,352	21.7%	Mexico	11,957	24.5%
Japan	35,972	37.6%	Korea	1,318	3.3%
United States	19,103	5.7%	Venezuela	1,131	4.1%
Switzerland	4,332	56.0%	Brazil	912	0.6%
Canada	3,292	7.4%	Israel	569	7.8%
Norway	1,385	39.5%	Thailand	563	1.6%
Australia	355	0.9%	Colombia	345	1.5%
New Zealand	202	1.3%	South Africa	147	0.7%
Iceland	182	63.1%	Argentina	75	0.2%
			Morocco	71	0.6%
			Papua New G.	34	na
			Tunisia	25	0.6%
			Costa Rica	16	0.3%
Sum	147,176		Sum	17,162	
Accession					
Russia	4,400	5.9%	Saudi Arabia	858	7.0%
Chinese Taipei	458	3.2%	Tajikistan	184	9.1%
Ukraine	115	0.4%	Viet Nam	178	0.4%
N. Macedonia	19	1.8%	Jordan	2	0.1%
Moldova	18	1.2%			
Montenegro	0	0.1%			
Sum	5,010		Sum	1,221	

Notes: Values are 2016–18 averages. Mexico's BTAMS scheduled in 1991 pesos multiplied by each year's notified deflator before USD conversion. Russia's 2016 BTAMS set equal to 2017 Final Bound Total AMS. Value of production for Venezuela refers to 2012–14. Not available (na); rounds to zero (0).
SOURCE: Authors' calculations from member schedules with USD conversion where applicable at annual average exchange rates. See Table 4.3 for source of values of production.

Table 4.2 provides additional overview information. It gives the USD values of the BTAMS for the 32 members with this flexibility in 2016–18. The positive BTAMS commitments are concentrated among developed country members and for these members among a few that provided the most support in their base period. The sum of the BTAMS of the EU, Japan and the United States amounted in 2016–18 to 80.6% of the USD 170.6 billion of BTAMS of all members. While the next largest BTAMS was Mexico's at USD 12.0 billion, the other 16 developing country BTAMS amounts were considerably less. Among members with smaller positive values of BTAMS, its value can correspond to a relatively high percentage of agricultural value of production (e.g., Iceland and Norway) or to a low percentage (e.g., Australia and Brazil). For members with the lowest BTAMS, the value of production of some products they support has increased to the point that the *de minimis* allowance for that product exceeds the member's BTAMS in which case the *de minimis* allowance becomes the binding limit.

4.2   Article 6 Support

Art. 6 support, that is, all domestic support other than green box support, showed a slightly declining linear trend between 1995 and 2016–18 (Figure 4.1), with the 2016–18 average total based on the 70 members that had submitted a domestic support notification for at least one of these years. Declines are seen for most years between 1996 and 2007, followed by years with mostly smaller increases. The 2015 peak in Art. 6 support was

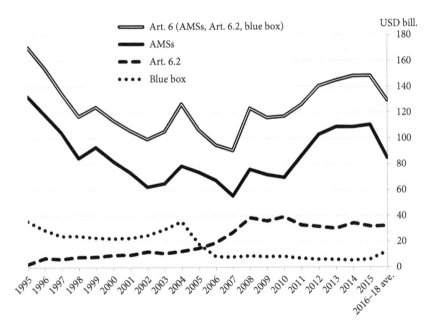

Figure 4.1   Article 6 support by category, 1995 to 2016–18 (USD billion).
Note: Positive AMSs only.
SOURCE: Member notifications with USD conversion where applicable.

still below the amounts of the mid-1990s. AMS support was the dominant category of Art. 6 support throughout the period. Art. 6.2 support has since 2006 replaced blue box support as the second largest category.

Table 4.3 shows the yearly Art. 6 support notified in total by members and by the five members with the largest support in 2016–18. Art. 6 support of the EU shows a sharp declining trend from the highest value in 1995 to fourth highest in 2016–18. Japan's Art. 6 support drops in the late 1990s then stabilizes, while Art. 6 support of the United States displays substantial variability but no evident trend. From 2005, Art. 6 support of all members rose from USD 106.6 billion to reach USD 148.5 billion in 2015 and then declined to USD 129.5 billion in 2016–18, particularly as China reported less support in 2016. India's Art. 6 support shows a strong upward trend from 1995 to become the largest of all during 2016–18. The sum for India and China of an average of USD 59.6 billion in Art. 6 support annually during 2016–18 exceeded the average sum of USD 42.9 billion of the United States, the EU and Japan.

Art. 6 support is concentrated among a relatively small number of members. The top five accounted for 79.2% in 2016–18, a decline from 90.0% in 1995. The sum of these five members' Art. 6 support and the USD 13.8 billion (Table 4.1) of the next five Art. 6 large-support members was USD 116.3 billion, accounting for 89.8% of all Art. 6 support in 2016–18.

Value of production in agriculture and Art. 6 support as a percentage of VoP are also shown in Table 4.3. World VoP more than doubled between 1995 and 2016–18, quadrupling in China and India, doubling in the United States and remaining stable or declining in the EU and Japan (a relatively low value of the euro explains the EU's relatively low VoP in USD in 2000).[7]

---

[7] Since many members' notifications do not give VoP, the review uses gross production values in agriculture in current USD from the FAO as the VoP measurement (FAO 2021). In mid-2021, this data included 114 of the then 136 WTO members with schedules. The differential set of 22 members are seen from other sources to have small or very small agricultural VoPs. The FAO VoPs in 2018 of the 114 WTO members summed to 96.4% of the FAO world VoP in agriculture, which includes several countries with a small VoP that were not members of the WTO. The difference between support as a percentage of the VoP of all WTO members and as a percentage of the world VoP is thus small in later years after declining since 1995 with the increase in the number of WTO members.

Table 4.3 Article 6 support, all notifications, India, China, United States, EU and Japan, 1995 to 2016–18

	1995	2000	2005	2010	2015	2016–18 average
	Article 6 support (USD million)					
All Art. 6 support	170,678	114,012	106,602	117,096	148,506	129,248
India	6,210	8,478	12,318	33,892	25,936	30,469
China	na	na	568	18,170	54,593	29,167
United States	14,729	24,184	18,923	10,113	17,185	19,486
EU	94,943	61,445	53,628	14,617	15,387	14,986
Japan	37,678	7,729	6,350	11,112	8,293	8,424
Sum of above 5 members	153,561	101,836	91,787	87,904	121,394	102,533
Share of above 5 in all Art. 6	90.0%	89.3%	86.1%	75.1%	81.7%	79.3%
	Value of production (USD million)					
World	1,563,301	1,418,805	2,025,403	3,392,843	3,794,029	3,707,070
India	100,606	101,420	152,583	331,574	351,777	402,719
China	271,744	301,759	472,112	891,003	1,196,725	1,201,742
United States	164,440	168,819	210,656	315,170	345,831	334,270
EU	312,486	232,349	313,794	385,628	362,960	378,776
Japan	128,446	90,865	87,489	104,475	81,513	95,690
Sum of above 5 members	977,722	895,211	1,236,635	2,027,849	2,338,805	2,413,198
Share of above 5 in world	62.5%	63.1%	61.1%	59.8%	61.6%	65.1%

Table 4.3 (*cont.*)

	1995	2000	2005	2010	2015	2016–18 average
			Article 6 support / Value of production			
World	10.9%	8.0%	5.3%	3.5%	3.9%	3.5%
India	6.2%	8.4%	8.1%	10.2%	7.4%	7.6%
China	na	na	0.1%	2.0%	4.6%	2.4%
United States	9.0%	14.3%	9.0%	3.2%	5.0%	5.8%
EU	30.4%	26.4%	17.1%	3.8%	4.2%	4.0%
Japan	29.3%	8.5%	7.3%	10.6%	10.2%	8.8%

Notes: AMSs (positive values) included whether *de minimis* or larger. World value of production in agriculture includes countries that were not WTO members in the given year (see text). China not a member (na).
Sources: Art. 6 support from member notifications with USD conversion where applicable. Value of production from FAO (2021) gross production values with USD conversion where applicable by FAO at official annual average exchange rates.

Art. 6 support declined from 10.9% of the world VoP in 1995 to less than 4% from 2010 through 2016–18. The declining percentage of trade-distorting support matches the long-term objective of the Agriculture Agreement. Among the five large-support members, only China with 2.4% was below the world percentage in 2016–18. The percentages of the United States and the EU exceeded the world level, and those of India and Japan were still larger at 7.6% and 8.8% of their agricultural VoP, respectively. While the EU percentages reveal a clear downward trend, the US trend, which started at a lower 1995 percentage than the EU, is less pronounced. Japan's percentage dropped sharply after 1995 then remained relatively stable. As further evidence of the concentration of Art. 6 support, the top five members' share of 79.2% of all Art. 6 support exceeded their 65.1% share of world agricultural VoP in 2016–18.

4.2.1 AMS Support

Only 48 of the 136 members had by mid-2021 notified AMS support other than nil in one year or more since 1995. They included members from combinations of the following categories: developed and developing country members, original and accession members and members with no or a nil BTAMS and those with a positive BTAMS. Out of this set of 48 members, 32 had by mid-2021 notified AMS support other than nil for 2016, 26 members had done so for 2017 and 19 for 2018.

AMS support followed a declining trend until about 2007 and then increased without reaching the levels of the mid-1990s. The pattern of AMS support drives the corresponding trend in Art. 6 support and the concentration of Art. 6 support among the large-support members. The start of an upward trend in AMS support in 2008 coincided with the sharp rise in world prices of many agricultural products and production inputs at that time. The yearly totals also include support of the growing number of accession members.

The yearly AMS support reported in total and by the five members with the largest AMS support in 2016–18, in descending order, China, United States, EU, Japan and India, is shown in Table 4.4. These five members accounted for 79.7% of all AMS support in 2016–18. The ten members with the largest AMS support included the five members mentioned plus Russia, Canada, Turkey, Brazil and Korea. Although these 10 members accounted for 92.4% of the AMS support in 2016–18, they represented only 71.8% of world agricultural VoP. Additional notifications will likely show that the concentration of AMS support remained pronounced.

Table 4.4 *AMS support, all notifications, China, United States, EU, Japan and India, 1995 to 2016–18*

	1995	2000	2005	2010	2015	2016–18 average
	AMS support (USD million)					
All AMS support	132,513	82,356	73,808	69,564	110,469	84,854
China	na	na	568	18,170	54,593	23,292
United States	7,699	24,184	18,923	10,113	17,185	19,486
EU	67,399	40,971	36,908	10,456	10,584	9,610
Japan	37,678	6,869	5,758	7,617	7,477	7,998
India	5,956	–	2	2,282	2,383	7,273
Sum of above 5 members	118,732	72,023	62,158	48,638	92,222	67,659
Share of above 5 in all AMS support	89.6%	87.5%	84.2%	69.9%	83.5%	79.7%
	AMS support / Value of production					
World	8.5%	5.8%	3.6%	2.1%	2.9%	2.3%
China	na	na	0.1%	2.0%	4.6%	1.9%
United States	4.7%	14.3%	9.0%	3.2%	5.0%	5.8%
EU	21.6%	17.6%	11.8%	2.7%	2.9%	2.5%
Japan	29.3%	7.6%	6.6%	7.3%	9.2%	8.4%
India	5.9%	–	0.0%	0.7%	0.7%	1.8%

Notes: AMSs (positive values) included whether *de minimis* or larger. China not a member (na); nil support notified (–); rounds to zero (0.0).
SOURCES: Member notifications with USD conversion where applicable.

Among the WTO's original members (which excludes China) those reporting the largest amounts of AMS support remained the same in 2016–18 as in 1995, although their relative ranking changed, partly explained by changes in policy. AMS support declined from 1995 in the EU and fell in the early years in Japan. China becoming the member reporting the largest AMS support by 2010 is part of a substantial shift in AMS support toward emerging-market members asserting developing country member status, although some developed members remain large-support members.[8] AMS support, in contrast to Art. 6 support, remains lowest for India among the top five AMS support providers.

The amount of AMS support in relation to VoP in agriculture is indicative of the emphasis members put on supporting producers through non-exempt measures, as distinct from other categories of support. Although this percentage declined significantly for the EU and Japan from 1995 to 2016–18, it remained higher for Japan than for other large-support members and the world level. The trends in AMS support as a percentage of VoP follow from changes in members' policies and VoPs in agriculture and also from changes in members' notification practices.

China's AMS support in 2016 exceeded the amount of any other member but, at 1.9% of China's agricultural VoP when extrapolated to 2016–18, it was the second lowest percentage in the group of five. Comparing 2016–18 to 1995, the AMS support of the United States more than doubled along with agricultural VoP. The percentage changed only little, with variability in intervening years. In contrast, the AMS support in the EU declined multifold as did the percentage although the VoP rose only modestly. Japan's AMS support and agricultural VoP were both on a flat trend from 2000, such that its percentage AMS support in 2016–18 remained higher than for members whose VoPs were trending up. The picture for India was different again. India's AMS support increased modestly between 1995 and 2016–18 although the intervening years saw less or no AMS support. As agricultural VoP quadrupled, India's percentage AMS support fell. All AMS support notified averaged USD 84.9 billion annually in 2016–18, which corresponded to 2.3% of the world VoP in agriculture and was well below the estimated theoretical maximum room for AMS support of USD 752 billion as calculated in Chapter 2.

AMS support can be further evaluated differentiating between product-specific and non-product-specific AMSs. Among product-specific AMSs, the distinctions between MPS, payment and other subsidy support and also the product concentration reveal members' policy

---

[8] Measuring China's MPS as determined for wheat and rice in *China – Agricultural Producers* would increase its product-specific AMSs during 2012–15, which would reinforce China's top rank. Whether China will revise its notifications through 2016, and how it will notify AMS support for 2017–19 in light of the dispute ruling, are unknown at time of writing. China's notification for 2020 may reflect steps it subsequently took to claim compliance with its obligations, discussed in Chapter 7. Issues that have been raised about India's MPS calculations are also discussed in Chapters 5 and 7.

choices. *De minimis* AMSs and CTAMS are the essential measurements for determining members' compliance with their commitments.

Product-Specific AMSs and Non-Product-Specific AMSs

While the distinction in the Agriculture Agreement between product-specific AMS support and non-product-specific AMS support is binary, in practice it is open to interpretation. The Agreement defines non-product-specific AMS support as being in favor of agricultural producers "in general" (Art. 1(a)) and the calculation of its *de minimis* allowance uses the total agricultural value of production. This might mean that this category should include only support measures offering support to all products. However, members often report as non-product-specific the support resulting from measures that benefit only some products (such as crops but not livestock or a group of crops but not all crops). Large amounts of support to the selected products can thus be included in the non-product-specific AMS that remains within its *de minimis* allowance.

Members who notify any AMS support often report both product-specific AMSs and a non-product-specific AMS, but some report only one or the other. From their first to their latest notified year, 23 members had by mid-2021 reported product-specific AMSs in every notified year, compared to 13 for non-product-specific AMS. Policies generating product-specific AMSs are thus used more consistently over time than those generating non-product-specific AMSs. The five members reporting the most product-specific AMS support in 2016–18 were in descending order China, United States, EU, Japan and India, followed by Norway, Turkey, Korea, Russia and Canada. The United States, China, Russia, India and Japan reported the most non-product-specific AMS support, followed by Brazil, Canada, EU, Turkey and Switzerland.

Product-specific AMSs account for the largest share of all AMS support. However, the share of product-specific AMSs in AMS support fell from over 90% in 1995 to less than 70% in 2016–18 both for the members with the most AMS support in 2016–18 and for all notifying members (Figure 4.2). The share of non-product-specific AMSs increased slightly through 2008 and more sharply thereafter. The large increase in non-product-specific AMS support was overwhelmingly the result of China rapidly increasing such support from 2007, although followed by an abrupt drop in 2016.

In 1995, the largest sums of product-specific AMSs, shown in Table 4.5, were those of the EU (USD 66.4 billion) and Japan (USD

USD bill.

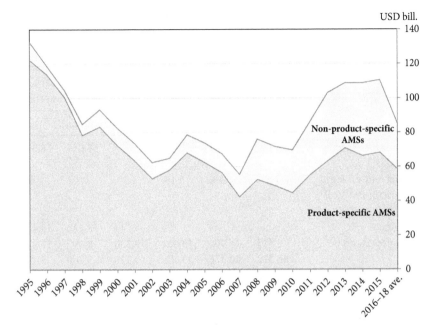

Figure 4.2   Product-specific and non-product-specific AMSs, 1995 to 2016–18 (USD billion).
Note: Positive AMSs only.
SOURCE: Member notifications with USD conversion where applicable.

37.4 billion), followed by the United States (USD 6.3 billion). In later years, China's USD 19.4 billion in 2016 was the most product-specific AMS support of any member even after declining from USD 33.2 billion in 2015. While these levels were much above the respective levels of the EU, Japan or the United States in 2015–17, the United States' product-specific AMS support was USD 17.4 billion in 2018, well above its 2016–18 average and of the same magnitude as China's support in 2016. India's product-specific AMS support stayed low for many years but then more than doubled from USD 2.3 billion in 2010 to an average of USD 4.8 billion in 2016–18, including USD 6.4 billion in 2018.

Regarding non-product-specific AMS support, in 1995 India reported the largest single such AMS (USD 5.8 billion) before it started to exempt

Table 4.5 *Product-specific AMS support and market price support, all notifications (AMS only), China, United States, EU, Japan and India, 1995 to 2016–18*

	1995	2000	2005	2010	2015	2016–18 average
	Product-specific AMSs (USD million)					
All product-specific AMSs	122,140	72,241	62,421	44,577	68,091	58,318
As percent of world agricultural VoP	7.8%	5.1%	3.1%	1.3%	1.8%	1.6%
China	na	na	300	3,744	33,150	19,415
United States	6,313	16,906	13,061	9,230	9,006	11,811
EU	66,372	40,476	35,590	9,528	9,760	8,491
Japan	37,422	6,675	5,593	6,868	5,288	6,013
India	184	–	2	2,282	2,049	4,770
Sum of above 5 members	110,291	64,056	54,546	31,653	59,254	50,500
Share of above 5 in all product-specific AMSs	90.3%	88.7%	87.4%	71.0%	87.0%	86.6%
	of which, MPS (USD million)					
China	na	na	–	212	23,505	15,714
United States	6,213	5,840	5,908	4,103	1,489	1,505
EU	61,836	28,596	20,027	7,406	7,551	6,977
Japan	34,779	4,676	3,581	4,489	3,661	4,201
India	184	–	2	2,282	2,049	4,770
Sum of MPS of above 5 members	103,013	39,112	29,518	18,492	38,255	33,166
Share of MPS in AMSs of above 5 members	93.4%	61.1%	54.1%	58.4%	64.6%	65.7%

Notes: Positive values of product-specific AMSs and MPS included whether *de minimis* or larger. China not a member (na); nil support notified (–).
SOURCES: Member notifications with USD conversion where applicable.

large amounts as Art. 6.2 support.[9] The non-product-specific AMS of the United States has shown significant annual variation and was the largest in the 1996–2006 period. China then for a period notified a larger non-product-specific AMS than any other member, but it fell from USD 21.4 billion to USD 3.9 billion between 2015 and 2016 due to declining non-product-specific input subsidies. This again made the non-product-specific AMS of the United States the largest, averaging USD 7.7 billion in 2016–18 and reaching USD 8.7 billion in 2018.

Market Price Support

MPS as distinct from producer payments and other subsidies was the dominant form of support of several of the participants in the Uruguay Round, which led in the negotiations to the inclusion of MPS in product-specific AMSs. MPS accounted for a large part of product-specific AMSs in the 1986–88 base period data submitted during that round, contributing to the BTAMS of the EU and Japan in particular. Table 4.5 (lower panel) shows MPS over time for the five members reporting the largest AMS support in 2016–18. In 1995, these members notified USD 103.0 billion in MPS, of which the EU accounted for USD 61.8 billion, Japan for USD 34.8 billion and the United States USD 6.2 billion. The top five providers of MPS in 1995 also included Switzerland (USD 3.6 billion) and Norway (USD 1.6 billion). Other members notified relatively small MPS amounts in their first notified year or in some or all later years, including Brazil, Canada, Indonesia, Mexico, Turkey and Viet Nam. Notified MPS in 1995 summed to around USD 109 billion.

The EU has reduced or eliminated support prices for many products over time, such that its MPS in 2016–18 was only about one-tenth of its 1995 level. This accounted for almost all of the decline in the EU product-specific AMSs. Japan's elimination of its support price for only rice in 1998 corresponded to almost all of the drop in Japan's product-specific AMSs after 1995. However, continued border protection meant that the domestic market price of rice did not decline significantly. Japan continued to report MPS for beef and, particularly, pork through 2018 in amounts only slightly below their 1995 levels. The United States revised its domestic dairy policy and by 2016–18 reported MPS only for sugar. After China raised its MPS from nil in 2002 to USD 23.5 billion in 2015 (not accounting for the panel rulings about MPS in *China – Agricultural*

---

[9] Non-product-specific support for selected years is AMS support in Table 4.4 minus the product-specific AMSs in Table 4.5.

Producers), it fell to USD 15.7 billion for wheat, rice and corn in 2016 and China then eliminated support prices for corn. India notified negative MPS for 10 products in 1995 and positive MPS only for sugarcane. By 2016–18 it calculated only one negative MPS and the number of products with positive MPS increased to eight. These MPS amounts accounted for all of India's product-specific AMSs in 2016–18. Switzerland had by 2015 abandoned MPS for a large number of products, while Norway kept its MPS amounts through 2018 only slightly less than in 1995.

The very large MPS reductions by the EU, Japan and the United States from 1995 levels explain much of the decline in all product-specific AMSs by 2016–18, although this effect was to some extent offset by the significant amounts of MPS observed in China and India. Altogether, the 15 largest Art. 6 support members showed more than 60 positive MPS products in their first notifications but only 29 such products in their notifications for 2016–18. The latest notified year by mid-2021 saw amounts of MPS larger than USD 2 billion for, in descending order, corn (China), rice (India), rice (China), butter (EU), pork (Japan), wheat (China) and wheat (EU).

The reporting by the EU and Japan and later by China of smaller amounts of MPS over time coincided with a shift to blue box and green box payments. Given that MPS is one of the potentially most distorting forms of support, the reduction or elimination of MPS, to the extent it corresponds to reduction or elimination of economic price support, is in line with the market-oriented objective of the Agriculture Agreement. Changing policy to support producers through blue box or green box compliant payments instead of MPS is thus a positive kind of box shifting, contrary to the negative sense sometimes given to this term.

Distribution of AMS Support among Product Categories

The sum of product-specific AMSs of the five large-support members declined by more than half over 1995 to 2016–18 and the distribution of this support shifted among them. The relative amounts of support among categories of products also changed noticeably. Table 4.6 shows the distribution of support across nine product categories in selected years for the five members providing in 2016–18 the most AMS support. These are percentages of quite different levels of product-specific AMS support, summing for the five members to USD 110.3 billion in 1995, falling to USD 31.7 billion in 2010 and increasing to USD 50.5 billion in 2016–18.

In 1995, cereals (mainly wheat, rice and corn) received about one-third of product-specific AMS support, four categories received between 13%

Table 4.6 *Product-specific AMSs by product category, large-support members summed, 1995, 2010 and 2016–18*

Product category	1995	2010	2016–18 average
	Percent of sum of positive product-specific AMSs		
Cereals	34%	33%	50%
Oilseeds	0%	5%	10%
Cotton and other fibers	1%	3%	7%
Fruits and vegetables	14%	2%	1%
Other crops	15%	11%	8%
Dairy	13%	27%	11%
Beef	19%	8%	5%
Pork	3%	12%	7%
Other livestock	0%	0%	1%
Sum	100%	100%	100%

Notes: Based on product-specific AMSs (positive values). Other crops include, *inter alia*, sugar, pulses, nuts and wine. Other livestock includes, *inter alia*, sheep and goats. Rounds to zero (0).
SOURCES: Notifications of China, United States, EU, Japan and India with USD conversion for China, EU and Japan.

and 19% each, and four other categories received no or little such support.[10] By 2010, the almost unchanged share of cereals AMSs masks large declines in the cereals AMSs of the EU and Japan, partially offset by increases in China and India. Policy changes in the EU explain the declines in the shares of fruits and vegetables, beef and other crops, mainly sugar. The increased percentage for oilseeds resulted from larger support in the United States and Japan. Although dairy AMSs in each of the EU, the United States and Japan declined, the larger declines in some other product categories resulted in a doubling of the dairy percentage. Japan maintained its AMS for pork almost unchanged between 1995 and 2010, which in combination with declines in other categories gave a large increase in the share of pork AMS in 2010.

Major increases in the cereals AMSs of China and India from 2010 contributed to this product category rising to account in 2016–18 for half of all

[10] The 1995 support was almost entirely that of the EU, United States and Japan, since China did not enter the summation and all of India's product-specific AMSs were negative except for sugarcane.

product-specific AMS support in the five large-support members. Increased oilseeds AMSs, primarily for soybeans in China and the United States, helped to double the share of this product category to 10%. Likewise, increased support for cotton, in China in particular, was part of the more than doubling to 7% of the fibers category. Less dairy support in the United States between 2010 and 2016–18 was a factor behind the large drop in the dairy percentage. While the amounts of beef and pork support, almost all in Japan, changed only very little, increases in other product categories made the beef and pork shares decline in 2016–18. The sums of support for other crops in the EU and the United States also changed only little between 2010 and 2016–18. While India raised support for pulses, increases in some other product categories dominated. The share of AMS support in the other crops category thus continued its decline in 2016–18.

Taken together, the support measured through product-specific AMSs became more concentrated on cereals, oilseeds and fibers (mainly cotton) over both the 1995 to 2010 period and the 2010 to 2016–18 period. These three product categories received 35% of all product-specific AMS support in 1995, which by 2016–18 had almost doubled to 67%. The sum of the shares of product-specific AMSs for fruits and vegetables, other crops and beef correspondingly fell during the 1995 to 2016–18 period.

De minimis AMSs and CTAMS

A member's whole amount of AMS support is informative but what matters for determining compliance with its limit or limits is the distribution of this support among a number of AMSs and in relation to any BTAMS entitlement. These limits differ among different groups of members.

The important distinctions between AMSs, their *de minimis* limits or thresholds and CTAMS and its limit are shown in Table 4.7 for the five members with the largest AMS support in 2016–18. The maximum theoretically available room for *de minimis* AMS support as calculated globally in Chapter 2 is divided for each member in Table 4.7 into room for product-specific and non-product-specific AMS support separately. China, with a nil BTAMS, and India, with no BTAMS, each used only minor shares of the available room within the respective sums of their *de minimis* limits on all potential product-specific AMSs.[11] The largest such share was the 33% of China in 2015 when its sum of product-specific

---

[11] The sum of *de minimis* limits or thresholds for product-specific AMSs in Table 4.7 is approximated as the member's *de minimis* percentage applied to its total agricultural value of production.

Table 4.7 *Use of* de minimis *allowances and BTAMS, China, India, United States, EU and Japan, 1995 to 2016–18*

	1995	2000	2005	2010	2015	2016–18 average
No or nil BTAMS						
China (8.5% *de minimis* percentage; nil BTAMS)						
Product-specific AMSs/ Sum of all potential limits	na	na	1%	5%	33%	19%
Non-product-specific AMS/Limit	na	na	1%	19%	21%	4%
India (10% *de minimis* percentage; no BTAMS)						
Product-specific AMSs/ Sum of all potential limits	2%	–	0%	7%	6%	12%
Non-product-specific AMS/Limit	57%	–	–	–	1%	6%
Positive BTAMS						
United States (5% *de minimis* percentage; BTAMS of USD 19.1 billion)						
Product-specific AMSs/ Sum of all potential thresholds	77%	200%	124%	59%	52%	71%
Non-product-specific AMS/Threshold	17%	86%	56%	6%	47%	46%
CTAMS/BTAMS	27%	88%	68%	27%	20%	36%
European Union (5% *de minimis* percentage; BTAMS of USD 82.4 billion)						
Product-specific AMSs/ Sum of all potential thresholds	425%	348%	227%	49%	54%	45%

Table 4.7 (*cont.*)

	1995	2000	2005	2010	2015	2016–18 average
Non-product-specific AMS/Threshold	7%	4%	8%	5%	5%	6%
CTAMS/BTAMS	64%	65%	42%	9%	10%	9%
Japan (5% *de minimis* percentage; BTAMS of USD 36.0 billion)						
Product-specific AMSs/ Sum of all potential thresholds	583%	147%	128%	131%	130%	126%
Non-product-specific AMS/Threshold	4%	4%	4%	14%	54%	41%
CTAMS/BTAMS	73%	18%	15%	15%	16%	16%

Notes: AMSs (positive values) included whether *de minimis* or larger. BTAMS of European Union and Japan converted to USD at 2016–18 annual average exchange rates. China not a member (na); nil support notified (–); rounds to zero (0).
SOURCE: Authors' calculations from notifications with USD conversion where applicable.

AMSs reached a peak of USD 33.2 billion, followed by a lower share in 2016. The corresponding shares for India were smaller but on an upward track, having reached 12% in 2016–18. For the non-product-specific AMS as a share of its limit, the percentages were generally lower for both China and India. China was an exception in 2010, while India's very large share in 1995 included types of support exempted under Art. 6.2 in subsequent years.

The US BTAMS is USD 19.1 billion and those of the EU and Japan average USD 82.4 billion and USD 36.0 billion, respectively, at 2016–18 exchange rates. Accommodated by their BTAMS entitlements, the sums of product-specific AMSs of the United States and of the EU greatly exceeded their respective summed *de minimis* thresholds of 5% of the VoP of all products in most of the first 10 years of the Agriculture Agreement but later remained well below these sums. Japan's sum of product-specific AMSs was not only much higher than the sum of their thresholds in the early years but also stabilized at levels that exceeded this sum. Regarding non-product-specific AMS, the United States used less than half of the threshold in 2016–18, a percentage below its level in the 2000s but above its level in 2010. The EU's non-product-specific AMS consistently accounted only for single-digit percentages of its threshold, while that of Japan rose to the neighborhood of half. As the non-product-specific AMSs of these three members were below their thresholds throughout the period to 2016–18, they did not enter their CTAMS.

The flexibility to exceed the thresholds on product-specific AMSs resulted in the early years in these three members using substantial parts of the room within the BTAMS. For the United States, while the share of CTAMS in BTAMS had stabilized at some 20–30% in the early 2010s, the 2016–18 average increased to 36%, reflecting a considerable increase to 68% in 2018. The increased use of the BTAMS room for product-specific support between 2015 and 2016–18 by the United States was in contrast to the stable use by the EU and Japan at significantly lower shares of 9% and 16%, respectively.

The United States, EU and Japan concentrated product-specific AMSs on a sub-set of all products in agriculture, although a larger sub-set than for China and India. There remained room to increase product-specific AMSs among the supported products and other products, whether within a product's *de minimis* threshold or entering CTAMS. Rising VoPs created more room within the AMS thresholds of the United States but less so for the EU. In Japan, the VoP in agriculture trended down from 1995, so at least some product-specific AMS thresholds declined along with the non-product-specific AMS threshold.

The analysis of AMSs of the five large-support members in selected years underscores observations that extend also to other members. This follows from members, by policy choice or for practical reasons, supporting only a sub-set of all the products in agriculture by means of AMSs and many of those AMSs not being close to their limits or thresholds. As the limits and thresholds rise along with VoP, AMSs have room to increase not only within present allowances but within larger future allowances.

Many members have reduced or eliminated AMS support and are far below their limits or thresholds on individual AMSs. However, there have been exceptions where members with no or a nil BTAMS have calculated an AMS in excess of its *de minimis* limit. Although mainly involving members with a smaller agriculture sector, China, India and Turkey, all with a large agriculture sector, have also reported excessive

AMSs for one or more products and years.[12] While several members with a positive BTAMS do not notify any AMSs or any that are large enough to enter the CTAMS, most report some product-specific AMSs in excess of their *de minimis* thresholds and include them in the CTAMS, which often remains well below the limit.[13] A few members have, however, notified a CTAMS in excess of their positive BTAMS commitments: Costa Rica, Iceland, Israel, Jordan and Norway.[14] An important factor behind the excessive CTAMS of most of these members was the amount of MPS for a small number of products rather than for a range of products or support in the form of payments and other subsidies.

4.2.2   Article 6.2 Support

About half of the number of developing countries used the Art. 6.2 exemption in at least one of the years between 1995 and 2018.[15] One-time or intermittent exemptions or highly variable exempted amounts reveal variability in subsidization or its reporting or both. Notifications of Art. 6.2 exemptions differ in level of detail and rarely describe how policies meet the criteria or how support is measured. While many exempted Art. 6.2 amounts were small compared to those of a handful

---

[12] China notified some excessive AMSs in 2011–16 for corn, cotton, soybeans, rapeseed and sugar; China's wheat and rice AMSs were notified within limit but were found in *China – Agricultural Producers* to exceed the limits for 2012–15. India calculated excessive AMSs for rice in 2018, 2019 and 2020, invoking shelter against a dispute challenge under the 2013 ministerial decision on acquisition of public stocks at administered prices. Turkey reported excessive AMSs in 2010–13 involving premium payments for certain oilseeds and cotton.

[13] Australia, Brazil, Colombia, Costa Rica, Moldova, New Zealand, Papua New Guinea, South Africa, Tunisia (calculated only with inflation adjustment) and Viet Nam reported a nil CTAMS in their latest notifications by mid-2021. The members with the largest BTAMS relative to VoP in agriculture calculated a CTAMS closely below BTAMS (Iceland and Norway) or at about one-third of BTAMS (Switzerland).

[14] Costa Rica's price support for rice made its CTAMS exceed BTAMS during 2007–14. Iceland's CTAMS in 2002 and 2003 exceeded BTAMS when calculating MPS without inflation adjustment but CTAMS was below BTAMS with inflation adjustment. Israel's price support for eggs and milk made its CTAMS exceed BTAMS during 2011–14. Jordan reported an excessive 2014 CTAMS without inflation adjustment but a nil CTAMS after inflation adjustment. While Norway's CTAMS exceeded BTAMS in 2008, Norway the following year revised its price support policy for beef to come into compliance

[15] Fifty-four developing country members have claimed Art. 6.2 exemptions. In addition, six members made Art. 6.2 exemptions in their base documentation in the Uruguay Round but have not reported such exemptions in yearly notifications. Romania exempted Art. 6.2 support prior to its EU membership.

of members, they can be a significant part of a member's total domestic support. Members classified most Art. 6.2 support as input subsidies, less as investment subsidies and still less as support to encourage diversification from growing illicit narcotic crops.[16]

Art. 6.2 support was rising only slowly at a low level from 1995 and then rose more rapidly from the mid-2000s. It reached two almost equal peaks in 2008 and 2010, coinciding with India exempting unusually large amounts of input subsidies in those years (India's fertilizer subsidies peaked in 2008). The amount of Art. 6.2 exemptions then stayed relatively stable at a higher level than before the peaks. At their peaks in 2008 and 2010, the Art. 6.2 exemptions were large enough to exceed by a small margin the peak amount of blue box exemptions in 2004.

The 10 members exempting the largest average annual amounts under Art. 6.2 during 2016–18 were, in descending order, India, Indonesia, Thailand, Turkey, Mexico, Brazil, Colombia, Philippines, Egypt and Viet Nam. Their yearly amounts ranged from India's USD 23.2 billion down to a few hundred million USD. While Mexico exempted USD 0.6 billion of such support in 2016–18, it had exempted USD 3.8 billion in 2002 pertaining to an overhaul of its rural credit system.

India is the outlier among the members using the Art. 6.2 exemption. Its exempted amounts increased rapidly from 1995, peaking at more than USD 31.6 billion in 2008 and 2010, and then declined in subsequent years (India's later 2019 and 2020 notifications reported USD 25.1 billion and USD 30.9 billion, respectively). India's Art. 6.2 exemption has been large enough to swamp the combined Art. 6.2 exemptions of the other members (Table 4.8). India alone accounted for 80.7% of all Art. 6.2 support in 2010 and 72.4% in 2016–18. India has reported a much larger share of members' input subsidies than of investment subsidies exempted under Art. 6.2 (Brink 2015b). While not shown in its notifications, India informed the Committee on Agriculture that its 2018 input subsidies included fertilizer (USD 10.5 billion), irrigation (USD 3.7 billion) and electricity (USD 10.0 billion). The relative shares by type of subsidy were similar in earlier years.

---

[16] Some support claimed as investment subsidies under Art. 6.2 relates to subsidized short-term or operating credit for current input use rather than investments in the sense of capital outlays with a return over several years. This support might be exemptible as input subsidies under Art. 6.2 if it is generally available to low-income or resource-poor producers. The distinction could matter if certain investment aids remain exemptible under the green box and Art. 6.2 support became subject to limit or if input subsidies but not investment subsidies became subject to limit.

Table 4.8 *Article 6.2 and Article 6.5 support, all notifications and large-support members, 1995 to 2016–18*

	1995	2000	2005	2010	2015	2016–18 average
	Art. 6.2 support (USD million)					
All Art. 6.2 support	2,444	9,450	14,874	39,144	31,764	32,040
As percent of world agricultural VoP	0.2%	0.7%	0.7%	1.2%	0.8%	0.9%
India	254	8,478	12,316	31,610	23,553	23,197
Indonesia	–	–	276	2,265	3,070	2,998
Thailand	215	67	0	nn	0	1,833
Turkey	–	–	124	609	877	828
Mexico	605	54	723	1,225	787	630
Sum of above 5 members	1,075	8,600	13,439	35,709	28,287	29,486
Share of above 5 in all Art. 6.2 support	44.0%	91.0%	90.4%	91.2%	89.1%	92.0%
	Blue box support (USD million)					
All blue box support (Art. 6.5)	35,721	22,206	17,921	8,388	6,273	12,355
As percent of world agricultural VoP	2.3%	1.6%	0.9%	0.2%	0.2%	0.3%
China	na	na	–	–	–	5,875
EU	27,545	20,474	16,720	4,161	4,803	5,376
Norway	1,123	871	608	727	649	671
Japan	–	860	592	3,495	815	426
Iceland	22	–	–	5	5	6
Sum of above 5 members	28,691	22,206	17,921	8,388	6,273	12,355
Share of above 5 in all blue box support	80.3%	100.0%	100.0%	100.0%	100.0%	100.0%

Notes: China not a member (na); not notified (nn); nil support notified (–); rounds to zero (0).
SOURCES: Member notifications with USD conversion where applicable.

The total yearly support exempted under Art. 6.2 during 2016–18 averaged USD 32.0 billion, as notified by 29 members by mid-2021. For most members, the amount exempted corresponded to less than 2% of VoP in agriculture, which is small relative to the limit or threshold of 10% of VoP applying to non-product-specific AMS. However, India's Art. 6.2 exemption averaged 5.8% of VoP in 2016–18, which freed up significant room for potential AMS support. It is not clear whether Art. 6.2 support, if it were not exemptible, would be only non-product-specific AMS support.

4.2.3 Blue Box Support

Art. 6.5 (blue box) support reached its highest amounts at almost the same levels in 1995 and 2004. From 2004, the amount declined to a relatively low level, which stayed flat for many years. Significantly more blue box support was then exempted in 2016, with much of the increase accounted for by China starting to exempt blue box payments. The amount of blue box support in 2016 nevertheless remained much below its 2004 peak. Only five members notified blue box support in at least one of the years 2016–18 (Table 4.8).

The EU and the United States were the initial large-support users of the blue box exemption. The EU over time exempted declining amounts of blue box payments, a result of policy changes under which the EU claimed large amounts of direct payments as green box exempt. Its blue box exemption started at USD 27.5 billion in 1995, peaked at USD 33.8 billion in 2004 before that year's policy change decision took effect and then declined to USD 5.4 billion in 2016–18, or 1.4% of VoP in agriculture. The decline occurred while the number of EU member states increased through EU enlargement. The United States exempted blue box payments of USD 7.0 billion only in 1995.

Only a small number of other members have utilized the blue box exemption. Five members reported blue box exemptions prior to joining the EU. Norway has exempted blue box payments since 1995, declining to an average of USD 0.7 billion in 2016–18 but still corresponding to 19.1% of VoP in agriculture. Iceland has exempted only small amounts. When Japan changed its price support policy for rice, it began making rice payments that it exempted from CTAMS as blue box, peaking at USD 3.5 billion in 2010. These rice payments averaged USD 0.6 billion in 2016–17, after which the payments ended, giving a

2016–18 average of USD 0.4 billion. China's policy changes in 2016 included making payments claimed as blue box exempt to corn producers, amounting to USD 5.9 billion, about 0.5% of VoP in agriculture and 9.0% of corn VoP.

The blue box exemption is thus important to China and particularly to Norway, which carefully manages blue box payments and CTAMS together in relation to BTAMS. It has become much less important to the EU, Iceland and Japan. The EU and Japan have much room within their BTAMS, which reduces the need to exempt payments from AMSs. As blue box payments tend to relate to specific products or groups of products, being able to exempt them can be significant for a member facing potentially binding limits on product-specific AMSs as China does. It remains to be seen whether future notifications include blue box claims by only a few members.

4.3   Green Box Support

Almost all members who have notified any domestic support to the Committee on Agriculture have reported support under Annex 2 (green box), at least in the form of expenditures on *General services*. Figure 4.3 shows all green box support and the part delivered as direct payments (paras. 5–13, Annex 2). Table 4.9 shows corresponding numerical detail, including the green box support of the members with the most such support in 2016–18, in descending order, China, United States, EU, India and Japan. Members exempted an annual average total of USD 464.9 billion as green box support in 2016–18, including USD 180.2 billion in direct payments, even with numerous notifications still outstanding. The green box support of USD 129.3 billion in 1995 was less than Art. 6 support at that time. From 2001, green box support increased through direct payments and even more through other expenditures. The continued increases made green box support in 2016–18 more than three times larger than Art. 6 support, shown for comparison in Figure 4.3. Green box support rose from 8.3% of world VoP in 1995 to 12.5% in 2016–18. This is a second substantial development toward less trade-distorting support, as envisioned under the objective of the Agriculture Agreement.

The evolution of green box support results from several factors. Including China's green box support of USD 30.5 billion in 2002 as its first full year as a member meant a 27% increase over the USD 112.3 billion notified for 2001 by all other members. China subsequently increased its

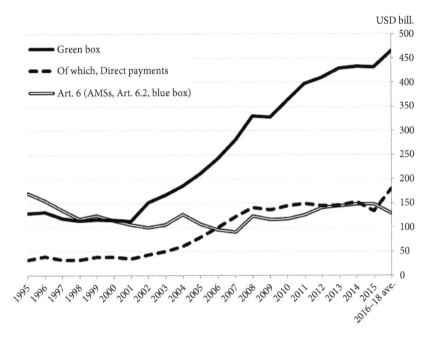

USD bill.

- Green box
- Of which, Direct payments
- Art. 6 (AMSs, Art. 6.2, blue box)

Figure 4.3 Green box support and Article 6 support, 1995 to 2016–18 (USD billion). Notes: Positive AMSs only. Direct payments are payments under paras. 5–13, Annex 2. SOURCE: Member notifications with USD conversion where applicable.

green box support by USD 167.1 billion from 2002 to 2016, making it the largest contributor to the total green box increase. Moreover, by increasing green box support and making policy changes that replaced earlier non-green-box support with green box support, other members increased the green box total, as did the accession of numerous more members. Changes in reporting practices to claim a larger share of domestic support as green box support also contributed marginally to the increase.[17]

[17] For example, before 2017 India accounted for its insurance premium subsidy entirely as AMS support but in 2017 split it into two parts with regard to production losses exceeding and not exceeding 30%. The former is reported as green box support and the latter as AMS support, despite the conceptual difficulty in measuring insurance subsidies by dividing indemnities paid on such an *ex post* basis. This reporting change, which might be questioned in terms of consistency with the Agreement, did not affect earlier years' amounts. Japan has reported separated crop insurance premium subsidies in a similar way since 1995.

Table 4.9 Green box support, all notifications, China, United States, EU, India and Japan, 1995 to 2016–18

	1995	2000	2005	2010	2015	2016–18 average
			Green box support (USD million)			
All green box support (Annex 2)	129,334	114,728	211,072	363,117	432,008	464,941
As percent of world agricultural VoP	8.3%	8.1%	10.4%	10.7%	11.4%	12.5%
China	na	na	37,778	78,968	173,941	197,631
United States	46,041	50,057	72,328	118,958	121,477	116,085
EU	24,814	20,129	50,092	90,129	67,917	74,192
India	2,196	2,851	5,907	19,479	18,391	24,539
Japan	33,691	24,083	17,386	17,349	14,448	16,935
Sum of above 5 members	106,742	97,120	183,492	324,883	396,173	429,383
Share of above 5 in all green box support	82.5%	84.7%	86.9%	89.5%	91.7%	92.4%

of which, Direct payments (USD million)

All Direct payments	32,227	38,693	79,814	143,892	134,216	180,202
As percent of world agricultural VoP	2.1%	2.7%	3.9%	4.2%	3.5%	4.9%
As percent of Green box support	24.9%	33.7%	37.8%	39.6%	31.1%	38.8%
China	na	na	11,306.8	30,648.3	53,743.5	89,040.9
United States	2,152	9,126	10,311	10,969	5,353	4,565
EU	17,817	15,492	42,558	77,866	58,843	65,844
India	228	136	207	4,542	21	4,044
Japan	4,180	3,506	3,840	6,501	4,785	5,300
Sum of above 5 members	24,377	28,260	68,223	130,527	122,745	168,793
Share of above 5 in all Direct payments	75.6%	73.0%	85.5%	90.7%	91.5%	93.7%

Note: China not a member (na).
SOURCES: Member notifications with USD conversion where applicable.

Sixty-three members had since 1995 claimed exemption by mid-2021 from their AMS calculations for support under one of the nine direct payment headings in Annex 2 in at least one year. Forty-one members had done so for at least one year during 2016–18. Direct payments accounted for less than 30% of all green box support in the 1990s, increasing by 2016–18 to 38.8%, having risen from 2.1% to 4.9% of world VoP in agriculture (Table 4.9).

China exempted the largest amount of direct payments in 2016 (USD 89.0 billion), of which one third was classified as *Payments under regional assistance programmes*. China's second largest direct payment category was *Decoupled income support* and *Payments under environmental programmes* were also large, mostly involving forestation. India's exempted direct payments varied greatly between years. The USD 4.0 billion average in 2016–18 included a USD 8.1 billion waiver of agricultural loans in 2017 (mainly short-term credit) under the green box heading relating to investment aids.

The EU average annual exemption of direct payments was USD 65.8 billion in 2016–18. This included BPS payments as *Decoupled income support* and SAPS payments as *Direct payments to producers* (USD 33.5 billion and 9.0 billion, respectively), both resulting from the shift away from AMS support, as well as payments referring to structural adjustment through investment aids and environmental programs. The United States exempted direct payments of USD 4.6 billion in 2016–18, almost all as *Payments under environmental programmes*, mainly in the form of conservation programs. Japan exempted direct payments of USD 5.3 billion, mostly involving maintenance of rice paddy fields in environmentally good condition under the environmental programs heading. Altogether, the sum of the amounts China, the United States, the EU and Japan exempted under this heading roughly doubled between 2005 (USD 18 billion) and 2016–18 (USD 35 billion). This was mainly because China's exemptions more than tripled, but the exemptions of the United States, the EU and Japan also increased significantly. India exempted little or nil support under environmental programs in these years.

The five large-support members reveal great diversity in the categories of *General services* to which they allocated their largest expenditures in 2016–18. While China reported the majority (54%) of its expenditure as Other, comprising mainly operating and administrative expenditures, its research expenditures were less than 4%. In contrast, research was India's largest share (28%) within a much smaller total expenditure than for China. Research was the second largest share of the EU (19%) and the United States (20%) but only a minor one of Japan (6%). Expenditure on infrastructural services was China's second largest share (26%), related to investments such as as for irrigation and transportation. Expenditure on infrastructural services was also India's second largest share (27%) but only a minor one in the EU. In the United States, infrastructural services was the largest *General services* share (29%), consisting entirely of crop insurance services (mainly reimbursement of private firms for insurance contract administrative and delivery costs). Japan's largest exemption was for physical infrastructure services pertaining to, for example, construction of irrigation facilities and roads (53%).

Only few members have reported green box expenditures under the headings of *Public stockholding for food security purposes* or *Domestic food aid*. India exempted the most expenditure under the public stock-holding heading, averaging USD 17.2 billion in 2016–18. The United States reported large expenditures as *Domestic food aid*, averaging USD 98.3 billion in 2016–18. With no requirement that eligible food be produced in the United States, it is not clear how this or similar expenditure by other members corresponds to the Agreement's notion of support in favor of agricultural producers. While notifying it makes this subsidy to food consumers more transparent, a separate estimate of the related amount that constitutes support for agricultural producers might be more relevant to domestic support measurement.

4.4 Summations of Support

4.4.1 Six Sums of Domestic Support

Summations of support using all members' notified data are shown in Figure 4.4 and Table 4.10. The first summation is the least inclusive. It is the sum of all AMS support, the measurement that is subject to limits under the Agreement which apply differently to different members.

The second summation adds blue box support to the AMS support. Participants in the Doha Round negotiations through 2008 often denoted this subset of Art. 6 support as the Overall Trade-Distorting Support (OTDS) in spite of not including Art. 6.2 support. Limiting the OTDS of many members was proposed but not agreed, as discussed in Chapter 6. As blue box exemptions declined, the difference between AMS support and the OTDS narrowed through 2015 and then increased with China's exemption of blue box payments in 2016.

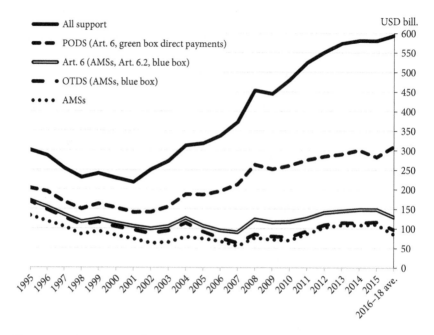

Figure 4.4   Summations of support categories, 1995 to 2016–18 (USD billion).
Notes: Positive AMSs only.
SOURCE: Member notifications with USD conversion where applicable.

The third summation is Art. 6 support: all support that is not exemp-tible on green box grounds. Larger Art. 6.2 exemptions caused OTDS to fall further below Art. 6 support over time, especially since 2005.

The fourth summation is a still more-inclusive indicator of the support that goes most directly to producers. The measurement of Producer-Oriented Domestic Support (PODS) is defined here as the sum of Art. 6 support and direct payments in the green box (paras. 5–13, Annex 2). PODS thus comprises all types of producer-oriented support without distinguishing between support with more and with less distorting effects. PODS is more inclusive than the OTDS by including not only all Art. 6 support but also green box direct pay-ments. The rationale is that, even though the green box allows the exemption of some direct payments to producers from limit, such

Table 4.10 *Summations of support categories, 1995 to 2016–18*

	1995	2000	2005	2010	2015	2016–18 average
	Summations of support (USD billion)					
Sum of AMSs	132.5	82.4	73.8	69.6	110.5	84.9
Overall Trade-Distorting Support (OTDS)	168.2	104.6	91.7	78.0	116.7	97.2
Art. 6 support	170.7	114.0	106.6	117.1	148.5	129.2
Producer-oriented domestic support (PODS)	202.9	152.7	186.4	261.0	282.7	309.5
All domestic support	300.0	228.7	317.7	480.2	580.5	594.2
Exempt support (Art. 6.2, blue box, green box)	167.5	146.4	243.9	410.6	470.0	509.3
	Summations of support / World agricultural VoP					
Sum of AMSs	8.5%	5.8%	3.6%	2.1%	2.9%	2.3%
Overall Trade-Distorting Support (OTDS)	10.8%	7.4%	4.5%	2.3%	3.1%	2.6%
Art. 6 support	10.9%	8.0%	5.3%	3.5%	3.9%	3.5%
Producer-oriented domestic support (PODS)	13.0%	10.8%	9.2%	7.7%	7.5%	8.3%
All domestic support	19.2%	16.1%	15.7%	14.2%	15.3%	16.0%
Exempt support (Art. 6.2, blue box, green box)	10.7%	10.3%	12.0%	12.1%	12.4%	13.7%

Note: AMSs (positive values) included whether *de minimis* or larger. See text for categories of support included in OTDS and PODS.
SOURCES: Authors' calculations from member notifications with USD conversion where applicable.

payments are nevertheless support going to agricultural producers. In contrast, green box expenditures on *General services, Public stockholding for food security purposes* and *Domestic food aid* are often not conceptually or in common parlance associated in a direct way with support received by producers.

Through 2000, PODS exceeded Art. 6 support by a stable amount of less than USD 40 billion. Subsequently, the increased direct payments in the green box made PODS rise, creating a large gap between PODS and Art. 6 support. Direct payments in the green box were the largest component of PODS since 2010.

The fifth summation is the sum of all Art. 6 and green box domestic support, that is, all non-exempted and exempted support, which gives the broadest perspective on the evolution of domestic support. It exceeds AMS support by the sum of the support exempted as Art. 6.2, blue box and green box support. The all-support summation exceeds PODS by the amounts of non-payment green box expenditures.

The sum of all domestic support rose from USD 300.0 billion in 1995 to USD 594.2 billion in 2016–18. While AMS support subject to limit has shown some variation and decline over time, these are minor compared to the near doubling of total support. The sum of all support also increased more sharply than PODS, attributable to increases in non-payment green box support.

The observed rise in all domestic support relates to it being a nominal amount and the number of WTO members having increased. While all support increased substantially since 1995, it was relatively stable from 2000 through 2016–18 at around 14–16% of world VoP in agriculture. China's sum of all support stood at USD 226.8 billion in 2016 (Table 4.1), which means that all other members' support (excluding China but including other accession members) only increased from USD 300.0 billion in 1995 to an average of USD 367.4 billion in 2016–18.

If all domestic support except China's had increased *pari passu* with the increase from 1995 to 2016–18 in the world's agricultural VoP excluding China, all support of members other than China would have increased by USD 281.9 billion. The actual USD 67.4 billion increase in the support of all members other than China was thus less than one-quarter of this counter-factual increase. All support of members other than China fell from 23.2% of their agricultural VoP in 1995 to 14.7% in 2016–18. Art. 6 support of these members fell by USD 70.4 billion and from 13.2% to

4.0% of their VoP, while their green box support rose by USD 138.0 billion, that is, a slight increase from 10.0% of VoP to 10.7%.[18]

A final summation in Table 4.10 (not in Figure 4.4) shows the evolution of all support exempted from limit as Art. 6.2, blue box or green box support. It tripled from USD 167.5 billion in 1995 to USD 509.3 billion in 2016–18. The major contribution to the increase came from larger green box exemptions, while increased Art. 6.2 exemptions were offset by reduced blue box exemptions. By 2016–18, exempt support summed to 85.7% of all notified support.

4.4.2   Comparing Notified WTO Domestic Support and OECD Measurements of Support

In the OECD measurements of policy support, calculated with different methods than under the Agriculture Agreement, a concept of producer orientation of support underlies the Producer Support Estimate or PSE (OECD 2021a). The OECD PSE includes most direct payments, while expenditures on many of the general services identified in Agriculture Agreement Annex 2, as well as the cost of public stockholding, are included in the OECD's General Services Support Estimate (GSSE). Domestic food aid of several kinds is accounted for in the OECD's Consumer Support Estimate.

In the PODS summation, the policy coverage and payments measurement are similar to those of the OECD PSE for budgetary transfers. However, the measurements of MPS differ in terms of products, price gaps and relevant quantities. The difference between a member's notified MPS, which enters PODS, and its economic MPS, which enters PSE, can be large.

With these differences in mind, interpreting the PODS summation benefits from relating it to its PSE counterpart. PODS amounted to USD 309.5 billion and the sum of positive PSEs of a group of 54 countries covered by OECD was USD 480.6 billion in 2016–18.[19] The ranking of

---

[18] The support amounts and percentages of VoP excluding China are not shown in Table 4.10 but can be computed for the selected years from the previous tables.

[19] The OECD (2021c) reported support through 2020 covering EU as an entity (including its OECD and non-OECD members), all other OECD members, and major non-OECD emerging economies. As many members' notifications to the WTO lag by years, the more timely availability of PSE and GSSE for many countries, and aggregation with other data for the AgIncentives (2021) consortium, contributes to transparency. Negative PSEs calculated by the OECD for some countries are excluded from the sum compared to PODS. The OECD coverage included South Africa and Ukraine that had notified domestic support to the WTO only for earlier years than 2016–18 by mid-2021 and thus are not included in PODS for these years.

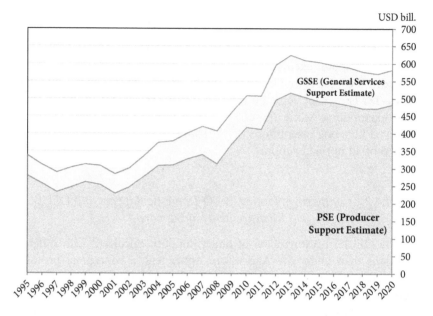

Figure 4.5 Support measurements of the OECD, 1995–2020 (USD billion).
Note: Positive PSEs only.
SOURCE: OECD (2021c).

members by the size of PSE also differs from the rankings in Table 4.1. The members with the five largest average PSEs in 2016–18 were, in descending order, China, EU, Japan, United States and Indonesia. In contrast, India ranked among the lowest countries because negative economic MPSs for some products made its PSE negative.

While PODS showed a declining trend to the early 2000s, followed by an increasing tendency, the PSE trend was flat from 1995 to the early 2000s, followed by a rising tendency (Figure 4.5). The two separate sources of support data, of which the PSE is more based on economic principles, thus consistently identify a trend shift in the mid-2000s. PODS increased in nominal terms by 53% from 1995 to 2016–18 and PSE increased by 72%, in part as the number of countries for which support was measured increased for both measurements. However, as world agricultural VoP more than doubled, the support directed at agricultural producers whether measured as PODS or PSE declined over time on a percentage of VoP basis.

The sum of expenditures exempted under the Agreement's headings of *General services, Public stockholding for food security purposes* and *Domestic food aid* can be compared to the support in the OECD's GSSE. The general services policies covered by those measurements are largely the same. The expenditures under these three paragraphs of Annex 2 declined for a few years from 1995 before commencing steady growth from 2002 with the inclusion of China's expenditures. GSSE showed only a slight upward trend. In 2016–18, the expenditures under these three paragraphs reached USD 284.7 billion, while GSSE amounted to USD 106.2 billion. The large difference is partly explained by the United States' inclusion of USD 98.3 billion as *Domestic food aid*, which is not part of GSSE. Another part of the explanation is the difference between India's USD 17.2 billion average expenditure in 2016–18 on *Public stockholding for food security purposes* and its USD 1.1 billion in GSSE as cost of public stockholding. The differences in trend and magnitude of support under these three paragraphs of Annex 2 and in GSSE underscore the differences in policy representations which can involve large amounts of support.

4.5   Increased Support by India and the United States, 2016–19

Art. 6 support of India and the United State increased after the mid-2010s, resulting in larger average support during 2016–18 than in 2015. The year-over-year increases in their respective Art. 6 support during that period continued in 2019.

Regarding India, the sum of support increased from USD 48.1 billion in 2016 to USD 68.7 billion by 2019. About half of the increase came from green box support. India's green box support reached more than USD 30 billion in 2017 and 2019, respectively due largely to renewed loan waivers (USD 8 billion) and expansion of a program of decoupled income support (USD 6 billion) that had been initiated in 2018.

About one-quarter of the increase of India's support arose from new agricultural credit subsidies included in the non-product-specific AMS and an increase of Art. 6.2 support (USD 2.1 billion and USD 2.3 billion, respectively). Another quarter of the increase arose from MPS, particularly for rice as higher AAPs increased the price gap when compared to the external reference price by 84% between 2016 and 2019, while eligible production rose from 38.1 million tonnes to 52.0 million tonnes. India's product-specific AMS support increased from USD 2.9 billion in 2016 to USD 8.5 billion in 2019, all accounted for by MPS. The issues related to measurement of India's MPS are evaluated throughout this book.

Regarding the United States, AMS support more than doubled from 2016 to 2019 and its CTAMS increased from USD 3.8 billion to a record level of USD 18.2 billion, eclipsing the previous highest level of USD 16.9 billion in 1999. Two developments drove the increase.

Starting in 2017, the United States initiated a set of tariff hikes on certain products and trade partners under laws that had not been applied unilaterally for many years.[20] These measures were aimed primarily at China for which US tariffs increased on a wide array of products. When this led to retaliation, including against agricultural exports, the US administration launched two consecutive compensatory support programs, the Market Facilitation Program (MFP) of 2018 and 2019. The MFP brought domestic support into the trade conflict. The 2018 MFP focused on compensation for revenue lost primarily because of tariff retaliation by China on just a handful of products. The 2019 MFP evaluated losses more broadly and put most compensation on a non-product-specific basis.

The global Covid-19 pandemic from early 2020 also drove increased US support. Agricultural markets faced significant displacements on both the supply and demand sides. Although these markets adjusted and rebounded with some resilience, supply disruptions remained notable two years after the pandemic began. The US economic relief responses to the Covid-19 disruptions enacted in 2020–21 included support for agriculture under the Coronavirus Food Assistance Programs (CFAP-1 and CFAP-2) and other measures. Payments were made to large numbers of products under various loss-assessment criteria.

The AMS support of the United States in 2016 to 2019 is shown in Table 4.11.[21] During 2016 and 2017, support of around USD 16 billion fit the stable general pattern of the mid-2010s. As a result of widely available

---

[20] See, *inter alia*, Irwin (2017), Bown and Kolb (2020) and Orden (2021).

[21] Green box support also increased by USD 26.7 billion from 2018 to 2019, mostly due to increased nutrition assistance to low-income consumers included in the US Covid-19 relief measures. Some of the aid, provided through purchase and donation of domestically-produced fresh fruits, meats and dairy products, was more closely tied to producer support than aid that raised retail food purchasing power regardless of the product source.

Table 4.11 *AMS support of the United States, 2016–19*

	2016	2017	2018	2019
	AMS support (USD million)			
All AMSs	16,039	16,352	26,068	34,497
Product-specific AMSs	8,634	9,450	17,350	21,273
of which, MFP	–	38	8,761	828
CFAP	–	–	–	11,352
Non-product-specific AMS	7,405	6,902	8,717	13,224
of which, MFP	–	–	5,191	8,399
CFAP	–	–	–	53
CTAMS	3,829	3,984	13,085	18,247
of which, MFP	–	6	8,091	363
CFAP	–	–	–	10,126
CTAMS / BTAMS (percent)	20.0%	20.9%	68.5%	95.5%
CTAMS / VoP of AMS products in CTAMS (percent)	16.5%	15.1%	20.8%	9.3%
De minimis AMSs	4,805	5,466	4,265	3,026
De minimis AMSs / VoP of AMS products not in CTAMS (percent)	1.1%	1.3%	1.1%	0.9%
	Support / US agricultural VoP			
All AMSs	4.5%	4.4%	7.1%	9.7%
Product-specific AMSs (sum of CTAMS and *de minimis* AMSs)	2.4%	2.6%	4.7%	6.0%
Non-product-specific AMS	2.1%	1.9%	2.4%	3.7%

Notes: MFP (Market Facilitation Program); CFAP (Coronavirus Food Assistance Program); nil support notified (–).
SOURCES: United States notifications.

subsidies on crop insurance premiums as many as 86 products received support. Product-specific AMSs summed to around USD 9 billion annually, over half of which was below the *de minimis* thresholds and exempt from CTAMS. The non-product-specific AMS was near USD 7 billion, averaging 2.0% of total production value.

AMS support increased by USD 9.7 billion in 2018 and by another USD 8.4 billion in 2019. Product-specific AMS support increased to USD 17.4 billion and USD 21.3 billion, respectively. The 2018 MFP support exceeded the net increase in product-specific AMS support from 2017 to 2018, going to only 13 products, primarily soybeans and cotton. The 2018 MFP added USD 5.2 billion of non-product-specific AMS support, also exceeding the net increase as other non-product-specific support declined. The 2018 CTAMS increased to USD 13.1 billion, a level 68.5% of BTAMS.

For 2019, product-specific MFP support was less than USD 1 billion, while non-product specific MFP support increased to USD 8.4 billion. With support reported over two years, the non-product-specific AMS was below the *de minimis* threshold each year.[22] CFAP added USD 11.4 billion to product-specific AMS support in 2019, spread over 76 products. Nearly 90% of the CFAP support entered CTAMS, which for 29 included products rose to 95.5% of BTAMS. The *de minimis* AMSs in 2019 for 55 products summed to USD 3.0 billion, amounting to only 0.9% of the sum of their *de minimis* thresholds.[23]

---

[22] Reporting the MFP non-product-specific AMS support over two years followed a change in US notification practice effective for 2017 support onwards. Under earlier practice, all MFP support was anticipated to be notified in 2019. For example, Schnepf (2020) projected USD 12.8 billion of non-product-specific 2019 MFP support, possibly making for the first time the non-product-specific AMS go slightly above 5% of total VoP and the CTAMS of the United States exceed BTAMS. Similarly, shifting the non-product-specific MFP support notified for 2018 to 2019 would result in an AMS of USD 18.4 billion which, at 5.1% of the total agricultural VoP, would enter CTAMS.

[23] The summed *de minimis* product-specific AMSs is expressed in Table 4.11 as a percentage of the summed values of production notified for each product. This sum includes the values of production of three groups of products in which the United States accounted for certain disaster assistance in a product-specific AMS for the group (livestock; orchards, vineyards, nursery and related crops; tree nuts). The VoPs of the three groups add on the order of USD 150 billion to the annual summed product values of production. This value largely overlaps with the VoPs of the individual products within the groups also receiving product-specific AMS support, e.g., beef cattle and calves, hogs and pigs (swine), poultry and sheep and lambs within livestock. Reporting some support as product-specific in individual product AMSs and other support as product-specific in group AMSs including the same products increases the amount of support that can be exempted from CTAMS on *de minimis* grounds, weakening the discipline on AMS support. The United States is the major user of this practice (Brink 2019). It notified AMS support summing between USD 0.3 billion and USD 0.6 billion annually for the three groups during 2016–19. While this practice has received little attention, it could become a larger concern if its use expanded or the limits on AMS support were tightened.

Several considerations arise from the increased AMS support of the United States during 2018–19. The support to offset losses resulting from retaliation against US tariff decisions underscores the interaction of border measures and domestic support policies and the need for limits on domestic support as part of the rules-based global trade policy regime.

The large space available for support under the Agriculture Agreement is illustrated by the expansion of US payments in 2018–19. Even with CTAMS approaching its limit, there was room for the United States to expand product-specific support by increasing payments up to *de minimis* thresholds for products already receiving some support and by supporting other products not previously supported on a product-specific basis. There was additional room to expand non-product-specific AMS support within the *de minimis* threshold.

A third consideration is that the United States is expected to include a large amount of Covid-19 relief payments in its 2020 notification, both as product-specific and non-product-specific AMS support. This could make 2020 CTAMS exceed BTAMS and the United States would violate a WTO obligation. The violation would result in part from support that proved transitory over only a few years and was initiated in response to an extraordinary global event. Many other members also included increased support in favor of agricultural producers within their Covid-19 relief measures, which later will be shown in their notifications, whether as AMS support or in other categories.[24] To the extent that pandemic-related support is Art. 6 support, the downward global trend of trade-distorting support may reverse. This will be a cautionary development to monitor.

4.6 Diverse Continued Support

A review of members' domestic support under the Agriculture Agreement demonstrates increased nominal support that has declined as a percentage of world agricultural value of production. Domestic support remains concentrated among as few as five or ten members providing the most support, with a substantial shift toward relatively more support offered by developing country members. There is also a substantial shift toward support that is less trade distorting. Green box

---

[24] OECD (2021a) reported that nearly 300 Covid-19 related support measures had been implemented among 54 countries under the OECD heading agriculture and food support, with nearly USD 75 billion of earmarked funding.

support accounted by 2016–18 for nearly 80% of all support, with China accounting for over 40% of the green box total. Many of the green box measures provide public goods and services that enhance members competitiveness over time; others deliver environmental benefits or income support less coupled to production than non-green-box measures. Numerous important caveats notwithstanding, these developments are broadly consistent with the objective envisioned in the Agriculture Agreement.

Compliance with their obligations requires different groups of members to meet different limits with different exemptions allowed. Among the five members with the most Art. 6 support in 2016–18, China's and India's AMSs face *de minimis* limits of 8.5% and 10% of values of production, respectively. The limits increase with rising production values and, formally, any number of agricultural products can be supported within their limits. In practical terms, support measures of China and India target only a small group of products. While these members have with notable exceptions notified AMS support within their *de minimis* limits, they have faced compliance disputes. Their use of the room available for AMS support across all of agriculture is relatively low. Art. 6.2 allows India but not China additional policy space, which India has used to an extent exceeding that of all other developing country members combined.

The United States, the EU and Japan, along with most other developed members and 17 developing members, have the additional flexibility for AMS support afforded by a positive BTAMS. The flexibility is concentrated among a handful of these members. In the late 1990s, the EU and Japan utilized around two-thirds of their BTAMS for product-specific AMSs exceeding their 5% *de minims* thresholds. The utilization of BTAMS by the EU and Japan has since fallen while remaining higher for Japan than the EU. The use of BTAMS by the United States has been countercyclical, with its CTAMS rising above 75% of BTAMS in 1999–2001 then declining before going up again in 2018–19. The United States and in later years Japan also utilized a larger part of their non-product-specific *de minimis* allowances than many other members.

Given the exemptions and the unused room for support subject to limits available in one way or another to different members, whether developed or developing, the Agriculture Agreement cannot be said to have required members to lower their support to producers. It has, however, provided guidance to policy evolution and a basis for benchmarking members' support decisions and levels of support. The trends and levels of Art. 6 support in later years reflect both members' policy changes and continuing differences in their chosen support measures.

The EU, Japan and the United States have substantially reduced use of MPS, which has become a key domestic support measure for China and India. The countercyclical payments and crop insurance subsidies of the United States follow a third track. Together with the differences among members in limits applying and exemptions available, the differences in measures through which domestic support is delivered suggest that the disciplines members seek to make effective will need to find balance in the degrees of constraint that apply in diverse settings. This process, whether under the Agriculture Agreement or through negotiated new rules and commitments, unfolds through discussions as the Committee on Agriculture reviews notifications, in proposals by members for changes to the Agreement that have as yet been far from finding common ground and in the few disputes that have been brought to challenge certain support measures of members.

5

Transparency

This chapter describes the review in the Committee on Agriculture of the implementation of domestic support commitments and the Committee's role as a forum for information exchange among members based on the submitted notifications and other materials and discussions. The mandate and procedures of the Committee are described and the barriers to transparency that arise from members' delays in notifications and different ways of applying the notification formats are examined. The chapter assesses the kinds of questions members have raised in Committee meetings regarding differences in interpreting the Agreement and the information provided in the review process by responses to those questions. Within certain limitations, the Committee has contributed to increased transparency about domestic support policies and levels of support on a multilateral basis, but there is room for substantial improvement.

5.1 Mandate and Procedures of the Committee on Agriculture

Members have an interest in seeing that other members follow the Agreement on Agriculture in classifying measures and measuring support and meeting their commitments. The Agreement established the WTO Committee on Agriculture and mandated it to review progress in the implementation of the commitments (Art. 17 and Art. 18.1). The Committee must base its review on notifications submitted by members on "such matters and at such intervals as shall be determined" and on any documentation the Committee requests the WTO Secretariat to prepare (Art. 18.2). The Agriculture Agreement sets out more explicit notification rules for new or modified domestic support measures that members claim as exempt from limit, that is, meeting the criteria of Art. 6.2, Art. 6.5 or Annex 2 (Art. 18.3). These measures "shall be notified promptly" with details about conformity with the criteria.

The Committee on Agriculture adopted its working procedures and notification requirements and formats in 1995 (WTO 1995a, 1995b). It identified domestic support as one of the matters requiring notification and specified the frequency and timing to which members should adhere in their notifications.[1] The Committee's use of "should" instead of "shall" could allow members some discretion regarding the timing and format of notifications. For domestic support, members with a BTAMS should submit yearly notifications "no later than 90 days following the end of the calendar (or, marketing, fiscal, etc.) year in question." An extension to 120 days is possible. Members without a BTAMS should submit "an annual notification." Still more lenient rules allow LDCs to notify only support under exempted measures and this only once every two years. In addition, the new or modified support measures members claim to be exempt from limits should under the Committee's decision be notified "as far as practicable before such measures are adopted and in any event within 30 days of adoption."

The yearly notification includes 10 tables in a format and numbering system that is common to all members. Table DS:1 is a concise statement of the BTAMS commitment level and the year's CTAMS. The formats of the nine supporting tables require information on the calculation of the amount of support under each measure and data sources. Members can choose the kind of year – such as calendar, marketing or fiscal year – they use for reporting support under various measures. Supporting Table DS:4 shows the calculation of the CTAMS as the sum of all AMSs except those claimed to be within their *de minimis* allowance. The substantiation of such a claim requires data on value of production, but the notification format does not explicitly require the submission of value of production data and many members have made *de minimis* claims without this data.

The Agriculture Agreement stipulates regarding the Committee on Agriculture that "In the review process Members shall give due consideration to the influence of excessive rates of inflation on the ability of any Member to abide by its domestic support commitments" (Art. 18.4). Members may "raise any matter relevant to the implementation" of the commitments (Art. 18.6), which is an avenue to pose questions and exchange information in a more timely setting than if tied to notifications. A member may bring to the attention of the Committee "any measure which it considers ought to have been notified by another Member" (Art. 18.7), allowing the submission of what are often termed

---

[1] The two types of notifications are identified as Table DS:1 and Table DS:2, respectively, as noted in Chapter 4.

counter-notifications. The points raised and the underlying arguments in the Committee signal to any member that others are paying attention to whether and how it abides by its commitment and follows the rules of the Agreement.

The Committee on Agriculture meets three or four times per year in regular session. The Committee meets separately in Special Session at varying frequency for negotiations. Delegates to the Committee are commonly generalists assigned from trade or agriculture ministries. Further expertise and guidance from members' capitals contributes to the focus and depth of the questions and answers, which can be shared in Committee meetings and related sessions.

In contrast to the Agriculture Agreement, under which the Committee on Agriculture established its own working procedures, the SCM Agreement lays down many of the working procedures of the Committee on Subsidies and Countervailing Measures (SCM Art. 24). The SCM Agreement also sets out explicit obligations regarding notification of subsidies in terms of both the timing and contents of notifications (SCM Art. 25). It directs the SCM Committee to every three years examine these notifications as well as notifications submitted under GATT 1994 Art. XVI (SCM Art. 26). The notification obligation extends to all specific subsidies in any sector, which includes agriculture. Domestic support measures in favor of agricultural producers are thus subject to notification under both the Agriculture Agreement and the SCM Agreement. Most of the discussion of agricultural domestic support occurs within the Committee on Agriculture given its sectoral focus, more specific notification requirements and the time constraints committees face.

5.2   The Transparency Dialogue

5.2.1   Timeliness and Comparability of Notifications

Notifications are critical for making members' support measures and levels transparent and assessing compliance with their commitments. The Secretariat circulates the notifications to members and makes them public shortly after they are submitted. However, many members' record of adhering to the notification deadlines is uneven or poor. Between 1995 and mid-2021 the Secretariat circulated 5,554 Agriculture Agreement notifications of which 1,594 or 29% were domestic support notifications. Of these, 1,384 were annual (or bi-annual) Table DS:1

notifications and 210 were Table DS:2 notifications. Twenty-eight members had by 2019 never submitted a Table DS:1 notification and 34% of such notifications that should have been submitted were still outstanding (WTO 2021j). Some members whose notifications had been outstanding for many years later brought their notifications more up to date, partly as a result of Secretariat efforts.

The lack of adherence to the notification requirements means that the information on many members' classification of measures and measurement of support is not up to date or complete. This has hampered the ability of the Committee or external analysts to timely monitor members' support measures and compliance with their commitments, as evident in the summations in Chapter 4. This problem has been compounded by members' different interpretation of the notification formats, although by 2020 initiatives of the Secretariat had also facilitated more comparable reporting of members' information.

Poor transparency has been a frequent topic for questions in both the Committee on Agriculture and other WTO committees.[2] Negotiating submissions have pursued the question of weak transparency in agriculture. Canada, the EU, Japan and the United States analyzed transparency issues based on notifications of domestic support during 2005–18 and in questions and answers in the Committee on Agriculture and, on this basis, proposed detailed changes to notification requirements (WTO 2020, 2021h, 2021k). Members would be required in domestic support to provide specific names and descriptions of individual notified measures, report the value of production of products receiving support and explain calculations of MPS including how the eligible production was determined. A member seeking consideration of the influence of excessive rates of inflation would be required to include such a request in its notification, along with statistics on rates of inflation and data not adjusted for inflation. The proposal reaffirmed notification requirements regarding cotton and public stockholding for food security purposes that were set out in ministerial decisions in 2013 and 2015. A group of 30 members proposed a general updating of the WTO's notification requirements and formats, including those under the Agriculture Agreement, to enhance transparency (WTO 2022a). Strengthened engagement in various WTO bodies would

---

[2] Beyond agriculture and the WTO, improved transparency is seen as important for addressing subsidies more broadly (Staff of IMF, OECD, World Bank and WTO 2022).

facilitate compliance with notification obligations, and technical assistance capacity building could play a larger role.

Meeting WTO notification requirements, including those in domestic support in agriculture, is seen by some developing countries as a difficulty that could be eased through constructive steps (e.g., Kwa and Lunenborg 2019, García Vargas 2021). Regarding the interval for notifying after the end of a year, Norway considered that the interval is unrealistically short and revising it to 12 months could reduce the recognized delays in notifications and increase transparency (WTO 2018d). Orden et al. (2011) proposed that coordination of some members' domestic support notifications with the annual agricultural support monitoring by OECD could improve timing.

5.2.2   Overview of Discussions

The level of activity of the transparency dialogue in the Committee on Agriculture in regular session since 1995 has varied inversely with the intensity of negotiations. Questions raised by members dropped sharply during the early 2000s through 2008 when the Doha Round negotiations were intense (Jackson et al. 2020). Subsequently, the number of questions trended upward as did the share of questions concerning measures not notified. While many members are involved in the discussions, Jackson et al. (2020) found that through 2016 the questions were mainly posed by and directed to developed country members and questions about domestic support dominated.

Members mainly report that their AMS support has remained within the applicable limit or limits in the notified year, with several exceptions as noted in Chapter 4. This refers to the CTAMS of the 33 members with a positive BTAMS and to individual AMSs of members with no or a nil BTAMS. Members' different interpretations both of the rules of the Agriculture Agreement and the notification formats underlie their questions and answers. Questions on notifications tend to focus on the classification of policies under the rules for exemption and the data and techniques for measuring support, especially the MPS component of an AMS. The large number of questions about domestic support in the Committee reveals that in many cases there is doubt about members' classification and measurement under the Agriculture Agreement rules. While the Committee does not have an adjudicatory function, the information exchanged can influence policy choices as well as notification practices.

5.2.3 Domestic Support Questions and Responses

Patterns over Time

The WTO Secretariat's Agriculture Information Management System (Ag-IMS), which includes notifications to the Committee on Agriculture and members' questions and answers in meetings, contributes to making both policy choices and the Committee's review process more transparent (WTO 2021a). The database assigns a number to each question, such as 98001, where 98 means the 98th meeting (the latest as of mid-2021) and 001 is the number assigned to the first question in the meeting. Modernization of the database has made it possible to search or aggregate questions in numerous dimensions. Systematic sorting of questions by keyword under the Agreement on Agriculture allows identifying the major areas of member interest. The Committee's summary reports of each meeting, which from 2020 include hyperlinks to questions and answers, facilitate an overview of the discussions.

In the 98 meetings of the Committee between 1995 and mid-2021, members posed questions on many of the 1,594 domestic support notifications and they also sought information under Art. 18.6, that is, raising any matter relevant to the implementation of commitments. From 2019, the Secretariat labels matters raised under Art. 18.6 as Specific Implementation Matters (SIMs) when not raised in connection with individual notifications. That label is adopted in this book for all Art. 18.6 matters from 1995 onwards. In the 1995 to mid-2021 period, members asked 4,051 questions on domestic support notifications (3,706) and SIMs (345). This was 53% of the total of 7,611 questions raised in the Committee on notifications and SIMs and contrasts against the smaller 29% share of domestic support notifications among all notifications. The difference indicates that members find domestic support issues to be complex and important but the submitted notifications apparently do not ensure satisfactory transparency. However, only 20% of a total of 1,687 SIM questions asked in the Committee concerned domestic support.

The numbers of questions on domestic support raised through mid-2021 are shown in Table 5.1 for seven categories of support and cross-cutting issues corresponding to the first-level keywords in Ag-IMS. One or more domestic support questions were raised toward 108 members (including those that later became member states of the EU) during meetings from 1995 through mid-2021. The full number of questions under each keyword is shown along with a breakdown between

Table 5.1 Questions on domestic support in the Committee on Agriculture, 1995–2021

Subject of question	In 98 meetings 1995 through mid-2021	In 80 meetings 1995 through mid-2016		In 18 meetings mid-2016 through mid-2021	
		directed to			
	108 members	5 large-support members	103 other members	5 large-support members	103 other members
AMS support	1,221	340	561	141	179
of which MPS	420	121	175	72	52
Claims for exemption					
Art. 6.2	194	28	94	26	46
Blue box	86	41	26	16	3
Green box	1,325	408	722	95	100
Classification of measures	106	15	53	26	12
Transparency issues	1,071	209	460	201	201
Other	48	10	32	5	1
Sum	4,051	1,051	1,948	510	542

Note: Large-support members (2016–18) are China, United States, EU, India, Japan.
SOURCE: Authors' compilation from Ag-IMS (WTO 2021a).

questions raised through mid-2016 (80 meetings) and those raised in later years (18 meetings). Within each sub-period, the questions directed to the five members that provided the largest amounts of all domestic support during 2016–18, in descending order, China, United States, EU, India and Japan, are distinguished from those directed to the 103 other members. SIMs relate to various keywords but are not broken out from other questions in the table.

Almost one-third (1,325) of the domestic support questions in the 98 meetings concerned green box exemptions, which corresponds to the large and growing amounts of support in this category. Questions on AMS support, identified using the Ag-IMS keyword Current Total AMS, numbered 1,221, of which 420 were questions about MPS, one of the second-level keywords. Questions on exemptions under Art. 6.2 and the blue box were asked in smaller numbers. Questions that are not specific to a particular Agriculture Agreement category of support measures fall under the keyword Classification of measures (106 questions). The keyword Transparency issues, which includes the SIM questions concerning members' outstanding notifications, comprises 1,071 of the questions.

Interest in domestic support intensified in the later years of the 1995 to 2021 period. In the 18 meetings in the five-year period between mid-2016 and mid-2021, members asked 1,052 domestic support questions, that is, 26% of all such questions in the 98 meetings from 1995. The interest in transparency was stronger in that 18-meeting period (38% of the transparency questions) than in the earlier meetings. This pattern of questions matched the absence of a notification by China after 2016 and the introduction of large payment programs by the United States from 2018 onwards.

As would be expected, the five members notifying the largest amounts of support faced many questions. In the 98 meetings, 1,561 or 39% of all domestic support questions were directed to these members. The share directed toward these five increased in the later period for each type of questions, with the percentage of all questions directed toward this group rising from 35% through mid-2016 to 48% percent in subsequent years. About equal numbers of questions were directed to the EU, United States and India, with fewer questions going to China and Japan. China was subject to questions only from 2002 onwards, which contributes slightly to the increased concentration of questions directed to this group.

Eight members received only one question each. Several other members received two questions each. The direction of questions to members with only a small role in agricultural trade indicates that members attach weight to comprehensively applying the Agreement's rules, which include special and differential treatment for developing countries.

AMS Support

Members' questions about AMS support in the 98 meetings of the Committee on Agriculture were directed most intensively to those members with the largest amounts of such support, although in total they were directed to about one-third of the 108 members. Given delays in Table DS:1 notifications, many questions seek up-to-date information on the functioning of policies providing AMS support. Measuring MPS can be contentious because members interpret differently the Agriculture Agreement rules on AAP, FERP and eligible production. The interest in the calculation of MPS is in many cases driven by an expectation that the market effects of the member's producer support are minimized by following the rules of the Agriculture Agreement.

In later years, questions on AMS support to the five large-support members focused on India: this included 78 of the 141 AMS questions and 57 of the 72 MPS questions to this group. This correlates with the 2018 and 2019 submissions of counter-notifications on India's MPS for several products and the initiation of *India – Sugar and Sugarcane*. The counter-notifications and dispute submissions showed much larger MPSs than India calculated, which would make India's AMSs exceed their limits and give India a higher rank among the largest providers of AMS support.

Members have raised questions about the negative AMSs resulting from negative MPS calculated by Brazil, China, EU, India, Pakistan, Switzerland and Tunisia. The use of fees, levies or other policy components to reduce AMSs without making them negative by Canada and Norway has faced questions, while the reporting of fees or levies by, for example, the United States does not seem to have been questioned. As many questions over the years have sought such elementary data as values of production needed to support claims that AMSs do not exceed *de minimis* allowances, more members have started including these values in their notifications. While India's notifications continued to lack this information, India in later years gave some values in answers in the Committee on Agriculture.

Under Art. 18.4, in the Committee's review process members are to give due consideration to the influence of excessive rates of inflation on members' ability to abide by their domestic support commitments. Some members (in later years, Iceland, Jordan, Tunisia and Ukraine) have unilaterally undertaken an inflation adjustment in the notifications on which the Committee's review process is based by deviating from Annex 3 in calculating AMSs. Following requests in the Committee that inflation-adjusting members' notifications show support with and without adjustment, three of these members have submitted dual notifications. While this increases the ability of the Committee to give consideration to the influence members attribute to excessive rates of inflation, the Committee as the forum for review does not establish members' compliance or non-compliance with their obligations.

Several technical issues arising in members' inflation adjustment of support calculations have been questioned in the Committee. While Art. 18.4 concerns excessive rates of inflation, inflation-adjusting members who use their full domestic inflation rates effectively claim that any inflation is excessive. Some members have switched from calculating support in one currency to another, which can reduce the nominal amount of support but does not clearly establish what constitutes an excessive rate of inflation. For example, while India does not assert that its use of different exchange rates over time is an inflation adjustment, it is one element of the difference between India's notified MPS and the MPS calculated in counter-notifications.

The commitments mentioned in Art. 18.4 are limits on support measured as CTAMS or AMSs under the rules of Art. 6.3 or Art. 7.2 (b). The four members noted above inflate the FERP when calculating MPS, that is, they do not deflate the CTAMS or an AMS as such to show the influence of inflation on their ability to abide by their commitments.[3] Such adjustments reduce the AMS, possibly bringing it below its *de minimis* level and thus reducing also the CTAMS. The issue of adjusting prices for inflation instead of adjusting measured support has not been raised in questions in the Committee.

Claims for Exemption

Of the 1,325 questions asked about green box support in the Committee meetings, 503 were addressed to the five large-support members, who were also the members that claimed the largest amounts as exempt from commitment on the basis of green box compatibility. The majority of

---

[3] The smaller price gaps resulting from higher FERPs differ from what they would have been if the gap had been deflated by cumulated inflation. These members do not deflate non-exempt payments or values of production.

questions relate to how a member's claim for green box classification is compatible with the fundamental requirement and criteria and conditions of Annex 2. Measurement issues do not arise often for green box exemptions, since measuring expenditures and direct payments is usually more straightforward than measuring other types of support.

As most green box questions seek further information than what is given in a notification, the questions and answers confirm that a full and timely Table DS:2 notification of the policy as new or modified would have avoided the need for an exchange in the Committee. Other answers take the form of claiming green box compatibility by assertion. Some questions seem designed to learn from another member's experience in designing policies that can be claimed as green box compliant, which may aid members in moving toward less-distorting policies.

The green box questions reveal a general concern that many exempted measures may not meet the requirement of having at most minimal trade-distorting effects or effects on production or do not satisfy the policy-specific criteria and conditions, particularly those for direct payments. In some instances, a member has retracted its green box claim for a policy but this is not common, since usually the only consequence for a member making an invalid green box claim is to be questioned about it in the Committee on Agriculture. The questions essentially signal to all members that their green box claims are being watched and that members do not hesitate to identify what they consider questionable classifications. Moreover, member concerns relate in some cases only to amounts of support for which disallowing the green box claim would not affect the member staying within its limit on AMS support. If disallowing a green box exemption were to generate excessive AMS support, a challenge could escalate into a WTO dispute.[4]

Between 1995 and 2021, members asked relatively few questions about Art. 6.2 exemptions. The 194 questions were directed to about two-thirds of the members claiming the exemption, including repeated questions that had not received an answer, even after several years. Questions directed to India accounted for 54 (28%) of the 194 questions, contrasting against its overwhelming share of support exempted under Art. 6.2, especially as

[4] In *US – Agricultural Subsidies* Canada (DS357) and Brazil (DS365) contended that fixed annual payments on base acres in the United States did not qualify for green box exemption. These disputes did not proceed past establishment of panels (see Table 2.3). In *US – Upland Cotton*, the panel and Appellate Body found that the US measures did not meet the relevant policy-specific green box criteria for exemption, as discussed in Chapter 7.

input subsidies. Brazil received 25 such questions. In the 18 meetings from mid-2016 to mid-2021, the 72 Art. 6.2 questions were directed to 23 of the users of this exemption. The most questions in this period were addressed to India (26) and Egypt (6), with many others receiving only one question. The questions often sought more description of the wide diversity of exempted subsidies and how they conform to the criteria of Art. 6.2, as well as explanations of significant increases in Art. 6.2 support in general or under particular policies such as input subsidization.

Many Art. 6.2 questions concerned a member's definition of low-income or resource-poor producers and any targeting of input subsidies to this group. In response to several questions, India has held that Art. 6.2 does not require such targeting. Information on members' distinction between investment subsidies and input subsidies under Art. 6.2 has also been sought. In a similar vein, Mexico's exemption of premium subsidies for many kinds of insurance, including crop insurance, under the heading of investment subsidies has been questioned.

Among the small number of questions on claims for blue box exemptions, the largest shares were directed to the EU (28 questions) and Japan (23). Nineteen questions were addressed to certain members before they joined the EU, while China's 2016 introduction of blue box payments elicited five questions. Large year-to-year changes in the amount of payments have attracted attention. Members have also been interested in the basis on which some payment programs meet the production-limiting requirement, particularly regarding the EU payments.

Classification and Transparency

As many as 1,177 domestic support questions in the meetings of the Committee on Agriculture through mid-2021 fell under the Ag-IMS keywords Classification of measures and Transparency issues. Classification includes a range of 106 questions that are not specific enough to connect uniquely to a particular domestic support category of the Agriculture Agreement, often involving alternative categories for a given measure. As this can stem from a paucity of explanation of a member's classification of its measure, the conceptual distinction between questions under the classification and transparency key words can be ambiguous. Of the 1,071 transparency questions, some sought more information about support exempted from AMS calculations or the sources of such information while others were SIMs raised under Art. 18.6 concerning policies in years not yet notified. Questions under the classification and transparency keywords are often open-ended and invite thorough explanations of a member's classification of a measure, including measures not explicitly identified in a notification.

Two examples illustrate the range of questions and responses that Ag-IMS places under the keyword Transparency issues. Australia asked Malaysia in 2019 about the subsidy available to each producer and the eligibility requirements under its paddy price subsidy program, notified as green box direct payments. The response mentioned low-income and resource-poor paddy farmers, not green box criteria, but the exchange did not lead to more discussion. In 2019, following up on an unanswered 2018 question, the United States asked India about its short-term crop loans at subsidized interest rates. Indicating the main website of a government department, India answered that a response would be provided in due course. Later in 2019, the United States asked for a more specific website location and inquired whether the program was included in India's notification and, if so, where and on what basis. The question was repeated in early 2020 without eliciting any further information at that time.

Specific Implementation Matters

The SIM questions under Art. 18.6 tend to relate to policy measures introduced or revised so recently that they have not yet been included in a notification. The United States was the respondent to the largest number (68) of the 345 SIM questions, while the EU faced 51 questions and India 50. Fewer questions were directed to China (16) and Japan (4).

Members seek recent information on not-yet-notified measures in order to evaluate the possible effects on trade. The responding member is not always able or willing to provide more information than what is available from, for example, government websites and media. Questions about classifying measures as exempt and measuring support often receive the answer that a future notification will give the information.

Some information sought through questions is publicly available from member governments themselves or from international organizations such as the OECD or the FAO. However, in view of the Committee on Agriculture's remit to review the implementation of commitments, members prefer to receive information directly from another government and in the context of the WTO. This may explain why some questions are formulated as seeking confirmation of a policy description or a policy parameter reported in media. The questions and answers in the Committee nonetheless gives information that otherwise would not be available and helps to assess a member's compliance with its commitments.

5.2.4 Imperfect Transparency through Questions and Answers

Altogether, while there have been many constructive question and answer exchanges in the review process of the Committee on Agriculture many questions have remained unanswered. This includes numerous questions about AMS support and measures claimed as green box exempt and smaller numbers of questions about Art. 6.2 or blue box exemptions. A similar lack of answers is evident for questions about classification and transparency including SIMs. Answers are in many cases unrelated to the question or do not provide the information sought. A member may be reluctant to share information that might undermine its preferred way of classifying policies and measuring support or to articulate a rationale for its measurement when doing so is at its discretion. The lack of answers weakens the Committee's ability to deliver on its responsibility to review progress in the implementation of members' commitments. This leaves much to be desired in terms of the transparency that could result from the Committee's attention to members' notifications.

5.3 Counter-Notifications

A member may bring to the attention of the Committee on Agriculture "any measure which it considers ought to have been notified by another Member" (Art. 18.7). While these submissions are often called counter-notifications, they are not necessarily submitted in opposition to a member's own notification and can be submitted in the absence of a member's own notification.

No counter-notifications were submitted on domestic support for many years until in 2018 and 2019 the United States, Australia and Canada made such submissions regarding the amounts of AMS support India provided to producers of wheat, rice, sugarcane, cotton and pulses. The counter-notifications concerned in particular the calculation of MPS but allowed also for the inclusion of other components in the products' AMSs. India's MPS for these products calculated in the counter-notifications exceeded the respective 10% limits on AMSs by wide margins, as summarized in Table 5.2.

An Art. 18.7 counter-notification documents a concern more formally and comprehensively than a written question for a meeting of the Committee. It alerts a member more strongly that another member disagrees with its reporting, or lack of reporting, in notifications and can lead to extended discussion in the Committee. The large differences

Table 5.2 *Counter-notifications in 2018–19 regarding market price support in India*

Product	Support years	Range of MPS	Date of circulation	Submitted by
Wheat	2010/11 to 2013/14	60% to 69%	9 May 2018	United States
Rice	2010/11 to 2013/14	74% to 84%	9 May 2018	United States
Cotton	2010/11 to 2016/17	54% to 81%	9 November 2018	United States
Sugarcane	2011/12 to 2016/17	77% to 100%	16 November 2018	Australia
Pulses	2016/17	47%	12 February 2019	Australia, Canada, United States
Chickpea		64%		
Pigeon pea		32%		
Mung bean		85%		
Black matep		52%		
Lentils		41%		

Note: MPS expressed as percent of product's value of production.
SOURCES: Counter-notifications WTO (2018b, 2018c, 2018e, 2019d).

between India's notified AMSs and the levels calculated in the counter-notifications for wheat and rice also underlie the tension related to sheltering excessive support from dispute challenge when developing countries acquire stocks at administered prices for food security purposes. In the case of sugarcane, India asserted that the counter-notification was "based on incorrect assumptions, faulty interpretations and flawed analysis, leading to erroneous conclusions," using similar wording about other counter-notifications (Permanent Mission of India to the WTO 2018). The calculation issues for wheat, rice and cotton as well as the issues that have been addressed in *India – Sugar and Sugarcane* are evaluated in Chapter 7.

5.4   Trade Policy Reviews

Outside of the review in the Committee on Agriculture, the WTO Trade Policy Review Body conducts a review for each member, which is essentially a peer-group assessment. Since 2016, the frequency of Trade Policy Reviews is three, five or seven years, depending on the member's share of world trade. The review produces a report prepared by the WTO

Secretariat with input from the reviewed member and a report prepared by the reviewed member itself. The Secretariat report usually has a chapter examining the member's trade policies and practices in agriculture, including domestic support. It draws on the member's notifications, complemented with both official and unofficial information.

Since preparing a Trade Policy Review involves thorough discussions with the member concerned, a certain level of authority attaches to the information and assessments documented. This adds transparency to how members are meeting their domestic support commitments, especially in terms of describing the policies providing support. Members may in the Trade Policy Review pose questions to the member under review, some of which reveal the nature of the concerns members harbor regarding the support other members provide in agriculture.

5.5 Improving Transparency

In reviewing the implementation of domestic support commitments under the Agriculture Agreement, members have in the Committee on Agriculture asked a large number of questions about, particularly, support claimed as exempt from limit on green box grounds, calculation of AMS support and its MPS component and transparency issues. The questions in the Committee are prompted by what members have and have not reported in notifications. There are substantial delays in the submission of notifications, and questions in the review process often do not receive informative answers. This detracts from the transparency that otherwise could result from the work of the Committee on Agriculture. The issues arising in measuring MPS are complex, can have a decisive bearing on the assessment of a member's compliance with its obligations to keep AMS support within its applicable limit and often are not resolved through discussion in the Committee. The contrasting notifications and counter-notifications submitted concerning India's AMS support demonstrate these aspects.

The exchanges in the Committee on Agriculture nonetheless add to members' understanding of other members' policy details and their interpretation of the Agreement's rules and commitments, which can in some cases resolve an otherwise contentious issue. While the Committee does not have a mandate to adjudicate differences in members' interpretation of the Agreement, its review process illuminates whether and how members implement their commitments. Unresolved issues remain on the table for discussion and subject to potential dispute settlement. The exchanges in the Committee, complemented by the Trade Policy Reviews, make available to members and the public much policy information that otherwise would be difficult to assemble. The information is official in the sense that it is submitted by governments but, as it is designed to demonstrate compliance with domestic support commitments, it does not always have a direct economic meaning. The coverage of the information in terms of years and number of members complements other public information, which adds transparency. Initiatives to enhance the timeliness, scope and relevance of the information members submit to the Committee are therefore in the interest of both the Committee's ability to carry out its mandate and the public interest in transparency regarding domestic support in agriculture.

6

Issues under Negotiation

The Agreement on Agriculture committed members to negotiations to continue the process of "substantial progressive reductions in support and protection resulting in fundamental reform" (Art. 20). These negotiations were launched in 2000 and integrated into the Doha Round the following year. Intense negotiations over draft modalities for new domestic support rules and commitments occurred through 2008 but members failed to agree on a comprehensive Doha Round outcome, in part due to differences over agriculture. This chapter reviews the domestic support issues raised in the negotiations that have continued from the year 2000 to revise the disciplines of the Agriculture Agreement. The 2008 failure to agree set the stage for subsequent negotiations with different views about the 2008 draft modalities' continued relevance. These piecemeal negotiations have achieved only a few decisions. The chapter reviews the 2008 draft modalities and the subsequent decisions through the 11th ministerial conference in 2017. It then turns to the domestic support issues pursued in the negotiations leading toward the 12th ministerial conference eventually held in June 2022. Two postponements due to the global Covid-19 pandemic had left four years without a meeting at the ministerial level. In the intervening years, members put forth numerous negotiating proposals but none gained consensus support. Thus, more than 20 years after members initiated negotiations to continue the reform process under the Agriculture Agreement, there has been almost no progress on new disciplines on domestic support. A ministerial decision in 2015 to eliminate export subsidies in agriculture and adopt rules on export financing is a substantial outcome of the negotiations with implications for managing domestic price support programs.

6.1   Scant Progress in Negotiations over Many Years

6.1.1   Negotiations Leading to 2008 Draft Modalities

Negotiations under Art. 20 of the Agriculture Agreement, titled Continuation of the Reform Process, progressed in the Doha Round from 2001. They take place in the Committee on Agriculture in Special Session, and decisions by ministers in ministerial conferences express what members have agreed. WTO rules require such conferences to meet at least once every two years. Ministers' decisions regarding the Agreement may differ in legal authority from an amendment under Art. X of the WTO Agreement (Marrakesh Agreement Establishing the World Trade Organization), but this question has not arisen concerning the Agriculture Agreement.

The agriculture negotiations in the Doha Round aimed, among other things, at achieving "substantial reductions in trade-distorting domestic support" (WTO 2001b). Special and differential treatment for developing countries was an integral element of the agriculture negotiations, also taking into account non-trade concerns such as environmental protection, food security and rural development. Negotiations, to be concluded by January 2005, were extended through 2006 and extended again to 2008. Major steps in the Doha Round process included agreeing on certain formulas and other modalities for domestic support in 2004 and 2005.

In 2008, the chair of the negotiations on agriculture prepared a detailed draft modalities document for an agriculture agreement (WTO 2008a). It proposed reductions of existing limits and new limits on various types of domestic support for different groups of members, and revised wording for many paragraphs of Annex 2. The draft modalities set out considerably more specific rules for the contents of notifications to the Committee on Agriculture. However, in the context of a deep global recession and financial crisis, members failed to reach an agreement to conclude the Doha Round in 2008 or the following years.[1]

Had the 2008 draft modalities been adopted, they would have expanded the rules and tightened the constraints on domestic support in several ways, particularly for developed countries. Commitments on BTAMS would have been reduced by up to 70% for developed countries and by

---

[1] Orden et al. (2011) examines in depth the domestic support proposals seen in the 2008 draft modalities. Martin and Mattoo (2011) discuss issues that remained unresolved in agriculture and other negotiating areas.

30% for a few developing countries. *De minimis* percentages would have been cut to 2.5% for developed countries and 6.7% for developing countries with positive BTAMS but maintained at existing levels for other developing countries. A cap would have been set on OTDS, a partial measurement of trade-distorting support including all AMSs and Art. 6.5 support but excluding Art. 6.2 support. The cap would have been reduced from a base level generally determined by BTAMS plus, for developed countries, 15% of total agricultural value of production during 1995–2000 or, for developing countries, 25% of that value during 1995–2000 or 1995–2004. The reduction from the base level would have ranged between 55% and 80% over a given number of years among developed countries, and would have been 37% for a few developing countries. No reduction would have applied for most developing countries. Caps on product-specific AMSs and total and product-specific blue box support would have been set. The draft modalities were assessed to reduce the space for OTDS support of developed countries from USD 274 billion to USD 60 billion, falling from 61% to 27% of the world total of such space (Brink 2011). China and India would need to keep OTDS within their base OTDS levels, keep AMSs below their *de minimis* limits and limit total and product-specific blue box support. Altogether, the 2008 Doha Round draft modalities were negotiated in substantial detail and would have significantly clarified and tightened the disciplines on domestic support.

6.1.2 Piecemeal Decisions after the Comprehensive Negotiations Faltered in 2008

The preparations for ministerial conferences in 2011, 2013, 2015, 2017 and originally planned for 2020 included consideration of issues in agricultural domestic support. Some members considered that negotiations should incorporate earlier progress in the Doha Round, others that the context for negotiations had changed such that the earlier progress had become out of date.

While the ministerial conference in 2011 (Geneva) did not address domestic support in agriculture, the 2013 conference (Bali) generated decisions on *General services* and *Public stockholding for food security purposes* under Annex 2 and on cotton. The decision on *General services* makes explicit that expenditures on land reform and rural livelihood security can be exempted if they meet the green box requirements (WTO 2013a). These expenditure programs can include land

rehabilitation, soil conservation and resource management, drought management and flood control, rural employment programs, issuance of
property titles and farmer settlement programs. The decision was that
these types of programs "could be considered as falling within the scope of
the non-exhaustive list of general services programmes in Annex 2." The
other Annex 2 decision and the cotton decision saw further elaboration at
the subsequent conference.

The 2013 and 2015 (Nairobi) conference decisions rule out, conditionally and on an interim basis, a dispute challenge of compliance
when a developing country member's excessive AMS support results
from acquisition of public food stocks at administered prices for food
security purposes (see Chapter 3). Ministers agreed to continue to
address cotton support issues "ambitiously, expeditiously and specifically." In 2017 the 11th ministerial conference (Buenos Aires) considered numerous proposals on public stockholding, cotton and other
dimensions of domestic support. However, in an increasingly fraught
world trade context, ministers did not take any decisions on agriculture nor even agree on an overall ministerial declaration.

Following the 2017 conference, members prepared for the 12th conference by discussing inputs in seven separately labeled negotiating areas
in agriculture, with transparency added in late 2021.[2] Negotiations
involving domestic support continued not only in the area with that
heading but also in the areas of public stockholding, cotton and transparency. Member engagement in the agriculture negotiations was
particularly active on these topics.

An important implication for the use of domestic price support
programs follows from a decision concerning export subsidization in
agriculture. Ministers decided at the 2015 conference to eliminate
scheduled export subsidy entitlements within given time frames and
to tighten the rules on export financing support under the Agriculture
Agreement. A member whose policies keep domestic prices above
world levels must therefore manage any resulting accumulation of
stocks within its domestic market rather than dispose of stocks internationally using export subsidies, subsidized export financing or food
aid outside set rules. This can make it more difficult to operate a price
support program.

---

[2] In addition to domestic support, public stockholding and cotton, the negotiating areas
included market access, export competition, export prohibitions or restrictions and an
import special safeguard mechanism for developing countries.

6.2 Ongoing Negotiations

Although negotiating progress had been scant, agriculture remained a high-profile issue in preparation for the 12th ministerial conference, originally scheduled for 2020 (Nur-Sultan). It was rescheduled for November 2021 (Geneva) and then rescheduled for June 2022 (Geneva), in both cases delayed because of the Covid-19 pandemic.

Among considerations of an overarching nature for ministers are the need to look forward and having regard to special and differential treatment for developing countries. The latter issue is controversial concerning the largest or highest-income developing country members. Moreover, agriculture negotiations take place in a context that includes, among other concerns, restoring the dispute settlement adjudicatory process, broad issues of WTO reform, trade and development and global adaptation to and mitigation of climate change.

In the years of preparing for the 12th ministerial conference, much of members' early input on domestic support under the Agriculture Agreement expressed views on ways to advance the negotiations on revising the rules and commitments. Members recognized that the pattern of which members support agricultural producers and how they do so had changed markedly since 2000. They also had more experience with members' different interpretations of the Agreement. The complexity and interactions of the rules contemplated for different categories of domestic support can be daunting as seen in the 2008 draft modalities. Member input concerned what limits and exemptions would apply to different categories of support provided by different groups of members and in what circumstances. Members exchanged views on technical details that could underpin decisions at a ministerial conference.

Some member input to the negotiations used information such as policy descriptions and data available from notifications and took the form of tabulation and organization of notified information to highlight particular issues. However, the completeness and specificity of the notified information did not always allow a thorough examination of issues. This motivated some members to focus on ways to improve transparency.

Members' input and discussions in the negotiating area of domestic support related to only a subset of the issues that fall within the Agreement's rules and commitments on domestic support. Discussions involving domestic support also continued in the areas of public stockholding for food security purposes, cotton and transparency. To illuminate the background for the chair's draft text of November 2021 for the 12th

ministerial conference (WTO 2021c) and the draft decision for the negotiating areas in agriculture formulated in June 2022 (WTO 2022e), the
following overview of member input draws mainly on submissions between
2018 and 2022 representing a diversity of views.[3] The chair's assessment was
that a substantive outcome on modalities for reducing entitlements to trade-
distorting domestic support was not achievable at the conference, nor were
other substantial decisions likely to be agreed upon.

6.2.1   Domestic Support

Members' suggestions in the domestic support area focused on
further limiting support within BTAMS and in *de minimis* AMSs, limiting
product-specific support and introducing limits on support the Agreement
exempts from limit as Art. 6.2 support and blue box support. Members'
perspective in negotiations was increasingly forward looking by considering
members' future entitlements to certain types of support in addition to
patterns of past support.

Members summarized and analyzed information under rubrics such as
trends in global trade-distorting support and analysis and observations
on product-specific support – the trends addressed in Chapter 4.
Submissions also concerned next steps toward reform, perspectives on
Art. 6.2 and blue box support and comprehensive domestic support data
in USD from 2001 onwards (e.g., JOB/AG/138 2018, JOB/AG/143 2018,
JOB/AG/195 2021, JOB/AG/196 2021, WTO [2021f]). Focusing on
members' past support in different categories, they paid relatively less
attention to differences in trade-distorting potential among measures,
such as between investment subsidies and input subsidies exempted
under Art. 6.2. Cairns Group members classified a variety of domestic
support options under the headings of reform through limits, clarification of rules and additional transparency (JOB/AG/160 2019).[4] Australia
and New Zealand highlighted and projected the future total of all
members' entitlements to support that is subject to limit (WTO 2019a).
Members observed that the amounts of product-specific AMSs within *de*

---

[3] In this chapter, many documents for the Committee on Agriculture in Special Session are
shown only with the WTO document symbol JOB/AG/### and year. They are available on
the searchable WTO Documents Online website https://docs.wto.org and are not included
in the book's references.

[4] The Cairns Group of WTO members pursues liberalization of global agricultural trade.
See www.wto.org/english/tratop_e/agric_e/negoti_groups_e.htm

minimis allowances were increasing and product-specific AMS support was concentrated among relatively few products and members (JOB/AG/150 2018, JOB/AG/157 2019).

China and India would reduce some members' entitlement to provide product-specific AMSs above *de minimis* levels, aiming to eliminate such AMS support (JOB/AG/137 2018). Those reductions and the eventual elimination would apply to developed country members only. A discipline incorporating special and differential treatment would apply for the 17 developing country members with a positive BTAMS. While the proposal seeks to address the asymmetry between most developed and most developing country members, it is silent on, for example, the asymmetry between the *de minimis* percentages that would govern members' AMSs after eliminating the entitlement to product-specific AMSs beyond their *de minimis* thresholds. A later proposal from India extended the same rules also to non-product-specific AMSs (JOB/AG/216 2021). Although these proposals would not eliminate the BTAMS entitlement, it would effectively be unusable because of the *de minimis* limits on individual AMSs.

While Cairns Group members repeatedly called for a focus on product-specific AMS support, they pointed at the same time to other forms of trade-distorting support. This includes non-product-specific AMS support, Art. 6.2 support, blue box support and possibly some green box payments. Seeing all Art. 6 support as trade-distorting, these members cautioned against setting limits only on certain categories of this support. The Cairns Group and other members proposed capping and reducing domestic support entitlements, taking into consideration all forms of support under Art. 6, which implies including the currently unlimited entitlements to Art. 6.2 and blue box support (JOB/AG/177/Rev.2 2021). The 2021 sum of global entitlements would be cut by at least half by 2030.[5] Without giving specifics, the proposal would require reductions by individual members in proportion to their existing entitlements and potential impact on markets. Similar in several respects, proposals by LDCs and the African Group appear to rule out AMSs larger than de *minimis* levels for members with a positive BTAMS (JOB/

---

[5] The global entitlements may refer to the sum for all members. The proposal is silent on how to establish the base levels for members' entitlement reductions and the global halving. As members' existing entitlements to any Art. 6.2 and blue box support are without limit, so are the global entitlements. Costa Rica suggested methods for establishing a base and determining reductions (JOB/AG/199 2021).

AG/159 2019, JOB/AG/173 2019, JOB/AG/203 2021). The proposals contemplated several variations for implementing this basic approach over time. The blue box exemption would be eliminated and direct payments exempted on green box grounds would be capped and be subject to stricter criteria.

Members saw a need to clarify some of the Agriculture Agreement's rules, such as calculation methodologies for MPS and definition of non-product-specific support. However, they put relatively little emphasis on updating FERPs so that MPS calculated under the Agreement more closely matches economic price support. An option suggested by the G-33 and African groups, representing many developing countries, would use a moving average of international prices as the external reference price in the case of calculating MPS resulting from acquisition by developing countries of certain stocks for food security purposes (or alternatively the G-33 proposed an adjustment for excessive rates of inflation), but the use of such a reference price would not extend more generally (JOB/AG/25 2013, JOB/AG/204 2021).

Given the diversity of views, the chair's November 2021 draft text for the 12th ministerial conference could suggest only that ministers agree to continue negotiating, taking into account and building on progress made in negotiations at that point. Among the large-support members, the EU, United States and Japan engaged very little in proposing possible reductions of domestic support commitments and tightening of the support rules.

6.2.2   Public Stockholding for Food Security Purposes

The treatment of MPS calculated under the Annex 2 rules for *Public stockholding for food security purposes* is a major unresolved issue in the negotiations. To recall the main points, developing countries' expenditures on accumulating and holding stocks can be exempted from AMS even if the stocks are acquired and released at administered prices. However, this requires accounting for the difference between the acquisition and reference prices in the AMS, which can make the AMS exceed its *de minimis* limit or cause CTAMS to exceed BTAMS even when the administered price differs little from current world market prices. The 2008 draft modalities had proposed that in certain circumstances, involving support for low-income or resource-poor producers or fighting hunger and rural poverty, the acquisition expenditure would be exemptible without accounting for the price difference in the AMS.

The 2013 ministerial conference decided on an interim solution. A developing country, which exempts expenditure on acquisition at administered prices and accounts for the price difference in the AMS, would not face a challenge under the WTO dispute settlement rules even if doing so makes an AMS or CTAMS exceed its limit (WTO 2013b). The WTO General Council in 2014 (under the pressure of India potentially blocking adoption of the Trade Facilitation Agreement) and the 2015 ministerial conference reaffirmed this decision (WTO 2015b). The opening to offer excessive price support to producers without dispute challenge is subject to notification and other conditions and requirements designed to reduce, and facilitate assessing, the likelihood that the accumulation and release of stocks distort trade or adversely affect the food security of other members.

The interim solution remains in place until a permanent solution is agreed and adopted. Committed to making efforts to achieve that end, members submitted analysis and proposals over several years. Some member input is not public. One group of members investigated which members had notified exemption of expenditures on stock accumulation as well as acquisition of stocks at administered prices, for which products and in which years (JOB/AG/210/Rev.2 2022). Four members (China, India, Indonesia and the Philippines) reported this practice in their latest notified year after 2013, which was 2016, 2019, 2018 and 2019, respectively, as of mid-2021. The number of identified members is strikingly few given the negotiating attention attaching to acquisition at administered prices for public stockholding, but each is a significant producer of some of the identified products. China, India and Indonesia were also among the G-33 group of members elaborating on earlier proposals on this issue (JOB/AG/214/Rev.1 2021).

Leading to the conference, some members saw a need to address urgently the acquisition for public stockholding issue to alleviate concerns about their food security situation and rural development needs, both heightened by the Covid-19 pandemic and global food price turbulence related to Russia's invasion of Ukraine in February 2022. Others failed to see how relaxing price support disciplines would help in this regard. The differences among members also concerned the type of permanent solution, its coverage in terms of products, programs and members, transparency and the safeguards to prevent excess purchased stocks from being offloaded on global markets. It was argued that making room for unlimited MPS in some situations would allow more trade distortion instead of reducing it, a potential effect of shielding compliance from dispute challenge. Introducing a permanent shelter against challenge would alter the balance between all rights and obligations in the WTO framework, including the settlement of disputes, in a more profound way than altering those specified for domestic support in the Agriculture Agreement.[6]

As members submitted input on the issue of acquisition at administered prices for public stockholding, they also met in sessions dedicated to this area. However, members had by late 2021 shown little movement. Brazil considered that the issue was not mature for a negotiating outcome (JOB/AG/209 2021). The chair interpreted the proponents as seeking a solution that was simple, efficient and broader in product and program coverage than the interim solution. The chair interpreted the non-proponents as being concerned about potential trade distortions and unlimited MPS beyond the Uruguay Round commitment levels. The chair's November 2021 draft text suggested only that ministers at the 12th conference undertake to make concerted efforts to agree and adopt a permanent solution at the 13th conference.

A few days before the 12th conference the African Group, the ACP (African, Caribbean and Pacific) members and G-33 proposed that any producer support under public stockholding programs would, subject to certain conditions, be deemed to be in compliance with the Agreement's limits on AMS support. The support would be calculated using an external reference price that was a moving average or adjusted for excessive inflation (WTO 2022f, discussed in Chapter 7). At the same time, Brazil proposed provisions that would make exemption from accounting for a price gap in CTAMS contingent on the member meeting certain development-related characteristics and also on its procured value as share of value of production and global export market share not exceeding given percentages (JOB/AG/230 2022). Appearing so soon before the finalization of the draft decision for ministers' consideration (WTO 2022e), the proposals would have had only minor influence in shaping that draft.

6.2.3   Cotton

Domestic support is a major issue in the cotton negotiating area, along with concerns about cotton market access and export subsidies. Earlier ministerial commitments to address cotton issues had involved agreeing

---

[6] The same outcome as when compliance is not challenged would eventuate, without a functioning Appellate Body, if a member found by a panel to have an excessive AMS appeals the finding and thus avoids policy change, as the situation at time of writing in *India – Sugar and Sugarcane*.

to substantially reduce domestic support, specifically reducing distorting subsidies for cotton by more than for other products. Without agreement on the size of any cuts for other products, the corresponding reductions in cotton support could not be agreed.

Material prepared by the WTO Secretariat supports the cotton discussions, drawing on data from notifications and replies to a cotton questionnaire (WTO 2021e). By 2021, only seven members showed cotton-specific AMS support in their latest notified year. Data also shows disbursements of cotton-specific development assistance along with agriculture and infrastructure-related development assistance over some years valued at hundreds of millions of USD (WTO 2021d). Receiving members report little, if any, of these funds in their domestic support notifications.[7]

The Cotton Four (Benin, Burkina Faso, Chad and Mali), supported by other members, champion the cotton issue. They proposed differentiated reductions in cotton AMS for developed and developing countries with a positive BTAMS and in blue box support for cotton, along with changes in the *de minimis* provisions (WTO 2021g). Members would not be allowed to support cotton producers with direct payments meeting the criteria of paras. 5–13 of the green box.[8] LDCs would be exempted from reduction commitments.

The chair's draft text suggested only that ministers agree to continue negotiations after the 12th conference and possibly later agree on modalities for reducing trade-distorting domestic support for cotton.

6.2.4 Transparency

In February 2020, the chair of the agriculture negotiations had singled out the longstanding issue of enhanced transparency in notifications as a critical element. Several members analyzed available information on domestic support from a transparency perspective and proposed improvements (see Chapter 5). In the process underlying the chair's draft text of November 2021, negotiators highlighted in all seven negotiating areas a need for greater transparency in relation to the negotiations, future disciplines or both (JOB/AG/201 2021). Transparency issues in

---

[7] The Agreement and the notification requirements do not exclude any support on the basis of origin of funds.

[8] Disallowing members' use of certain measures contrasts against disallowing exemption of support under certain measures from limit as seen in some proposals.

the domestic support area concerned particularly the timeliness and quality of information available from notifications.

Members suggested that revising the language in Annex 2 would increase transparency about measures qualifying for the green box exemption. There was caution against making notifications more burdensome or changing the timelines. Concerns in the area of public stockholding for food security purposes centered on whether the, at the time, two available notifications by India invoking the interim solution included adequate information. There were contrasting views on the need for and effects of stringency in such notifications. In the cotton area, members recognized that the regular dedicated discussions on cotton contributed to transparency and foresaw ways to improve the accuracy, timeliness and completeness of information. Taking the members' submissions into account, the chair saw fit to add transparency to the draft text as a cross-cutting negotiating area, focusing particularly on notifications.

6.2.5   Chairs' Preparations for the 12th Ministerial Conference

Based on member input through 2019 the then chair of the agriculture negotiations had summarized the elements in domestic support on the table for the conference scheduled for 2020 (JOB/AG/180 2020). They included, expressed with some ambiguity, establishing a new overall limit, eliminating AMS entitlements above *de minimis*, further limiting the categories of the Agreement, using a formula reduction, limiting product-specific support and capping and halving the sum of members' entitlements to trade-distorting domestic support between 2020 and 2030. He recognized member divergence on addressing all Art. 6 support or only some of its categories. On public stockholding for food security purposes, he suggested work on core provisions (no challenge of compliance), product coverage, program coverage, transparency, anti-circumvention and safeguards and monitoring, without ruling out other initiatives and possibly treating some member groups or some programs differently. On cotton, the then chair recognized, along with specific modalities proposed by the Cotton Four, suggestions to limit trade-distorting support as a percentage of cotton value of production or to a fixed monetary value and to address first the AMS granted to cotton beyond the *de minimis* level.

By November 2021, when the new chair circulated a draft text on agriculture for the 12th ministerial conference planned for that month

(WTO 2021c), several members saw it as the first such text circulated in more than a decade (JOB/AG/225 2022). The chair's basic premise for the draft text was that members shared a commitment to continue the agricultural negotiations. In the domestic support negotiating area, the draft text suggested a decision to negotiate toward agreeing at the subsequent conference on modalities to substantially reduce trade-distorting domestic support in a time frame to be determined. The contributions of members would be fair and underpinned by the principle that members who distort the most contribute more in the reform process (i.e., reduce by more) while taking into account special and differential treatment and non-trade concerns. On acquisition of public stocks for food security purposes, ministers would undertake to make all concerted efforts to agree and adopt a permanent solution. On cotton, ministers would associate a decision with their corresponding broader decision on trade-distorting domestic support and later agree on modalities for reduction. Ministers would commit to collecting and circulating cotton-related data and at the subsequent conference adopt any necessary decisions. On transparency, ministers would agree on a process toward adopting by the end of 2023 a revised version of the document setting out notification contents and timing of notifications. This would involve streamlining and updating the notification requirements for domestic support and taking due account of the capacity constraints of some developing countries.

Although building on the draft text of November 2021, member input to the 12th conference in the form of a draft ministerial decision on agriculture in June 2022 in the main suggested only that negotiations be continued and intensified with a view to achieving modalities and other outcomes at the 13th conference (WTO 2022e).[9] On domestic support rules and commitments it differed remarkably in ambition, substance, and specificity from the draft modalities of 2008, which had been negotiated in substantial detail but were never finalized. Preparing for the 12th conference, some key members were far from forceful in seeking agreement to strengthen the disciplines on domestic support. The draft decision might, if agreed, have engendered some negotiating momentum following the conference. However, with members so divided, particularly in the domestic support and public stockholding negotiating areas, ministers did not reach any decision on any of the negotiating areas in agriculture. Ministers did adopt a decision committing members not to

---

[9] This assessment applies generally to the seven negotiating areas. Transparency would be improved in the Committee on Agriculture on an ongoing basis.

impose export prohibitions or restrictions on purchases for humanitarian purposes by the World Food Program and declarations on emergency responses to food insecurity in a broad manner without specific new obligations and on modern sanitary and phytosanitary challenges (WTO 2022b, 2022c, 2022d).

6.3   Rethinking the Basis for Support Entitlements

The positive BTAMS concentrated in the schedules of only few members based on support measured in an outdated period and the resulting flexibility to exceed AMS *de minimis* levels, particularly for product-specific support, are concerns of many members. The exemptions of trade-distorting support under Art. 6.2 and Art. 6.5 also concern many members in terms of the effectiveness of the Agreement and, in the case of Art. 6.2, its equity among members. Explorations of a more even distribution of support entitlements under Art. 6 could be instructive in seeking to address member concerns. Such efforts by interest groups and independent analysts paralleled the negotiating inputs into the 12th ministerial conference, although the influence of the resulting findings was minor. Continued negotiations could draw on analysis such as summarized in the following studies and analysis by, for example, Musselli (2016) or Sharma et al. (2021), who explore domestic support disciplines particularly through developing country lenses. Some efforts identify a need to improve transparency, often referring to timeliness of notifications and inclusion of value of production and other relevant data.

Konandreas (2020) suggested summing for each product its AMS and its blue box support (all blue box support would be assigned to individual products) in an up-to-date base period. Those sums, expressed as percentages of the product's value of production, would constitute product-specific support entitlements with a corresponding non-product-specific support entitlement established. Entitlements larger than a given percentage level would be reduced, with relatively larger reductions of large percentage entitlements and for developed country members. The reductions would not apply to Art. 6.2 support. The author nonetheless contemplated including Art. 6.2 support in the non-product-specific entitlement in the base period and reducing that entitlement less than if not inclusive of Art. 6.2 support.

Ford (2021) built on Konandreas (2020) to suggest a reduction of the difference between a member's existing commitments and applied support by capping and reducing all Art. 6 support based on recent years, including Art. 6.2 support. The definitions of support in Annex 2 would be sharpened to ensure that exempted measures have at most minimal trade-distorting effects or effects on production.

Glauber et al. (2020, 2021) suggested setting a cap on a member's trade-distorting support based on a percentage of the member's total agricultural value of production. The cap would apply to all Art. 6 support and be reduced to an agreed level. Support counting toward this cap would be measured as a moving average over three to five years, in contrast to the current annual basis. Limits would apply to support to any product or group of products. MPS would not be calculated under public stockholding programs for food security purposes by developing country members when administered prices are set below international market prices. Special and differential treatment would take the form of a relatively higher initial cap on support, a longer phase-in period for reductions or both. The criteria of the green box would be reviewed to ensure they do not accommodate support causing more than minimal distortions to global markets and updated to address new policy challenges.

The New Pathways group suggested a menu of options (Cahill and Tangermann 2021). The common starting point would be to measure average Art. 6 support (including at least the input subsidy part of Art. 6.2 support) in a recent three-year period. MPS in that measurement would be calculated only where the AAP exceeded the external reference price, which would be a lagged moving average of international prices. Eligible production would equal total production.[10] The resulting measurement of Art. 6 support, expressed as a percentage of the total agricultural value of production, would be capped and undergo reductions differentiated by groups of members. Rules could be designed to prevent concentration of support on only a few individual products. Alternatively, separate limits would be set on budgetary non-price support and on price support, with the latter measured not by a price gap but by public expenditure. In a situation where significant progress had been made in reducing border measures, another alternative proposed would be to limit only certain budgetary expenditures. In the green box, the fundamental requirement and some policy-specific criteria would be revised for clarity and to reinforce the non-distorting character of the measures. A further alternative would differentiate between most direct payment programs versus social, development and public goods programs subject to differentiated notification provisions.

---

[10] The MPS methods parallel the proposals, with calculated examples, in Chapter 7 and earlier in Brink and Orden (2020). The New Pathways group includes Brink.

Brink (2021) reported a counter-factual analysis where each member was allowed a fixed BTAMS equal to 4% of total agricultural value of production in a recent year, not based on past levels of applied support. The *de minimis* percentages for developed countries would be reduced to 4% and 3%, respectively, for product-specific AMSs and non-product-specific AMS. The percentages for developing countries would be 10% for product-specific AMSs and be reduced to 5% for non-product-specific AMS. Art. 6.2 and Art. 6.5 support would be exemptible from CTAMS only if no AMS (measured without Art 6.2 or Art. 6.5 support) exceeds its *de minimis* level. Taken together, these latter provisions would tighten the support space for both developed and developing members.

The evaluation of this set of changes covers the five members with the largest Art. 6 support in 2016–18 plus Mexico, using their latest notification by mid-2021. The sum of these members' BTAMSs declines by 22% from USD 152.6 billion to USD 119.4 billion. The sum of room for *de minimis* support of the United States, EU and Japan falls from USD 90.4 billion in the measured years to USD 63.3 billion. The shift in the distribution of room for Art. 6 support exceeding *de minimis* levels is even more striking. China obtains a BTAMS of USD 60.5 billion and India of USD 20.4 billion, while the sum of BTAMS of the United States, EU and Japan falls by USD 104.2 and for Mexico by USD 10.1 billion. China thus gains substantial room for additional Art. 6 support. Its CTAMS calculated under the counter-factual assumptions is USD 18.1 billion including blue box support, as AMSs for corn, soybeans and cotton exceed the 10% levels (using 2016 notification data). The EU and Mexico also have CTAMS below BTAMS, although room for additional Art. 6 support is sharply curtailed. In contrast, India's CTAMS is USD 31.4 including Art. 6.2 support, as AMS for rice exceeds the 10% level (using 2019 notification data). This CTAMS goes above India's counter-factual BTAMS. The CTAMS of the United States and Japan also exceed BTAMS (using 2019 and 2018 data, respectively). This is because the US non-product-specific AMS exceeds its counter-factual 3% *de minimis* threshold and enters CTAMS, while for Japan the BTAMS based on value of production is much smaller than when based on 1986–88 support.[11]

---

[11] In addition to the six members mentioned, the analysis extended to Georgia, Chile, Nigeria and Nepal to illustrate possible effects for members without BTAMS, including accession members, developing country members and an LDC. Their AMSs were nil or small, so CTAMSs were nil. The BTAMS of LDCs is 8% in this analysis and their *de minimis* percentages remain at 10%.

In an alternative scenario, the external reference prices in MPS calculations were updated with a lagged three-year moving average replacing the FERPs (see Chapter 7). This updating of FERP reduced or eliminated positive MPS for the products for which the five large-support members calculated MPS.

The counter-factual analysis demonstrates several broad points. Determining BTAMS support space equitably in proportion to the size of each member's agricultural sector can be compatible with a reduced global BTAMS sum, consistent with the objective of reducing trade-distorting domestic support. This depends, however, on the percentage of value of production determining BTAMSs being low enough. The distribution of BTAMSs and the room for *de minimis* AMS support could be markedly different from its existing distribution, again depending on the percentages adopted. The large counter-factual BTAMS of China demonstrates that on its own such a reallocation would not remove the risk of substantial market distortions if, for example, China were to concentrate AMS support on only a few products. The analysis also demonstrates that being able to exempt Art. 6.2 support from limit only if all AMSs are *de minimis* can be an incentive to reduce AMSs or Art. 6.2 support or both, also in line with the objective of reducing trade-distorting support. Basing the reference price in MPS calculations on more up-to-date international prices would reduce or eliminate the often large artificial price gaps calculated under the Agriculture Agreement. This could be relevant when discussing excessive AMSs in the context of acquisition at administered prices for public stockholding.

6.4   Dialogue and Impasse in Domestic Support Negotiations

After members failed to reach a comprehensive Doha Round agreement in 2008, the continued negotiations on domestic support prepared input for consideration by ministers at conferences held every two years but postponed in 2020 and 2021 due to pandemic circumstances. Ministers reached a final decision on only one domestic support issue: expenditures related to land reform and rural livelihood security in developing countries were made explicitly exemptible as *General services* under the green box. Ministers decided on an interim solution to effectively expand the room for developing countries' MPS. The decision means that under the green box heading of *Public stockholding for food security purposes*, contingent on the member meeting certain conditions and requirements, the member's compliance with its obligations cannot be challenged under the WTO dispute settlement rules even when MPS makes an AMS or CTAMS exceed its limit. Securing a permanent solution with broader coverage of products and future programs remains a priority for many members, while others are concerned about potential market distortions.

In preparing for the 12th ministerial conference in 2022, members continued to bring forward a variety of ideas on what new constraints, if any, would apply to different types of domestic support and different groups of members. Reaching a negotiated outcome on domestic support for cotton was a priority for many members, and members also prioritized enhanced transparency. Given the divergent views among members, input on agriculture for ministers' consideration at the 12th conference proposed only advancement toward subsequent decision making, and ministers were unable even to agree on this.

The Agriculture Agreement's Art. 20 commits members to continued negotiations on agriculture. Substantial fault lines run through these negotiations, with members far apart on the priorities and future direction for rules and commitments. Little prospect is on the horizon for early agreement on comprehensive new domestic support disciplines. Meanwhile, the Agreement on Agriculture continues to define the disciplines to which members are committed and by which other members can scrutinize domestic support and seek compliance.

7

Disputes Involving Agricultural Domestic Support

The Agriculture Agreement, the SCM Agreement and related provisions of GATT 1994 place domestic support measures in favor of agricultural producers under different and overlapping sets of WTO obligations. Only few of the disputes initiated under the Dispute Settlement Understanding (DSU; Understanding on Rules and Procedures Governing the Settlement of Disputes) have involved domestic support. Brazil has been particularly active initiating five such disputes, followed by the United States and Australia (three each). Five other members have each initiated a single dispute. Nine of these sixteen disputes raised issues about compliance with domestic support obligations under the Agriculture Agreement, particularly involving MPS measurement. *Korea – Various Measures on Beef* (DS161 and DS169) and *China – Agricultural Producers* (DS511) advanced to having reports adopted by the Dispute Settlement Body (Table 2.3). Three other of these disputes are inactive: either the dispute did not proceed past a request for consultations (DS507) or a dispute panel was never composed (DS357 and DS365). The disputes *India – Sugar and Sugarcane* (DS579, DS580 and DS581) address India's MPS and subsidies for sugarcane and export subsidies for sugar but the panel report is under appeal, which, with the Appellate Body not functioning, leaves the disputes unresolved.

Of the remaining seven disputes involving agricultural domestic support, two involved domestic support measures primarily under the SCM Agreement, namely *US – Upland Cotton* (DS267) and DS451, the latter not proceeding past the request for consultations. Five disputes addressed whether domestic support measures resulted in the provision of export subsidies through cross-subsidization, *Canada – Dairy* (DS103 and DS113) and *EC – Export Subsidies on Sugar* (DS265, DS266 and DS283).

This chapter reviews the disputes involving MPS in relation to applicable limits on support under the Agriculture Agreement, that is, MPS for beef in Korea, wheat, rice and corn in China and sugarcane in India. Because the MPS measured under the Agreement differs from an economic measurement of price support, questions arise regarding the calculation parameters and circumstances in which the Agreement's obligations can effectively constrain the trade-distorting effects of such support. The chapter also reviews the long dispute under the SCM Agreement about US domestic support measures causing adverse effects to the interests of Brazil through significant price suppression in the world cotton market, as well as the dispute about EU domestic support measures causing export subsidization for sugar. The review places the economic circumstances, main arguments and consequences of these disputes in context. Members' motivation to initiate and pursue the disputes, how the outcomes help to clarify the WTO disciplines for domestic support measures in favor of agricultural producers and the policy reforms members undertook in light of the dispute outcomes are considered.

7.1   The Dispute Settlement Process

The WTO Agreement foresees members' possible use of the DSU to settle disputes. The outcome of dispute settlement is more powerful and can have greater consequences than the information exchange in the committees. The DSU recognizes good offices, conciliation and mediation, possibly engaging the Director-General of the WTO, as steps to settle a dispute before it escalates. Alternatively, or if these fail, the complaining member can request consultations with the responding member. If they fail to resolve the dispute, the complainant can request the Dispute Settlement Body to establish a panel to examine the matter at issue and generate findings to assist that body in making recommendations to the disputing members. Once the panel is established, the appointment of panelists constitutes its composition. The disputing parties can appeal the panel report on issues of law and legal interpretation, in which case the Appellate Body can uphold, modify or reverse the legal findings and conclusions of the panel.[1]

   If the panel or the Appellate Body concludes that the respondent has violated its obligations under an agreement such as the Agriculture Agreement, it recommends that the respondent bring its measures into

---

[1] This describes the role of the Appellate Body as defined in the DSU. Resulting from blockage by the United States of the replacement of Appellate Body judges whose appointment expired, the Appellate Body ceased to function in December 2020. At time of writing the impasse was not resolved.

conformity with its obligations. The Dispute Settlement Body's adoption of the report of the panel or Appellate Body makes the recommendations effective. The DSU specifies procedures to follow if there is disagreement over a member's implementation of the recommendations within a reasonable period of time. This can include compliance panel and Appellate Body proceedings (DSU Art. 21.5) and/or requests that the Dispute Settlement Body authorize the suspension of concessions (DSU Art. 22.2), which involves permission for the complainant, for example, to temporarily raise tariffs on imports from the respondent. If the level of suspension is contested by the respondent in the dispute, requests for suspension are settled by an arbitrator (DSU Art. 22.6).

7.2 Disputes about Market Price Support and AMSs

7.2.1 Korea – Various Measures on Beef

The dispute *Korea – Various Measures on Beef* was brought by the United States and Australia (WTO 1999c, 1999d). It clarified some issues in measuring MPS under the Agriculture Agreement and addressed measures alleged to restrict beef imports (WTO 2000a, 2000b). The Appellate Body was unable to determine from the panel's factual findings whether Korea's beef MPS was large enough to make Korea exceed its BTAMS commitment levels in 1997 and 1998.[2] However, several of the panel and Appellate Body arguments are instructive beyond this outcome.

The Agriculture Agreement stipulates that an AMS be "calculated in accordance with the provisions of Annex 3 of this Agreement and taking into account the constituent data and methodology used in the tables of supporting material incorporated by reference in Part IV of the Member's Schedule" (Art. 1(a)(ii)).[3] This is relevant where certain aspects of a member's AMS calculation for the base period, performed during the Uruguay Round or accession negotiations, remain relevant to

---

[2] The panel's calculated MPS did not base FERP on the years 1986–88, which was incompatible with para. 9 of Annex 3.

[3] Part IV, Section I, of members' schedules (Domestic Support: Total AMS Commitments) includes an entry for relevant supporting tables and document reference. The tables show base period data supporting the member's entry for annual and final bound commitment levels. The supporting tables of original members carry a WTO document symbol that includes AGST. The corresponding documents of accession members carry different symbols. In either case, the document is usually called the member's AGST tables.

the calculation of current AMS. The Appellate Body concluded that "in accordance with" the Agriculture Agreement reflects a more rigorous standard than "taking into account" the constituent data and methodology when calculating an AMS.

Both the panel and Appellate Body also expressed views on what constitutes eligible production in calculating MPS. The panel considered that eligible production comprises the total marketable production "even though the quantity purchased by a government agency is small or even nil" (WTO 2000b, para. 827). The Appellate Body modified that finding and concluded that eligible production refers to production that is "fit or entitled" to be purchased rather than the quantity actually purchased (WTO 2000a, para. 120). The Appellate Body reasoned that a government is able to define and to limit eligible production. As Korea had announced a maximum quantity it would purchase in its beef support program, the Appellate Body determined that this was the quantity of eligible production, even though Korea purchased a lesser quantity.

7.2.2   China – Agricultural Producers

The early dispute about MPS for beef in Korea was the only adjudication on this type of support until the United States initiated a complaint over China's MPS for wheat, rice and corn in September 2016 (WTO 2016b). The panel found that China's MPSs for wheat and rice (evaluated separately for Indica and Japonica varieties) had exceeded its AMS limits of 8.5% of value of production in each of the years 2012 through 2015 (WTO 2019c). The report was not appealed and the Dispute Settlement Body adopted it in April 2019.

The United States initiated a related dispute, *China – TRQs*, in December 2016 concerning China's administration of TRQs for wheat, rice and corn (WTO 2016a). The panel found that China had failed to ensure that its administration of TRQs would not inhibit the filling of each TRQ (WTO 2019b). Again, the report was not appealed and the Dispute Settlement Body adopted it in May 2019.

The United States initiated both disputes at a time when world market prices had fallen back from relatively high levels during 2007–11 and in circumstances where China in 2012 continued to raise AAPs, providing a rising floor under domestic market prices. The OECD (2021b) estimates of China's economic MPS at the farm level averaged 32.2% of value of production at domestic prices for wheat, 32.0% for rice and 22.6% for corn during 2012–15.[4] The large economic MPS and associated border protection coincided with declining US exports to China of these grains and growing Chinese grain stocks.[5]

Adjudication and Implementation

The *China – Agricultural Producers* panel examined two critical measurement issues. First, the United States argued that China's quantity of eligible production of wheat, rice and corn was the entire production in the provinces and regions where the support programs operated. For wheat and rice, this covered nearly 80% of national production and for corn about 45% during 2012–15. In contrast, China used the smaller quantities actually purchased under the support programs, which it asserted was the measurement it had used in its WTO accession to determine its Base Period AMSs. Second, the United States argued that China's FERPs in CNY/tonne for wheat, rice and corn should be based on the three-year averages of 1986–88 world prices, as specified in the Agriculture Agreement (para. 9, Annex 3). In contrast, China used the much higher 1996–98 prices as it had in its accession. For example, the FERP for wheat was 431 CNY/tonne if based on 1986–88 versus 1,698 CNY/tonne if based on 1996–98. The different interpretations resulted in vastly different MPSs. The United States held that China's MPSs exceeded its summed AMS limits for wheat, rice and corn by an average of CNY 604 billion (USD 97 billion) per year during 2012–15. China claimed it was within its 8.5% *de minimis* limits.

The panel determined that the FERPs from the years 1996–98 used in China's accession were appropriate for calculating China's subsequent MPSs which "should be based on the same years used to calculate China's Base Total AMS" (WTO 2019c, para. 7.275). The panel reasoned that the stipulation of 1986–88 as the base years for FERP needed to be read in proper context and in light of the objective and purpose of the

---

[4] OECD MPS can be expressed as a percentage of value of production at domestic prices, like expressing the MPS calculated under the Agriculture Agreement as a percentage for comparison to *de minimis* percentages. Economic price support is often expressed alternatively as the percentage by which the domestic farm level price exceeds the international reference border price. Such border protection adjusted to farm level averaged 47.7% for wheat, 47.2% for rice and 30.0% for corn during 2012–15 using OECD data.

[5] China's wheat, rice and corn end-year carryover stocks reached the quite-high levels of more than half of annual production at the end of the 2015/16 marketing year, having increased by 56%, 43% and 86% from 2011/12 (data from Agriculture Market Information System [AMIS] www.amis-outlook.org/).

Agreement. The panel concluded that using a member's Base Total AMS as the basis for reduction commitments under the Agriculture Agreement implied a need for consistency in the way base period AMSs and subsequent AMSs were calculated and that this consideration was relevant even where no reduction from Base Total AMS was required. This did not mean the data and methodologies in the base period and subsequent calculations had to be identical in every respect. In particular, the panel rejected China's argument that eligible production used to calculate MPS must correspond to the approach taken in its accession base-period calculations. The panel established that for wheat and rice eligible production was production in the relevant provinces and regions, not quantities purchased, because the legal instruments for China's price support programs did not provide "any explicit or implicit limits" on the quantities eligible for the support price (WTO 2019c, para. 7.315).[6] The panel made a minor adjustment for ineligible grain of low-quality but did not reduce eligible production because the program operated only part of the year or some grain was consumed on-farm, as China had argued.

Drawing on these determinations, the panel found that China exceeded its AMS limits for wheat and Indica and Japonica rice in each year 2012–15 and therefore was not in compliance with its obligations under Art. 3.2 and Art. 6.3 of the Agriculture Agreement. Table 7.1 gives annual values of the panel's determination of China's MPS. Market price support is in this chapter often expressed as a percentage of value of production, or %MPS, to facilitate comparison to a member's *de minimis* percentage for AMS, such as China's 8.5%.

The panel findings have several implications. Figure 7.1 facilitates discussion of three key points. It illustrates the %MPS for wheat (on average over the four years) under alternative quantities of eligible production using the 1996–98 FERP and also using 1986–88 to determine the FERP.[7] Two limits are illustrated: China's AMS limit of 8.5% of value of production and a lower effective limit on MPS during those years taking into account input subsidies (for improved crop strains and seeds), which China included in its AMSs for

---

[6] China did not calculate corn AMSs arguing it had terminated the corn price support program in March 2016. The panel concluded that a ruling on corn MPS was not required. The panel indicated that a significant drop in producer prices of corn in China in 2016 helped it reach its conclusion because it confirmed that China had terminated its corn price support program. The panel found no compelling evidence that a corn price support program would be reintroduced.

[7] Annual calculations for wheat, Indica rice and Japonica rice are reported in Brink and Orden (2020).

Table 7.1 *Panel determination of China's AMSs, 2012–15*

	2012	2013	2014	2015
	Percent MPS			
Wheat	12.1%	18.2%	21.7%	22.4%
Indica rice	23.6%	30.3%	31.3%	31.9%
Japonica rice	13.3%	18.9%	20.7%	21.3%

Notes: Panel's AMS includes MPS but not subsidies. Entries for rice are averages of panel's two alternative calculations which differed only slightly.
SOURCE: WTO (2019c).

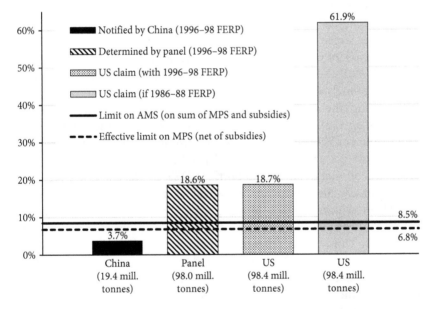

Figure 7.1   China's wheat market price support using alternative quantities and reference prices, 2012–15 averages (percent).
SOURCE: Brink and Orden (2020) based on WTO (2018a, 2019c) and US submissions posted on website of the US Trade Representative.

2012–15. China notified these subsidies to the WTO only in December 2018 (WTO 2018a) and they were not under consideration in *China – Agricultural Producers*. The input subsidies reduce the effective limit on MPS from 8.5% to 6.8% on average for wheat and similarly for rice.

China's notified purchases of wheat at support prices averaged 19.4 million tonnes, with a %MPS each year below the effective AMS limit and averaging 3.7% as shown by the first column of Figure 7.1. The second column illustrates that eligible production as determined by the panel required the AAPs to be lower in order to make MPSs fit within China's AMS limits.[8] Had domestic market prices moved down with the lower AAPs, they would have exceeded border prices but economic price support would have been less than reported by OECD.

The panel's adoption of the FERP from 1996–98 and not 1986–88 reduces the extent to which support prices would have had to be lower. This is illustrated for the US-claimed eligible production of wheat in the last two columns of Figure 7.1. The %MPSs for wheat are more than three times larger when calculated with the lower 1986–88 FERP. Wheat AMSs compliant with China's limits using the 1986–88 FERP would have required AAPs set below border prices and precluded any economic support through a price support program.

Following the earlier Appellate Body ruling in *Korea – Various Measures on Beef*, the panel also left open the possibility that eligible production could be determined by a maximum quantity of purchases at the support price "defined in the legal framework that regulates the provision of market price support" (WTO 2019c, para. 7.284). The maximum eligible production of wheat averaged 37.3 million tonnes for AMSs within China's limits during 2012–15 at the announced AAPs, the 1996–98 FERP, and accounting for the subsidies included in the AMSs. Thus, China potentially could have complied with its wheat AMS limits during 2012–15 without reducing support prices if its legal framework had defined maximum purchase quantities that were no larger than the quantities exhausting the effective AMS limits, yet larger than the quantities of wheat purchased. The results are similar for Indica rice. The potential maximum purchases averaged 25.6 million tonnes, while actual purchases averaged 11.6 million tonnes. For Japonica rice,

---

[8] Compliance at the eligible production determined by the panel would have required reductions of wheat AAPs of about 8% in 2012 to 20% in 2015 (Brink and Orden 2020). AAPs for Indica rice would have needed to be 24–30% lower and for Japonica rice 8–17% lower.

the potential maximum exceeded actual purchases in 2012 and 2013. However, the maximum would have been binding in 2014 and 2015 when China's Japonica rice purchases rose to 18.2 and 20.1 million tonnes, respectively, compared to 4.0 and 13.5 million tonnes the previous two years. At the purchases in 2014 and 2015, AMS for Japonica rice exceeds the 8.5% level when the input subsidies are included.[9]

Use of the two policy parameters enables a government to manage the combination of AAP and eligible production such that a product's AMS stays within each year's limit. China began reducing its wheat and rice support prices in 2016. The support price for wheat had been reduced by 5.1% (to 2,240 CNY/tonne) by 2019, Indica rice by 9.9% (to 2,460 CNY/tonne averaged over early and mid-to-late varieties) and Japonica rice by 16.1% (to 2,600 CNY/tonne). If these lower support prices had been applied in 2012–15 in conjunction with the eligible production determined by the panel the MPSs for Japonica rice would have been within the AMS limits. These support price reductions alone would not have been sufficient to bring support into compliance for wheat and Indica rice.

To claim compliance with its commitment as determined by the dispute panel, China announced the maximum quantities of wheat, Indica rice and Japonica rice that would be purchased in 2020 at 37 million tonnes, 20 million tonnes and 30 million tonnes, respectively (NDRC 2019, 2020). The maximum quantities were above past purchases and anticipated 2020 purchases but low enough that China's 2020 AMSs could be expected to be below their limits.[10]

Setting maximum purchases to define eligible production breaks the correspondence of the quantity variable in the Agriculture Agreement legal calculation of MPS and the economic measurement of price support. China can choose a combination of AAPs and maximum purchase quantities anywhere on a compliance curve where the combination meets the product's AMS limit (with the given FERP).

Altogether, the outcome of *China – Agricultural Producers* places only modest constraint on China's levels of AAPs and accordingly on its levels of economic price support. It is nonetheless a legal constraint clarified by a

---

[9] China's notifications calculate MPS separately for Indica rice and Japonica rice then include both in a single rice AMS, which, including the subsidies, was notified as remaining below the 8.5% level in 2014 and 2015.

[10] As noted in Chapter 4, whether China will revise its notifications for 2012–16 and how it will notify MPS for wheat and rice for 2017–19 during which no caps on purchases were announced was unknown at time of writing.

dispute ruling. The constraint is a disincentive for China to provide AMS subsidies to wheat and rice, especially if the authorities seek to maintain a distance between announced maximum quantities eligible to be purchased and actual purchases and also between the expected levels of AMS at the maximum purchases and the 8.5% limits on AMSs. In 2016, China ended the product-specific input subsidies for wheat and rice paid during 2012–15, leaving more room for MPS within its AMS limits.

The consequences of legal compliance in *China – Agricultural Producers* for economic price support are specific to China's circumstances. The broader context of the dispute includes other ongoing controversies around MPS measurement under the Agriculture Agreement. One concern is that, while the outcome achieves consistency between China's measurement of Base Total AMS and Current Total AMS, the use of different base periods for FERPs by original members and accession members creates inconsistency of obligations among the membership. Negotiators in the Uruguay Round could have explicitly addressed such potential inconsistency in the Agriculture Agreement but did not do so, even though many countries applied for accession to the GATT during the 1986–94 negotiations (Ahn and Orden 2021).

TRQ Administration and Post-Dispute Policy

Seeking WTO compliance on MPS and TRQ administration are complementary means to similar ends. Larger TRQ fill makes maintaining any given AAP more difficult for China – more grain has to be purchased to maintain the support price – but it does not explicitly preclude any AAP level. A lower AAP makes it easier to allow TRQs to be filled but lessens the arbitrage incentive for imports. Ahn and Orden (2021) and Glauber and Lester (2021) note that during 2012–15 high support prices and large grain carry-over stocks were disincentives to allowing imports within the TRQs.

China committed in its 2001 WTO accession to allow global access at a 1% in-quota tariff for 9.6 million tonnes of wheat, 5.3 million tonnes of rice and 7.2 million tonnes of corn (approximately 7%, 4%, and 3% of its mid-2010s production, respectively). Over-quota imports face a prohibitive tariff of 65%. China committed to administering its TRQs "on a transparent, predictable, uniform, fair and non-discriminatory basis using clearly specified timeframes, administrative procedures and requirements that would ... not inhibit the filling of each TRQ" (cited in WTO 2019b, para. 7.3). China may apportion the use of 90% of the wheat TRQ, 60% of the corn TRQ and 50% of the rice TRQ to COFCO

(China National Cereals, Oils and Foodstuffs Import and Export Corporation), a state trading enterprise for grains. Each year, China made an initial allocation of TRQs among COFCO and private trading enterprises, then later in the year reallocated unused amounts only of the private firm TRQ allocations. Despite China's high internal prices, the fill rates of its TRQs so administered were well below full utilization.[11]

The panel in *China – TRQs* considered the legal instruments by which China established and administered its TRQs and its administrative procedures and practices. The panel determined that the practice of allocating the entire state trading enterprise portion of the TRQs to COFCO and not requiring its unused allocations to be reallocated to private trading enterprises violated China's obligation to administer TRQs in a manner that would not inhibit the filling of each TRQ. It found that China was inconsistent "as a whole" with its obligations for TRQ administration (WTO 2019b, para. 7.173).

The extent to which the United States as the complainant might benefit from expanded export opportunities from compliance responses to *China – Agricultural Producers* and *China – TRQs* came to be overshadowed by the larger trade frictions that arose between the United States and China in the period when these disputes were adjudicated. To dampen the trade conflict, from January 2020 China undertook to expand its imports of agricultural and other products from the United States to levels above previous years (USTR 2020). China's elimination of its corn price support program in 2016 and subsequent lowering of AAPs for wheat and rice signaled some movement in grain policies. The outcomes of the two complementary disputes enhanced the incentives for continued movement. International grain markets subsequently strengthened, in part as China's imports of corn and wheat at in-quota tariff rates for the first time rose above its WTO commitments on TRQs.[12]

---

[11] For wheat, the average fill rate of the COFCO portion of the TRQs was 29%, whereas the annual private trading enterprise portion fill rates were 90% or higher (Grant et al. 2022, see also Gale 2021). For rice, the averages were 21% and 70%, respectively, and for corn 21% and 86%. Chen et al. (2020) estimate that if TRQ administrative obstacles were removed, the fill rates in 2017 would have been higher for all three grains.

[12] Despite the improved market circumstances and China's larger imports, the United States sought authorization to suspend concessions for non-compliance in both disputes and then indicated it had paused those proceedings. China took in both disputes the unusual step for a respondent of requesting establishment of compliance panels. Following their establishment in 2020 and 2021, respectively, proceedings were paused at time of writing.

7.2.3 India – Sugar and Sugarcane

India is a second large agricultural producer and developing country member to have faced challenges regarding its domestic support, particularly MPS. The United States, Australia and Canada in 2018 and 2019 submitted counter-notifications to the Committee on Agriculture concerning India's domestic support (Table 5.2). Brazil, Australia and Guatemala subsequently initiated *India – Sugar and Sugarcane* addressing domestic support and export subsidies during marketing years 2014/15 to 2018/19. This led to the establishment of three panels, composed of the same persons, and the circulation of three identical panel reports (WTO 2021b).

Market Price Support in India

The complexities in applying the rules of the Agriculture Agreement affect its capacity to constrain economic price support differently for India than China. India's notifications calculate MPS for crops where, in India's view, government agencies have purchased a quantity. They do not calculate MPS for sugarcane where sugar mills, not government agencies, purchase sugarcane at minimum prices set by the central and some state governments. India has in most years calculated negative MPS for wheat and positive MPS for rice, cotton and pulses within its 10% AMS limits. In its AGST document India, as an original WTO member, based its external reference prices on 1986–88 border prices expressed in INR/tonne and used value of production in INR. India's subsequent annual notifications convert the external reference prices into USD/tonne at a fixed 1986–88 exchange rate but converts the AAPs at subsequent yearly exchange rates. This substantially narrows the price gap in the MPS calculation. India uses only quantities procured (purchased) by government at administered prices as eligible production. In contrast, the counter-notifications use AAP and FERP in INR/tonne and total production as the eligible production, yielding much larger MPSs.[13]

However the price gap in India's MPS might be properly measured in legal terms, India's conversions of AAPs, and values of production to calculate %MPS, from INR to USD at yearly exchange rates incorporates three adjustments compared to 1986–88. First, the conversions adjust for the inflation occurring in India after 1986–88 to the extent it

---

[13] Table 5.2 gives the range of counter-notified MPS. Brink and Orden (2020) provide comparisons through 2017 of notified MPSs and those similar to the counter-notifications.

is offset by a corresponding depreciation of the INR. Second, inflation also occurs in the United States and, if the INR/USD exchange rate adjusts in purchasing power parity terms, its increase reflects the excess of rates of inflation in India compared to the United States, not the full extent of inflation in India. Finally, an exchange rate change deviates from a pure monetary adjustment, whether real (inflation adjusted) appreciation or depreciation. This real exchange rate movement compared to the real 1986–88 exchange rate is also incorporated in the AAPs and values of production when they are converted from INR to USD at yearly exchange rates. None of these adjustment components applies to the external reference price.[14]

Differences in economic context are also important for assessing the role the Agriculture Agreement commitments on domestic support can have in constraining support that distorts markets. The OECD (2021b) calculates that India's economic price support for wheat, rice and cotton was mostly negative during the 21-year period 2000–20. India kept producer prices for both wheat and rice well below the border prices (adjusted to farm level) during the years when world prices rose sharply in the late 2000s and early 2010s. India later narrowed the gap as world prices declined by raising support prices. Economic MPSs became less negative and positive for wheat in 2016 and 2019.

---

[14] To evaluate these effects on MPS as percent of value of production during 2010–17, Brink and Orden (2020) compared two alternative measurements to the notified and counter-notified MPSs for wheat, rice and cotton. Both alternatives used total production as eligible production. The first alternative used the USD price gap and value of production as calculated by India. The second alternative adjusted the price gap to offset only the effect of inflation in India since 1986–88 by expressing AAP and value of production in INR deflated by India's wholesale price index for all commodities. In the first alternative measurement, wheat MPS, when positive, remained below 10% of value of production but rice MPS exceeded 10% in all years. The deflation adjustment gave negative MPS for wheat for all years and for rice until 2014. The outcomes for cotton depended in both alternatives on the seed cotton-to-lint conversion factor, which differs between India's notifications and the counter-notification. The results highlight the contrast between MPS in the counter-notifications and calculated with these two inflation-related adjustments. This empirical observation potentially relates to but is separate from the legal issue of how members in the Committee on Agriculture review process under Art. 18.4 are to give their due consideration to the influence of excessive rates of inflation on a member's ability to abide by its domestic support commitments. These alternative measurements are also informative in the context of considering the influence of excessive rates of inflation as suggested in negotiations over acquisition at administered prices of public stocks for food security purposes (WTO 2013c, WTO 2022f).

When comparing MPS calculated under the Agriculture Agreement with economic support, the contrast between India and China is striking. India's administered prices for wheat, rice and cotton have regularly been below international reference border prices. If India were to calculate MPS for these products with the price gap in the counter-notifications, bringing MPS within its limits would require setting even lower AAPs or constraining eligible production at levels far below past purchases. In contrast, China, with AAPs considerably higher than international prices, faces only modest constraint on its price support.

The incongruence between MPS measured under the Agriculture Agreement and its economic implications spills over into ongoing negotiations about the consequences of using administered prices when acquiring public stocks for food security purposes. With India's purchases under the rice support program at or above 38% of total production, even using its particular calculations made India's rice AMS exceed its 10% limit in 2018 (11.5%), 2019 (13.7%) and 2020 (15.2%). India claimed shelter against dispute challenge under the ministerial decision in relation to the Annex 2 rules for *Public stockholding for food security purposes.*

The Sugar and Sugarcane Dispute

Indian sugar mills buy sugarcane from producers subject to government-set minimum prices. Because a government agency is not the buyer of sugarcane, India argues that its government-set minimum prices are not a MPS measure because there is no government expenditure or revenue forgone.[15] The fact that the government operates several measures that assist sugar mills to pay the minimum prices does not in India's view negate this stance.

Australia argued in contrast through its counter-notification on sugarcane that India's minimum prices are AAPs and that all of India's sugarcane production is eligible to receive the AAP. It calculated MPS and %MPS using AAP, FERP and value of production in INR/tonne and total sugarcane production as eligible production (WTO 2018i). This gave an annual %MPS between 77.1% and 99.8% during 2011–16 based

---

[15] In the Committee on Agriculture, India explains not including MPS for many crops in notifications by an absence of purchases at administered prices. For example, India did not notify MPS for cotton in 2010 or 2016 because there were no purchases in those years, whereas the United States' counter-notification contended that with total production as eligible production MPS exceeded India's limits.

on the value of production of sugarcane used to produce sugar reported by India. In comparison, the OECD (2021b) estimates the economic %MPS for sugar is slightly positive in almost all years, increasing sharply to average 25.5% during 2017–19 then falling to 14.3% in 2020 as world market prices increased. Although not as large as the MPS in the counter-notification, the increased economic support helps explain why a dispute was initiated for sugarcane in 2019.

The submissions of the complainants to the dispute panel calculate India's MPS and AMS for sugarcane for 2014–18 (WTO 2021b). Whereas the MPS in the counter-notification derived only from the mandatory minimum price (Fair and Remunerative Price, FRP) set by the central government, the complainants' submissions also account for price premiums based on the recovery rates of sugar from sugarcane and the minimum price applied by some states (State Advised Prices, SAPs). This gives higher %MPSs for sugarcane, in the range of 105.1–117.9% during 2014–18.

Several other measurement issues arise in the dispute over the level of India's MPS for sugarcane. First, the complainants adjusted the 1986–88 external reference price to account for productivity gains that increased recovery rates of sugar per tonne of cane. This raised the FERP from 156.2 INR/tonne to 183.6 INR/tonne by 2018. More conse-quentially, building on the rulings in *Korea – Various Measures on Beef* and *China – Agricultural Producers*, and as in Australia's counter-notification, the complainants view was that with no cap set on eligible production all sugarcane produced was eligible for the minimum prices. India's crop statistics report a value of production under each of the headings of sugarcane and of gur (a sweetener produced differ-ently than sugar). Interpreting these two values as the value of sugar-cane used to produce sugar and to produce gur, respectively, the complainants suggested two options for the total value of sugarcane: with or without the sugarcane used for gur. Including the value of sugarcane production used for gur raised the total value of production by an average of nearly one-quarter, bringing the calculated %MPS down to a range of 86.1–93.6% during 2014–18.

Table 7.2 shows the annual %MPS calculated for sugarcane in Australia's counter-notification for 2011–16 and its dispute submission for 2014–18 with the two alternative values of production. The dispute submission using all sugarcane value of production is compared to two illustrative alternative measurements that India could have raised. Calculating the price gap and value of production in USD as India does in its MPS for other products, and with total production of sugarcane

Table 7.2 *Measurements of India's market price support for sugarcane, 2011–18*

	2011	2012	2013	2014	2015	2016	2017	2018
					Percent MPS			
Economic MPS (OECD; sugar)	−15.6%	6.4%	5.8%	13.3%	8.3%	−0.9%	28.0%	23.5%
India's notification: no sugarcane MPS	–	–	–	–	–	–	–	–
Australia's counter-notification	77.7%	77.1%	94.1%	94.4%	99.8%	94.4%		
Australia's dispute submission								
Excluding gur from value of production				115.2%	117.9%	112.5%	108.4%	105.1%
Including gur in value of production				93.6%	91.8%	86.1%	91.4%	90.2%
Alternative measurements								
Price gap as India measures it for other crops				70.2%	67.2%	65.4%	69.9%	65.0%
Adjustment of AAP and value of production for inflation				63.1%	63.1%	61.8%	64.0%	59.9%

Note: Alternative measurements by authors use values of production including gur.
SOURCE: Authors' compilation and calculations from WTO (2018b), OECD (2021b) and DFAT (2021).

as eligible production, the first alternative lowers the range of %MPS to between 65.0% and 70.2% during 2014–18. The second alternative deflates the AAP and value of production by the wholesale price index for all commodities to account only for inflation in India, which gives a %MPS ranging from 59.9% to 64.0%. For sugarcane the nominal AAP in INR/tonne had by 2018 been raised to about 18 times the 1986–88 FERP, which was proportionately more than the INR depreciated or India experienced inflation.[16] In contrast, corresponding AAPs for wheat, rice and cotton were on the order of 5–8 times the FERPs. Each alternative measurement thus reduces the %MPS relatively less for sugarcane than for the other products. Even with the alternative adjustments, bringing sugarcane MPS within the 10% AMS limit would require substantially lower AAPs, eligible production defined as less than total production or some combination of lower support prices and eligible quantity.

Panel Rulings on MPS and AMS

India argued before the panel that the mandated minimum prices that sugar mills were required to pay for sugarcane were not a MPS measure and should not be included in an AMS. The argument rested on India's interpretation of the Agriculture Agreement para. 1, Annex 3, in light of its para. 2. Para. 1 states that for each basic agricultural product "receiving market price support, non-exempt direct payments, or any other subsidy not exempted from the reduction commitment" an AMS shall be calculated. Para. 2 states that subsidies under para. 1 "shall include both budgetary outlays and revenue foregone by governments or their agents." In India's view, the phrase "or any other subsidy" in para. 1 implied MPS also had to be a subsidy. Read in context of para. 2, MPS as a subsidy had to entail budgetary outlays or revenue forgone, which were not entailed in India's sugarcane minimum prices. In India's view, although its mandated minimum prices were not an exempted measure in the context of the Agriculture Agreement, they would nonetheless not have to be included in the residual measures accounted for in an AMS.

The panel rejected India's argument on several grounds. It found that the plain meaning of MPS included mandatory prices fixed by governments and that such measures could provide support to producers of agricultural products. The panel found the textual analysis of para. 1 and

---

[16] The INR/USD exchange rate rose to about 4–5 times its 1986–88 value. Wholesale prices increased to about 5–6 times their 1986–88 levels.

para. 2 open to various interpretations, such that they did not require India's reading. The panel then found the rules for calculation of MPS in para. 8, Annex 3 of the Agreement, pertinent to its investigation. The panel concluded that para. 8 describes the circumstances in which MPS can be said to exist, namely where there is an AAP and rules to determine a quantity of eligible production, and it includes no limitation of MPS only to measures involving purchases by governments or their agents. The panel considered inclusion of minimum-price measures in which payments are made by private entities in MPS consistent with the object and purpose of the Agriculture Agreement, because those measures were apt to cause distortions in markets. Overall, the panel concluded that "the Agreement is clear that market price support does not require government procurement of or payment for the relevant agricultural product" (WTO 2021b, para. 7.59).

Having found that India's minimum price constituted MPS, the panel turned to calculation of the annual levels of support provided during 2014–18. India did not present any calculations, nor did it contest the accuracy of the data, evidence and calculations presented by the complainants. This was unlike in *China – Agricultural Producers* where the values of AAP, FERP and eligible production were all contested by the parties to the dispute and determining the appropriate values of these parameters under the Agriculture Agreement was critical to the panel findings. The *India – Sugar and Sugarcane* panel found that the complainants had sufficiently demonstrated that the FRP and SAPs constituted AAPs for sugarcane and had provided sufficient evidence to determine the AAPs, the FERP and the quantities of eligible production taking into account differences in recovery rates, grading and pricing schemes among the Indian states where sugarcane was produced.

The panel's determination of India's annual MPSs essentially matched those of the complainants and the panel's value of production of sugarcane included sugarcane used for gur.[17] The panel found, for example, that for the 2018/19 sugar season India's sugarcane MPS was INR 1,110.1 billion compared to its AMS limit of INR 123.0 billion (USD 16.2 billion and USD 1.8 billion, respectively, converted here at the 2018 annual exchange rate). The resulting %MPS values ranged from 86.1% to 93.6% as shown in Table 7.2.

---

[17] The Appendix, an integral part of the panel reports, contains the panel's calculations of annual MPSs by state, which it used to calculate annual AMSs for India. The discussion here shows rounded aggregate data.

In conjunction with the minimum prices mills were required to pay for sugarcane, the complainants identified three measures through which the government of India provided payments to mills to meet the cost of cane, particularly for arrears where full payment had not been made. These measures were India's Production Assistance Scheme, Buffer Stock Scheme and Marketing and Transportation Scheme. While the panel took into account that the specific payment criteria of each scheme differed, in each case payments went directly into accounts set up for cane producers with a mill retaining any residual funds only after it had met its obligations to those producers.

Although the three schemes assisted sugar mills in paying the AAP for sugarcane, the panel considered that the benefit accrued to sugar mills and not to cane producers. In assessing domestic support compliance, the panel recognized that the complainants' identified these measures as payments that might be made to maintain the price gap in MPS and that the complainants did not include them in calculating sugarcane AMS. The panel did not identify these payments under domestic support or include them in calculating AMS for sugarcane, in line with its recognition that such payments "should not be taken into account" (WTO 2021b, para. 7.72). Measures directed to processors are only to be included in AMS to the extent that such measures benefit the producers of the basic agricultural product (para. 7, Annex 3). With processors required to pay the government-set minimum prices in any case, no additional benefit accrued to cane producers from the three schemes. Moreover, the Agreement stipulates that budgetary payments, such as buying-in costs, to maintain the price gap between the AAP and the external reference price shall not be included in the AMS (para. 8, Annex 3). The exclusion of the payments under these schemes from AMS eliminates the redundancy that would arise from including not only the MPS calculated using a price gap but also the budgetary payments made to maintain that gap.

The complainants also asserted that three state-level support measures provided small amounts of non-exempt payments or support from other non-exempt policies that should be included in AMSs. While this bolstered their arguments on domestic support and the levels of India's AMSs, the amounts of support added were small. The panel found that the complainants had presented sufficient evidence only to include in AMSs the payments made in Tamil Nadu in 2017/18 (INR 1.4 billion) and 2018/19 (INR 1.0 billion).

The panel findings in *India – Sugar and Sugarcane* provide further judicial interpretation on how the rules of the Agriculture Agreement on domestic support should be applied. In finding levels of MPS under the Agreement that are quite high compared to levels of economic price support, the panel report adds validity to assertions in a counternotification. The ruling is substantial in finding that "India provided non-exempt domestic support to sugarcane producers in excess of the permitted level" (WTO 2021b, para. 7.112) and thus acted inconsistently with its obligations under Art. 7.2(b).

However, the ruling also raises questions about the usefulness of the measurement of MPS under the Agriculture Agreement in achieving the objective of establishing a fair and market-oriented agricultural trading system by reducing support and protection. As noted, an alternative sugarcane calculation indicates that, without a cap on eligible production, even using a price gap adjusted the way India has done for other products, would have indicated support above India's limits and above estimated economic price support. The sugarcane dispute did not address issues involving price gaps or levels of eligible production seen in India's calculation of MPS for other products, as India did not raise them. India's decision not to submit MPS calculations in this dispute may, given the panel's reasoning about those put forth by the complainants, leave India's MPS for other products more vulnerable to challenge, even when economic price support is negative or low.

Australia also claimed that were the minimum sugarcane prices found to constitute MPS then India had violated its obligation to notify this support to the Committee on Agriculture. Beyond its argument that the minimum prices were not a subsidy and were not required to be included in AMS, India argued that Art. 18 of the Agriculture Agreement does not impose mandatory notification requirements and the Committee requirements are not binding on members. The panel found that Art. 18.2 includes an obligation of members to notify all their support measures to the Committee on Agriculture and agreed with Australia that India had violated this notification obligation (WTO 2021b, para. 7.354).

India appealed the panel reports in *India – Sugar and Sugarcane*, whereas in *China – Agricultural Producers* neither party appealed and the Dispute Settlement Body adopted the panel report. The decisions in *China – Agricultural Producers* left room for a government to combine the settings of the AAP and eligible production to generate an MPS within the AMS limit, and China lowered its support prices to some extent. In India, the government in late 2021, after year-long farmer protests, repealed changes in the laws governing agricultural marketing. This context could make it more challenging for India to change its sugarcane policy as required to bring the MPS measure into conformity with its obligations as interpreted by the panel. India's appeal was therefore not surprising since, with the Appellate Body not functioning, it became an appeal into the void. The dispute is thus left unresolved, allowing India to continue its sugarcane support programs at least until resolution.

Export Subsidies

Payments under India's Production Assistance Scheme and Buffer Stock Scheme were made on condition that a mill met a given minimum export quantity and under the Marketing and Transportation Scheme on condition that a mill exported at least 50% of a given maximum export quantity. The complainants claimed that the payments under these schemes were export subsidies that violated both the Agriculture Agreement and the SCM Agreement.

The panel examined the consistency of the three schemes and a fourth scheme (Duty Free Import Authorization) with Art. 9.1(a) of the Agriculture Agreement, which describes certain forms of export subsidies subject to reduction commitments as:

> the provision by governments or their agencies of direct subsidies, including payments-in-kind, to a firm, to an industry, to producers of an agricultural product, to a cooperative or other association of such producers, or to a marketing board, contingent on export performance.

Examining the evidence, and drawing on SCM Art. 1 as relevant context for determining what constitutes a subsidy (particularly there being a financial contribution that provides a benefit), the panel concluded that India's government through the four schemes granted to sugar mills, as producers of an agricultural product, direct subsidies contingent on export performance. Since India does not have a scheduled ceiling commitment for sugar export subsidies, the panel concluded that India's subsidies contingent on export performance were inconsistent with Art. 3.3 and Art. 8 of the Agriculture Agreement.

Turning to the SCM Agreement, the panel rejected India's claims that the export subsidy transition period under SCM Art. 27 for certain developing country members had not expired for India and that SCM Art. 3.1(a) therefore did not apply to its subsidies. The panel found that the complainants having established the existence of a subsidy within the meaning of SCM Art. 1 and its contingency on export performance in the context of Art. 9.1(a) of the Agriculture Agreement was sufficient to conclude the four schemes violated the prohibition of export subsidies under SCM Art. 3.[18] The panel also concluded India violated its notification obligations on export subsidies under both agreements. As it did on the sugarcane support conclusions, India appealed into the void the panel conclusions on sugar export subsidies. Finally, it bears mention that the panel decisions on the four schemes did not involve an argument that they were domestic support measures that caused the export subsidization found to exist, even though three of the schemes made payments to assist sugar mills in paying the AAP to sugarcane producers.

7.3 An Option for Improving the Measurement of Market Price Support

The difference between the measurement of MPS under the Agriculture Agreement and an economic measurement is problematic in terms of achieving substantial progressive reductions in agricultural support and protection. The diversity of measurements of MPS under different interpretations of the Agreement in notifications, counter-notifications and dispute arguments adds complexity to the problem. While recognizing that the Agreement's measurement of MPS relies on using the policy-determined variables of AAP and eligible production, a major part of the difference between it and an economic measurement is the use of a reference price that has remained constant for a long time. This motivates examining ways to reduce the difference between the Agreement's MPS and an economic MPS.

Revising the MPS calculation under the Agriculture Agreement to base the reference price on price observations from lagged recent years would in many situations make it and the economic MPS more similar without making them identical. A further step in making the rules-based MPS more like an economic MPS would be to apply the calculated price gap to all production, whether purchased under the price support program or not. This is because all production benefits when the AAP exceeds the border price in a situation where a significant percentage of national output can be sold at the AAP and where arbitrage across geographically dispersed

---

[18] The panel rejected India's argument that the Marketing and Transportation Scheme provided export subsidies permitted under Art. 9.4 for developing countries. Only Australia challenged the Duty Free Import Authorization Scheme for sugar. The panel rejected India's argument that this scheme for sugar qualified under footnote 1 of the SCM Agreement not to be deemed to be a subsidy.

domestic markets at the farm level ensures the support price determines the minimum producer price nationally.

A lagged reference price (LRP) option for measuring MPS would replace the FERP with a moving average of lagged world market border prices adjusted for transportation costs and stage of processing for comparability with the basic agricultural product to which the AAP applies. The LRP MPS using, for example, a three-year moving average of lagged prices, would be:

$$LRP\ MPS_t = [AAP_t - LRP_t] \times [Total\ Production_t]$$

where LRP_t is the moving average of lagged border prices (average $[t - 1, t - 2, t - 3]$ or an Olympic moving average from five lagged years dropping the lowest and highest values). The LRP MPS enables the government to use an administered price to benchmark producer prices in the domestic market within the space that is available within the applicable border protection. Some members see this as an essential policy option. Since the LRP MPS uses AAP in the price gap, there is room for the domestic price to exceed the AAP without raising the LRP MPS. This would accommodate the effects on domestic prices of tariffs or other border or behind-the-border policy measures, without subjecting these effects to the domestic support discipline. As the panel in *China – Agricultural Producers* noted when considering corn prices after the price support program was terminated in 2016, domestic prices can differ from border prices not only because of an administered price but for reasons that are not disciplined by AMS limits.

Comparing three MPS measurements (Agreement MPS, Economic MPS and LRP MPS based on three lagged years) in percentage terms for wheat in China and India over the period 2008–18 illustrates their differences (Figure 7.2). With eligible production and value of production from year *t*, the measurements differ only by the different price gaps in their numerators.[19]

The measurements for China prompt several observations. First, the Agreement %MPS rose sharply after 2010 from earlier negative or low

[19] The quantity of production and value of production in year *t* are not known when the AAP for year *t* is determined. However, not having final information on these variables when government sets the AAP for year *t* has not been a concern in members' *ex post* calculations of MPS under the Agriculture Agreement and an *ex post* evaluation is applied here as well. For China these calculations use total national production as eligible production, not the dispute panel's production in the provinces and regions where the price support program operated. For India, the currency of AAP, FERP and value of production is INR.

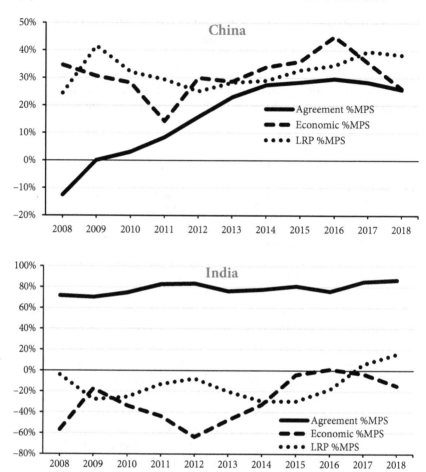

Figure 7.2 Measurements of wheat market price support of China and India, 2008–18 (percent).
SOURCE: Authors' calculations using data on support prices and from OECD (2021b).

positive levels as China raised AAPs. The Agreement %MPS exceeds 25% by 2014 and remains at similar levels through 2018. Second, the economic %MPS and LRP %MPS exceed Agreement %MPS in all years, although the three measurements come closer together in the later years of higher AAPs. The economic %MPS and LRP %MPS move together in most years, although there are also year-to-year differences due mostly to deviations of time t references prices from their lagged average. A given limit applying to MPS would generally constrain the economic MPS and LRP MPS to a similar extent. It would, especially in the earlier years, constrain these MPSs more than the Agreement MPS calculated with total production.

The corresponding assessment for wheat in India has quite a different narrative. The key observation for India is the large difference between the Agreement %MPS and the economic and LRP %MPSs. The Agreement %MPS is nearly 80% in all years, similar to the levels in the counter-notification for wheat. Conversely, the economic %MPS and LRP %MPS are negative as domestic prices are generally below year t border prices and AAPs below lagged border prices.[20] Unlike the Agreement MPS, with the LRP MPS India would not need to lower wheat support prices or cap eligible production to meet its AMS limits, which is more consistent with its negative economic MPS.

A second observation for India is that economic MPS and LRP MPS move along a common track although less closely so than for China. The largest difference occurs in 2012, primarily because the 2012 border price increased to exceed lagged border prices. The subsequent trend of economic %MPS becoming less negative comes from domestic prices increasing while border prices fall. The negative LRP %MPS declines to become more negative through 2015 as lagged border prices rise by more than AAPs.

The above comparisons reinforce the idea that improving the measurement of MPS under the Agriculture Agreement could bring the effect of the Agreement's discipline on AMS closer to what it would be if its MPS was the economic MPS. Using a moving average of lagged border prices as the reference price is not ideal compared to using the current border price. However, it brings the reference price in many situations closer to the current border price than using a FERP based on increasingly distant past years.[21]

The use of a moving average reference price in MPS calculations was discussed in the Uruguay Round negotiations as was the idea of a FERP being fixed only for five years. Introducing a moving average reference price or adjusting the base years for FERP then received only scant

---

[20] OECD (2021b) sets MPS to zero in years (2008–10 and 2017–18) when India imports wheat while domestic producer prices are below the border reference prices. Figure 7.2 retains any negative values in economic and LRP MPSs.

[21] Using an average of lagged border prices would have reduced or eliminated price gaps for the notified MPS products of China, India, EU, United States and Japan in a recent year, as noted in Chapter 6.

attention in negotiations, with somewhat more focus on this issue at the 12th ministerial conference. The G-33 group had earlier suggested calculating an external reference price as a moving average or reducing AAP for excessive inflation (WTO 2013c), but discussion waned as attention focused on the proposed interim solution. In more recent years the African Group highlighted the problems with the outdated FERP and proposed a moving average of past prices as the external reference price when higher than the FERP from 1986 to 1988 (WTO 2021i). The African Group proposal would make permanent the insulation from dispute challenge of compliance when MPS resulting from stock acquisition at administered prices generates an excessive AMS even with the modified reference price.

The African Group, the ACP members and the G-33 then proposed that a year's external reference price be the Olympic moving average price of the preceding five years, or the Agreement's external reference price adjusted for excessive inflation (WTO 2022f). Instead of there being an explicit shelter against dispute settlement regarding compliance of support with limits, any producer support under public stockholding programs would, provided that certain conditions were met, be deemed to be in compliance with the Agreement's limits on AMS support. Thus, in both of these proposals by groups of members adjusting the reference price is a secondary consideration to continuing the insulation of MPS from acquisition of stocks for food security purposes at administered prices from dispute challenge or limit. The permanent insulation is problematic as a solution to the public stockholding issue because it would leave output price support for major crops in developing countries exempt from being capped. With investment and input subsidies also exempt under Art. 6.2, distorting producer support would essentially be completely unconstrained, which is inconsistent with the objective of the Agreement.

The Committee on Agriculture in Special Session formulated draft decisions for the 2022 ministerial conference as it convened in June. On the public stockholding issue the draft decision suggested only that members continue negotiations and "work towards agreeing and adopting a permanent solution" by the following conference (WTO 2022e). The draft decision suggested that the negotiations consider "an assessment of the external reference price" along with other issues. This is the first mention of assessing the reference price in a document at this level, which also noted that the reference price issue "would be considered more broadly in the context of current AoA disciplines." Outside of the negotiations, the New Pathways group of independent observers recommended a lagged moving average reference price (Cahill and Tangermann 2021). Glauber and Sinha (2021), writing for the International Institute for Sustainable Development, also discuss the option of an updated or moving average reference price while, like the African Group, their main recommendation is an extension of the interim solution.

The experience gained over time of implementing price support policies and applying the rules of the Agreement warrants all of the recent consideration and further analysis of using a moving average of lagged border prices instead of a FERP to calculate MPS. Retaining the economically misleading FERP-based indicator of price support when negotiating new legal rules on domestic support does not seem a fruitful route to correcting and preventing distortions in world agricultural markets.

7.4 Disputes Addressing Other Constraints on Domestic Support Measures

7.4.1 US – Upland Cotton

In *US – Upland Cotton*, initiated in 2002, Brazil asserted that certain US measures related to the export of upland cotton (and other agricultural products) during 1999–2002 violated US export subsidy obligations under the Agriculture Agreement and the SCM Agreement and certain other US cotton subsidies were actionable under the SCM Agreement and caused serious prejudice to its interests due to significant price suppression in world markets (WTO 2002b). The economic context of this dispute was that after a brief spike in 1996–97, agricultural commodity markets experienced a broad multi-year trough with relatively low world prices. The dispute proved complex and extended (Table 7.3 gives a chronology of the key developments). This section reviews the main arguments and outcomes in the comprehensive adjudication regarding both export subsidization and domestic support and their interrelated effects on world markets.[22]

---

[22] Earlier reviews of *US – Upland Cotton* include McMahon (2006), Sapir and Trachtman (2008), Davey and Sapir (2010), Grossman and Sykes (2011), Glauber (2018b), and Mazza de Andrade and Flores Schmidt (2019).

Table 7.3 *Key developments in* US – Upland Cotton, *2002–18*

Year	Developments
Initial proceedings	
2002–03	Consultations requested; Panel composed
2004–05	Panel and Appellate Body reports adopted
Delayed adjudication and negotiations	
2005	US announces new rate structure for GSM–102, terminates applications for GSM–103 and ceases issuing SCGP export credit guarantees
	Brazil requests authorization of countermeasures; US notifies its objections; referred to arbitration; Brazil and US jointly request suspension
2006–07	Step 2 payments program terminated
	Brazil requests DSU Art. 21.5 panel; Compliance report circulated
2008	2008 US farm bill extends cotton support programs, terminates GSM–103 and SCGP programs, modifies GSM–102 loan conditions
	Panel and Appellate Body compliance reports adopted; Brazil requests resumption of arbitration
2009	Decision of arbitrator circulated; Brazil authorized to take countermeasures
2010	Temporary agreements: US to make annual payment to Brazilian Cotton Institute; steps agreed toward ultimate negotiated solution; Brazil postpones countermeasures
2013	US terminates payments to Brazil, having paid nearly USD 500 million
Subsequent US policies	
2014	2014 farm bill makes cotton ineligible for countercyclical support programs; cotton base acres reclassified; new cotton loan rate formula; transition payments of $478 million to cotton producers; payments to domestic users of cotton from any source; new STAX (Stacked Income Protection Plan) insurance program for cotton; GSM–102 program contract length capped at 24 months
	Brazil and US *Memorandum of Understanding* to terminate the dispute: US pays additional USD 300 million; GSM–102 program contract length capped at 18 months and fees to cover long-term operating costs and losses; Brazil not to request dispute consultation on cotton support or GSM–103
2018	2014 farm bill amended to establish a seed cotton countercyclical support program; acreage enrolled in the seed cotton program not eligible for STAX
	2018 farm bill continues the cotton lint marketing loan program and extends the seed cotton countercyclical program

SOURCE: Authors' compilation.

Initial Arguments and Findings

The main argument on export subsidies was that three export credit guarantee programs of the United States, known as GSM–102, GSM–103 and SCGP, provided subsidies that were inconsistent with its export subsidy obligations under the Agriculture and SCM Agreements (WTO 2004b).[23] Two main questions were addressed. First, did Art. 10.2 of the Agriculture Agreement exempt the US programs from the stipulation of Art. 10.1 that export subsidies "shall not be applied in a manner which results in, or which threatens to lead to, circumvention of export subsidy commitments; nor shall non-commercial transactions be used to circumvent such commitments." Second, if not exempt, did the US credit guarantee programs violate Art. 10.1 and consequentially provide export subsidies in violation of the Agriculture Agreement and prohibited under the SCM Agreement. Agriculture Agreement Art. 10.2 states that:

> Members undertake to work toward the development of internationally agreed disciplines to govern the provision of export credits, export credit guarantees or insurance programmes and, after agreement on such disciplines, to provide export credits, export credit guarantees or insurance programmes only in conformity therewith.

The United States argued that Art. 10.2, taken in context of the negotiating history, excluded its export credit guarantee programs from the stipulation in Art. 10.1 against circumventing export subsidy commitments until disciplines were agreed, which at the time had not been achieved. With one member dissenting, the Appellate Body rejected the US argument. With Art. 10.1 found applicable, the panel and Appellate Body concurred that the US programs provided prohibited export subsidies for cotton and other products without scheduled export subsidy commitments and circumvented the US export subsidy commitment for rice, a scheduled product.

Brazil also argued that US payments known as Step 2 payments, to defray differences between world market prices and higher domestic prices, made to cotton exporters upon export of domestic cotton and users upon its utilization in cotton-based products were prohibited subsidies. The United States argued that since these payments were made for both export or

---

[23] General Sales Manager (GSM)–102 and GSM–103 offered guarantees on repayment of credit made available from foreign banks to finance commercial exports of agricultural products on credit between 90 days and 3 years and 3–10 years, respectively. The Supply Credit Guarantee Program (SCGP) guaranteed the repayment of credit extended by a US exporter for a period up to 180 days.

domestic use, covering the universe of uses, they were not prohibited subsidies and were notified under the Agriculture Agreement as part of AMS support. The applicable discipline, the United States argued, was that support remain within its domestic support commitment, including support from measures directed at processors to the extent that such measures benefit producers of basic agricultural products. The panel rejected the US argument that the domestic support commitment was the only discipline applicable to Step 2 payments. The panel found the Step 2 payments to cotton exporters were inconsistent with US obligations under Art. 3.3 and Art. 8 of the Agriculture Agreement that it not provide export subsidies except as specified in its schedule and were prohibited export subsidies under Art. 3.1(a) and Art. 3.2 of the SCM Agreement. It also found that the Agriculture Agreement made no provision for, nor specifically allowed, subsidies contingent on use of domestic over imported goods and that the Step 2 payments for domestic use of domestic cotton therefore violated Art. 3.1(b) and Art. 3.2 of the SCM Agreement.

The argument about actionable subsidies in *US – Upland Cotton* concerned support measures that Brazil asserted resulted in significant price suppression, causing adverse effects in the form of serious prejudice to its interests in violation of SCM Art. 5. The panel found three types of payments to be price contingent: (i) those made on each year's output when the domestic cotton market price fell below the legislated loan rate (support price) of USD 0.52 per pound (the US marketing loan program, notified as product-specific AMS support); (ii) Step 2 payments (found to be both prohibited and actionable subsidies); and (iii) payments made on base acreage and fixed yields per acre determined by past cotton production, with current planting flexibility not requiring cotton be grown, when current domestic cotton prices fell below the higher legislated target price of USD 0.724 per pound (the 2002 US CCP program, notified as non-product-specific AMS support, and similar ad hoc Market Loss Assistance [MLA] payments during 1999–2001). Two other support measures were found not to be price contingent: (iv) fixed payments decoupled from both prices and cotton production made on base acreage and yields determined by past production (the US PFC and Direct Payments, notified as green box *Decoupled income support*) and (v) programs providing premium subsidies on crop insurance which at the time primarily covered only yield risk.

An initial procedural issue concerned whether the challenged measures were subject to the SCM Agreement even though Art. 13 (Due Restraint) of the Agriculture Agreement before 2004 excluded from

SCM challenge measures fully compliant with Annex 2 (Art. 13(a)) and measures that did not "grant support to a specific commodity in excess of that decided during the 1992 marketing year" (Art. 13(b)(ii)).

Two issues were considered on compliance of the US PFC and Direct Payments with the Annex 2 criteria for exempt payments. They arose in assessing whether the Art. 13 rule against challenge, conditional on support not exceeding that decided during the 1992 marketing year, applied to non-exempt US measures. The panel first considered whether a prohibition on producing fruits, vegetables or wild rice on base acres failed the criterion that payments not be "related to, or based on, the type or volume of production" after the base period (para. 6(b), Annex 2). The panel concluded that the prohibition was inconsistent with this criterion and hence the US payments decoupled from prices and current cotton production did not fully conform with Annex 2. Having found the US payments not conforming on these grounds, the panel considered it unnecessary also to make findings on whether updating of base acres allowed between the 1996 and 2002 farm bills met the Annex 2 condition that eligibility for payments be determined by "clearly-defined criteria . . . in a defined and fixed based period" (para. 6(a), Annex 2).

Whether support "to a specific commodity" was provided in excess of that during the 1992 marketing year raised the question of whether US payments made on base acres and fixed yields, either price-contingent or at fixed rates not affected by current prices, should be included in that comparison. The panel subsequently evaluated the question of whether either of these types of measures contributed to significant price suppression.

The panel found that both types of US measures making payments based on past output provided support to the specific commodity of cotton. The Appellate Body overturned a panel finding that payments on any base acreage on which cotton was grown should be counted in each year, instead ruling that only cotton base acreage payments on acres planted to cotton should be counted, a so-called cotton-to-cotton methodology. The Appellate Body nonetheless concurred with the panel that US support each year during 1999–2002 exceeded support decided in 1992 such that the measures could be challenged under the SCM Agreement.

The panel determined that price suppression could be evaluated at the world market level. It took two market circumstances into account to assess whether significant price suppression had occurred. First, the panel found that US cotton exports increased from 23.5% of world total in 1999 to 39.9% in 2002, with a substantial proportionate influence on the world market. Second, the panel found a close temporal correspondence between the US cotton support and declining world prices, concluding the correspondence was relevant to its adjudication but not "in and of itself, conclusive for a determination of price suppression" (WTO 2004b, para. 7.1288).

On the structure, design and operation of the subsidies, the panel viewed as critical a distinction between those that were price contingent and those not contingent on prices. The panel concluded that the structure, design and operation of the marketing loan and Step 2 programs had "enhanced production and trade-distorting effects" (WTO 2004b, para. 7.1295).[24]

The panel concluded that the nature of the measures providing price-contingent payments based on past output reduced revenue risk and also had a nexus with the subsidized product and the world market cotton price. Moreover, the panel found that market revenue did not cover total costs of cotton production. Overall, the panel concluded that the nature of the price-contingent subsidies taken into consideration with the magnitude of the subsidies "constitutes strong evidence supporting a finding of price suppression" (WTO 2004b, para 7.1308).

Conversely, the panel concluded that the non-price-contingent payments decoupled from prices and cotton production and premium subsidies on crop insurance had effects that were not as easily discernable. The panel excluded these measures from its determination of price suppression, stating that Brazil had not established on the basis of their structure, design and operation that these measures

> had a sufficient nexus with the marketing of the subsidized product and the price suppression effects as to render their inclusion or non-inclusion in our price suppression analysis legally determinative in respect of the significant price suppression that we have found (WTO 2004b, para. 7.1350).[25]

---

[24] Although not quantified in the panel report, payments under these two programs exceeded USD 2.0 billion in 1999 and 2001 and averaged 40.4% of the value of production of cotton during 1999–2002, compared, for example, to 8.7% from similar measures for corn and wheat.

[25] In making this determination, the panel asserted that the SCM Agreement permitted an integrated examination of effects of any subsidies with a sufficient nexus with the subsidized product and the particular effects-related variable under examination. Later WTO cases have confirmed that it is appropriate for panels to use categorizations of subsidies, such as price-contingent and non-price-contingent subsidies, when structuring their causation analysis. The Appellate Body in US – Large Civil Aircraft (DS353), for example, emphasized that a panel must take due account of all subsidies that provide a relevant and identifiable competitive advantage to the recipient and its product (WTO 2012). Where one or more categories of subsidies are shown to supplement or complement the effects of other subsidies that, by themselves, cause adverse effects, they should

While the United States appealed nearly every key decision of the panel, the Appellate Body upheld the panel's procedural and substantive findings in nearly every regard (WTO 2005c).

Delayed Further Adjudication

The Dispute Settlement Body called upon the United States to withdraw its prohibited subsidies without delay (by 1 July 2005) and to take appropriate steps to remove the adverse effects or withdraw the actionable subsidies by 21 September 2005. Instead, adoption of the reports led to a protracted 11-year period of negotiations, adjudication and policy revamping.

Initially, Brazil sought authorization of countermeasures for US non-compliance with the rulings on both prohibited and actionable subsidies. The matter was referred to arbitration then Brazil and the United States jointly requested suspension of the arbitration proceedings. The United States announced modifications to the GSM–102 program, moved toward termination of GSM–103 and SCGP and terminated the Step 2 program in 2006. It made no changes to the other subsidies for upland cotton. These only partial responses prompted Brazil to request establishment of a compliance panel.

The compliance panel scrutinized the US measures under updated market conditions of 2002–05 (WTO 2007). The panel found that the United States continued to provide export subsidies under the modified GSM–102 program. For its finding, the panel drew on item (j) of the Illustrative List of Export Subsidies in Annex I to the SCM Agreement, finding that GSM–102 premiums charged failed to cover long-term operating costs and losses under the program. The provision of GSM–102 export credit guarantees for cotton and other unscheduled products as well as for rice, pig meat and poultry meat above scheduled levels meant that such export subsidies were inconsistent with Agriculture Agreement Art. 10.1 and Art. 8. The panel also concluded that these export subsidies were prohibited under SCM Art. 3.1(a).

be included in the adverse effects finding where their contribution is meaningful or non-trivial. This suggests a panel ruling in more recent years on the US cotton non-price-contingent subsidies might find differently than the panel did in 2004. Where subsidies are found to supplement or complement the adverse effects of other subsidies, a respondent may under Article 7.8 of the SCM Agreement choose to withdraw all subsidies determined to result in adverse effects or to take steps to remove the adverse effects. These steps might include moving toward relying more on those measures with less effects, whether they supplement or complement the adverse effects of other subsidies.

On actionable subsidies, the compliance panel made a "but for" assessment of the effects of the US marketing loan and CCP programs (WTO 2007, para. 10.46). The panel found the United States had a substantial influence on the world market and that the price-contingent nature and revenue-stabilizing effects of the US programs insulated domestic cotton producers from low prices. It was more explicit than the original panel about the magnitude of the subsidies, noting marketing loan payments of USD 1.26 billion in 2005 and countercyclical payments, calculated using the cotton-to-cotton methodology, of USD 838 million. The panel found that market revenue did not cover total costs of cotton production except during 2003. It concluded that during the more recent period there continued to be significant price suppression as a result of the US price-contingent support programs, resulting in present serious prejudice to the interests of Brazil. Again the United States appealed many of the panel findings.

The Appellate Body upheld that the GSM–102 program provided export subsidies that were inconsistent with the Agriculture Agreement and prohibited under the SCM Agreement. The Appellate Body also upheld that the marketing loan and CCP programs caused significant price suppression (WTO 2008b). The US farm bill of 2008 extended the cotton domestic support programs. It terminated the GSM–103 and SCGP programs and modified some GSM–102 program elements. Brazil then sought resumption of the countermeasures arbitration. The limited changes to GSM–102 and absence in the 2008 farm bill of material change in the marketing loan or CCP programs as they applied to cotton informed Brazil's decision, taken while tighter limits on US domestic support were being pursued but not agreed in the Doha Round negotiations.

Brazil based its countermeasure claims on economic analysis it had earlier presented to the compliance panel.[26] Evaluation of price suppression rested on three types of parameters of the economic model: the elasticities (responsiveness) of US and rest-of-world supply and demand for cotton in response to changing prices, the relative degree to which countercyclical payments made on cotton base acres and past yields increased cotton production incentives (coupling factor) and the harvest-time prices expected when the cotton crop was planted. Under Brazil's assumptions, the analysis suggested that for the 2005/06 marketing year US

---

[26] Coppens (2014) discusses the compliance panel reasoning and the arbitrator's evaluation of Brazil's economic simulation model in determining the level of countermeasures.

cotton production was 18.8% higher and world prices were suppressed by 10.8% due to the price-contingent support programs.

Overall, the arbitrator accepted the economic parameters proposed by Brazil. The supply response of US producers, where a permanent change in support policy was argued to be well-understood, was modeled as more elastic (0.8) than in the rest-of-world (0.2) where various factors could mute price perceptions or transmission. Demand for cotton was assumed to be price inelastic in both cases (−0.2). These parameters influence the simulated world market equilibrium price in absence of the US support programs. The arbitrator found the elasticity values proposed by Brazil consistent with the range of estimates seen in various previous studies and relevant to the issues under its consideration. The arbitrator also accepted the coupling factor of 0.4 for countercyclical payments proposed by Brazil rather than 0.25 proposed by the United States as consistent with relevant literature. Finally, the arbitrator determined that post-harvest futures prices at time of planting were the best representation of the price expectations of US cotton producers. The expected future prices mattered because a historically estimated distribution of subsequent prices around this expectation was used in the model to simulate the producers' assessment about the subsidies they might receive and hence the effects of those subsidies on their production decisions.

Taking these determinations into account, the arbitrator concluded that adverse effects of USD 2.9 billion on cotton producers in the rest of the world resulted from the US price-contingent support programs. Seven years after consultations were requested, the arbitrator determined that worldwide adverse effects were close to the effects Brazil had claimed. The arbitrator also found that Brazil, as the sole complaining member, was only entitled to impose countermeasures commensurate with the impact of those adverse effects on its own cotton producers. This came annually to USD 147.3 million.[27]

Brazil was authorized to impose countermeasures in November 2009. This led to the announcement in 2010 of two interim agreements toward ultimately reaching a negotiated solution. That solution rested on changes in US farm support legislation expected through a 2012 farm bill, eventually enacted in 2014. In the interim, the United States made annual payments of USD 147.3 million to the Brazilian Cotton Institute for certain cotton-sector development activities. With the 2014 farm bill

---

[27] The arbitrator also determined countermeasures of USD 147.4 million due to the effects of GSM–102 (WTO 2009).

enacted, Brazil and the United States agreed to terminate the dispute (WTO 2014). The United States made a final payment of USD 300 million and the agreement circumscribed more tightly some elements of the operation of the GSM–102 program. Brazil agreed not to request new dispute consultations regarding the US support programs through September 2018 and on GSM–102 as long as it operated as specified. The circumscribed condition under which Brazil and the United States agreed GSM–102 would operate became a basis for the subsequent decision on export credits, export credit guarantees or insurance programs at the 2015 WTO ministerial conference.

Subsequent US Cotton Policies

The United States substantially altered its crop support programs in the 2014 farm bill. The fixed Direct Payments, which had become politically unpopular in an era of higher market prices, were terminated for all crops and the countercyclical CCP program was renamed as Price Loss Coverage (PLC). A new Agriculture Risk Coverage (ARC) program was created with payments made on base acres when revenue fell short of an Olympic moving average of the five previous years. Base updating was again allowed, and farmers were permitted to choose between the ARC and PLC programs for the duration of the farm bill. Crop insurance by 2014 primarily consisted of revenue insurance providing protection against both yield and price risk.

The 2014 farm bill changed the cotton support programs even more substantially. Cotton was excluded from eligibility for ARC and PLC. The 17.6 million cotton base acres were reclassified as generic base acres on which ARC and PLC payments were contingent on production of an eligible crop in a given year, not determined by earlier production. Marketing loan rates for cotton were changed to a moving average of two years of past adjusted world market prices, within a specified range. Cotton remained eligible for subsidized crop insurance. The Stacked Income Protection Plan (STAX), an insurance program exclusively for cotton, replaced eligibility for ARC and PLC. It covered losses between 10% of insured revenue and the coverage level of the producer's other cotton insurance. STAX premiums were heavily subsidized, with only 20% paid by the producer.

Removing cotton from eligibility for the countercyclical ARC and PLC programs was a historic break from having support programs for cotton operate in tandem with programs for other crops. *US – Upland Cotton* can be viewed as an essential catalyst for this revamping of cotton domestic support. Analysis similar to that used in arbitration suggested that the new STAX program could be highly distorting, although Brazil had agreed not to challenge it through 2018 (Lau et al. 2015). The issue never arose as the STAX program proved unpopular.

By February 2018, cotton eligibility for the ARC and PLC support programs was restored based on seed cotton (prior to ginning) instead of cotton lint (Schnepf 2018). The 2018 farm bill then extended the seed cotton program. The regulations for reverting generic base acres back to cotton resulted in a drop to 12.9 million base acres, reducing eligibility for seed cotton payments from the higher previous cotton base acreage.

Almost all seed cotton base acreage was enrolled in PLC, under which payments totaled USD 1.7 billion for the three years 2018–20. Counterfactual simulation suggests that payments would have reached USD 1.5 billion annually during 1999–2002 had the seed cotton program existed, a level of payments similar to that of the cotton lint counter-cyclical programs in those years (Glauber 2018b). Thus, some 15 years after Brazil first requested consultations, the nature – the structure, design and operation – of US price-contingent domestic support programs for cotton had not fundamentally changed. World market prices were strong enough that the legislated parameters of the marketing loan program and new seed cotton program resulted in lower levels of subsidies than in the years for which significant price suppression was found. Neither Brazil nor any other WTO member has sought dispute settlement consultations about the US domestic support programs for cotton, or for any other crop, in these circumstances.

7.4.2   EC – Export Subsidies on Sugar

A dispute over export subsidies resulting from a domestic support regime also arose in 2002. The EU sugar policy regime of domestic support and trade measures had regulated almost every aspect of its sugar market for more than three decades when Australia, Brazil and Thailand initiated *EC – Export Subsidies on Sugar* (WTO 2002c, 2002d, 2003).[28] In the EU sugar sector, primarily sugar beets are produced at the farm level, which are processed into raw or processed (white) sugar that is consumed domestically and traded on world markets. Under the EU's Common Market Organization for Sugar, domestic sugar prices, and the related prices of

---

[28] This section refers to the EC as the EU except when quoting or directly discussing WTO dispute documents.

sugar beets, were held about three times higher than world market levels through the 2005/06 marketing year. Intervention prices, at which the government would make purchases, set a floor for domestic sugar prices, and quotas on production for the domestic market were restricted sufficiently to keep prices above the intervention levels. Production was controlled through two categories of quota allocations (A and B sugar, respectively about 11.9 million tonnes and 2.6 million tonnes in the early 2000s). Only limited transfer was allowed between quota holders either among EU member states or among producers within a member state. Sugar produced above the quotas (C sugar) faced stiff penalties unless exported under license or carried over in limited quantities that would apply toward the production quotas in the following year.

Any A and B sugar sold on world markets was exported with refunds from the government making up the difference between domestic and world prices, while C sugar exports were priced at world market levels. The refunds for A and B sugar were funded by beet and sugar producers based on levies applied against the prices received for A sugar (up to 2%) and B sugar (up to 37.5%). The EU's WTO schedule at the time limited export subsidies on sugar to no more than EUR 499.1 million and 1.3 million tonnes. The EU also made annual concessional purchases of sugar at zero duty from ACP countries under the ACP/EC Partnership Agreement. These imports received the high EU domestic prices as a form of development assistance. The EU exported an equivalent amount of sugar at world market prices, so the preferential imports did not alter the net availability of sugar from quota production in its internal market.

The *EC – Export Subsidies on Sugar* dispute centered on two main issues: exports of sugar equivalent to its ACP imports with taxpayer-financed refunds and alleged subsidization of exports of C sugar. None of these exports were incorporated into its scheduled commitments.

Exports Equivalent to Imports from ACP Countries

With respect to the first issue, a footnote in the schedule merely indicated that the commitment "Does not include exports of sugar of ACP and Indian origin on which the Community is not making any reduction commitments. The average of export in the period 1986–1990 amounted to 1,6 mio t" (1.6 million tonnes).

The EU argued that the footnote in its schedule allowed export of the equivalent sugar in excess of its commitment, that the complainants had understood this during the Uruguay Round negotiations and that their acceptance of inclusion of the footnote implied that they accepted that it altered the EU obligation. The panel and Appellate Body dismissed these arguments, finding that the footnote did not enlarge or otherwise modify the commitment levels in the schedule (WTO 2005b, para. 225). The panel and Appellate Body then found in favor of the complainants that exports of the equivalent to ACP (1.3 million tonnes) and Indian (10,000 tonnes) sugar received direct subsidies provided by government as described in Art. 9.1(a) of the Agriculture Agreement. This violated the commitment if either the scheduled subsidy value or quantity were exceeded. The panel and Appellate Body found there were excesses and that the EC violated Agriculture Agreement Art. 3.3 and Art. 8. The ruling did not involve the effects of the domestic quota and price support measures on the level of subsidized exports of sugar.

Cross-Subsidization of Exports through Support of Production for Domestic Consumption

The second issue was whether exports of C sugar, varying from 1.3 to 3.3 million tonnes annually between 1997 and 2002, were cross-subsidized by the support provided through domestic production quotas and high domestic prices and were thus subsidized exports within the meaning of the Agriculture Agreement. The EU argued that C sugar exports did not receive any subsidies and that the complainants did not act in good faith, asserting it had never before been argued that C sugar exports were subsidized. The Appellate Body upheld the panel's finding that the complainants acted in good faith.

Before the panel and Appellate Body, the determination of whether C sugar exports were subsidized rested on arguments related to Art. 9.1(c), which identifies export subsidies arising from

> payments on the export of an agricultural product that are financed by virtue of governmental action, whether or not a charge on the public account is involved, including payments that are financed from the proceeds of a levy imposed on the agricultural product concerned or on an agricultural product from which the exported product is derived.

The wording of Art. 9.1(c) relates closely to programs along lines of the EU sugar regime. The determination hinged on whether there were payments within the meaning of Art. 9.1(c), whether they were on the export, and whether they were financed by virtue of governmental action.

The panel found, and the Appellate Body upheld, that there were in effect two types of payments-in-kind that were covered by the word payments in Art. 9.1(c). This followed the logic of the panel and Appellate Body in *Canada – Dairy*, where sales of milk at below average total cost of production for processing into dairy products for export had been found to provide export subsidies (WTO 2002a, 2002e). The two forms of sugar payments were "through sales of C beet below the total costs of production to C sugar producers" (WTO 2004a, para. 7.293), and internally to sugar processing firms "in the form of transfers of financial resources, through cross-subsidization resulting from the operation of the EC sugar regime" (WTO 2004a, para. 7.338). Because of the restrictions on disposition of C sugar and the entire market regulatory structure of the sugar regime, the panel and Appellate Body held these payments were on the export and arose by virtue of governmental action. By providing export subsidies within the meaning of Art. 9.1(c) for C sugar in excess of its commitments the EC was in violation of Art. 3.3 and Art 8. of the Agriculture Agreement.

While the panel used the word cross-subsidization only for the second type of payments it found within the meaning of Art. 9.1(c), the issue for each type of payment is the same: whether beet producers or sugar processors used revenue received from their domestic sales under the A and B quotas at high domestic prices to make it profitable to sell C beets or sugar at a price below the average total cost of production. This subsidization can occur when there are fixed or quasi-fixed factors of production and the quota quantity is less than the level of output that minimizes average total cost of production per unit.[29] In this case, it can be profitable to produce beyond the quota amount and sell that add-itional output at marginal cost of production (in the case of C sugar production at the world market price) even when that sale price is below average total cost. This occurs because the fixed cost of each unit of output declines with the added production, so total profits increase. The panel found that beet producers were selling beets processed into C sugar at less than their average total cost of production and that this constituted

---

[29] De Gorter et al. (2008) develop the theory of the full set of conditions under which cross-subsidization can occur, including both by expansion of output of firms profitable at the quota levels and high domestic prices and by deterring exit of firms that are unprofitable at quota output levels even with high domestic prices but are profitable with their quotas and an expanded level of output. Gohin and Bureau (2006) discount the fixed-factors cross-subsidization argument in the long run where quasi-fixed factors would adjust to optimal levels for quota output. They highlight two other ways the EU sugar regime could have cross-subsidized C sugar production: to ensure that A and B quotas could be filled even as annual yields vary and to be able to retain quota in the event that future levels were reduced. The dispute panel acknowledged both of these possible effects. Gohin and Bureau contrast the subsidization incentives with the possibility that efficient EU sugar producers could produce C sugar without subsidy. In their empirical analysis, they find evidence of cross-subsidization of C sugar production. See also Hoekman and Howse (2008).

a payment to sugar processors. Likewise, the panel found that the transfer by sugar processors of financial resources from the high-revenue sales of A and B sugar to cover part of the fixed costs of their processing of beets bought at the C beet price constituted a second export subsidy. The panel concluded that the price of C sugar did not "even remotely cover its cost of production" (WTO 2004a, para. 7.301).

In both *EC – Export Subsidies on Sugar* and *Canada – Dairy* the Appellate Body affirmed that there is a boundary between the domestic support and export subsidy disciplines but the economic effects of domestic support may spill over to export production. A concern was expressed in *Canada – Dairy* that the export subsidy disciplines of the Agriculture Agreement would be undermined if there was no limit on the exportation of products subsidized under certain domestic measures. The contrary view was also expressed, namely that it was not for the panel to collapse domestic support disciplines into export subsidy disciplines.

The Appellate Body in *Canada – Dairy* explained that if WTO-consistent domestic support measures were automatically characterized as export subsidies because they produced spill-over economic benefits for export production, the distinction between the domestic support and export subsidy disciplines of the Agreement would be eroded. However, the Appellate Body also considered that the distinction between the domestic support and export subsidy disciplines would be eroded if domestic support could be provided without limit for exports. The domestic support provisions of the Agriculture Agreement along with high levels of tariff protection allowed extensive support to Canadian milk producers under its domestic production quotas and high prices, compared to the limits imposed through export subsidy disciplines, the Appellate Body explained. An approach that it said maintained the export subsidy discipline without erosion while best respecting the integrity of the two disciplines was to rely upon the total cost of production to determine whether there were payments in the meaning of Art. 9.1(c) (WTO 2001a, para. 92).[30] Giving further attention to the distinction

---

[30] The Appellate Body reasoned that if producers do not recoup the total cost of production over time they incur losses that must be financed from some source, possibly by virtue of governmental action (WTO 2001a, para. 87). In determining that average total cost of production was the appropriate standard of comparison to evaluate whether payments were made, the Appellate Body rejected use of the domestic price, which could be influenced by domestic support measures but not indicate producer costs. It also rejected use of the international price at which exports would have to compete. Janow and Staiger (2004) provide a critical analysis of the Appellate Body decisions.

between domestic support and export subsidy disciplines, the Appellate Body later explained that under the Agriculture Agreement subsidies may be granted in the domestic and export markets, provided that the disciplines imposed by the Agreement on both levels of subsidization are respected. Specifically, Art. 9.1(c), the Appellate Body reasoned, brings "in some circumstances, governmental action in the domestic market within the scope of the 'export subsidies' disciplines of Article 3.3" (WTO 2002a, para. 148). Thus, in some circumstances, particular measures may provide both domestic support and export subsidies, in which case both the domestic support commitment and the export subsidization commitments need to be complied with.

The parties in *EC – Export Subsidies on Sugar* also expressed concern about any redrawing of the boundary between domestic support and export subsidies or they invoked the Appellate Body's view, stated earlier in *Canada – Dairy*, of the distinction between domestic support and export subsidy disciplines. The Appellate Body considered that its interpretation concerning export subsidization in *EC – Export Subsidies on Sugar* did not erode the boundary between domestic support and export subsidies recognized under the Agriculture Agreement. Its interpretation, it said, respected the boundary between the two and operated to ensure that members provide domestic support and export subsidies in conformity with their obligations. Given the Appellate Body findings, the arbitrator summarized that domestic support "under the complex and integrated sugar regime of the European Communities, for beet farmers and sugar producers" was the source of the export subsidy that was found to exist in *EC – Export Subsidies on Sugar* (WTO 2005a, para. 70).

Alternative and Additional Arguments

In the event that exports of C sugar were not found to be subsidized by virtue of governmental action under Art. 9.1(c), the complainants put forward the alternative argument that the EU sugar regime violated Art. 10.1, which prohibits export subsidies not listed in Art. 9.1 from circumventing a member's commitments. The main argument was that the two forms of subsidies fell within the meaning of SCM Annex I Illustrative List item (d) which is (footnote omitted):

> The provision by governments or their agencies either directly or indirectly through government mandated schemes, of imported or domestic products or services for use in the production of exported goods, on terms or conditions more favourable than for provision of like or directly competitive products or services for use in the production of goods for

domestic consumption, if (in the case of products) such terms or conditions are more favorable than those commercially available on world markets to their exporters.

The complainants argued that because Art. 10.1 might cover export subsidies which did not satisfy some element of an Art. 9.1 export subsidy, the term "directly or indirectly through government mandated schemes" should be interpreted more broadly than "by virtue of governmental action" in Art. 9.1(c). The EU argued to the contrary that "government mandated" gave the phrase a narrower meaning. Going further in the alternative argument, Australia argued that, if it were found also that the EU sugar regime did not provide export subsidies under the SCM Illustrative List, it still provided subsidies as defined in SCM Art. 1.1(a)(2) and these were export subsidies and thus fell under Agriculture Agreement Art. 10.1. Having concluded that the EC sugar regime provided export subsidies within the meaning of Art. 9.1(c), the panel did not examine the alternative claims under Art. 10.1, and neither did the Appellate Body.[31]

The complainants in *EC – Export Subsidies on Sugar* also made the alternative argument that the sugar regime provided export subsidies prohibited under the SCM Agreement, again relying firstly on SCM Illustrative List item (d) and secondly on SCM Art. 1. They argued that the Agriculture and SCM Agreements applied cumulatively and therefore, in the event that the EU was found in violation of the Agriculture Agreement, failure to make a determination under the SCM Agreement would deprive them of securing all of their rights. This concerned particularly having the panel determine the time frame for the EU to come into compliance, rather than possibly complex and lengthy arbitration determining that period. The panel nonetheless exercised judicial economy and did not examine the SCM claims.

The Appellate Body found the panel had erred in doing so but declined to complete the legal analysis, stating it was not persuaded that the relevant provisions of the Agriculture and SCM Agreements were closely related "because the issues presented under the two

---

[31] As the complainants noted in their arguments, on three occasions the panel in *Canada – Dairy* had found that supply of milk at below domestic prices to export processors together with prohibition on diversion of that milk back into the domestic market fell within the meaning of SCM Illustrative List item (d) and thus constituted an export subsidy (WTO 1999b, 2001c, 2002e). In that dispute also, the Appellate Body determined that considerations of arguments in the alternative were not germane given its concurrence that the dairy support regime provided export subsidies under Art. 9.1(c) (WTO 1999a, 2002a) or indicated it could not make a determination (WTO 2001a).

Agreements are different in several respects" (WTO 2005b, para 338).[32] It also concluded that a number of complex issues arose in light of Art. 21 and the SCM Art. 3 prohibition of export subsidies except as provided in the Agriculture Agreement. The Appellate Body reasoned that the lack of requisite factual findings precluded a full exploration of the issues.

Reform of the EU Sugar Regime

Adoption of the panel and Appellate Body reports in *EC - Export Subsidies on Sugar* in May 2005 came at a propitious time. Reform of various aspects of the CAP had been underway for more than a dozen years, bringing lower intervention prices and reduced export subsidies for many products compensated by support less coupled to market conditions than the earlier EU measures. The EU also committed in 2001 that, after a delay until 2009, duty-free quota-free access for sugar imports from LDCs would apply as part of its Everything But Arms (EBA) development assistance agenda. The WTO requirement to bring its export subsidies within its commitments catalyzed a reform of the EU sugar regime that involved substantial adjustments.[33]

The initial thrust of the reform was to lower intervention prices in two steps from EUR 632 per tonne to a reference price of EUR 404 per tonne in 2009/10. The A and B quotas were combined, and this quota was reduced from 17.5 to 13.5 million tonnes. The beet production area fell from 2.2 million hectares to less than 1.5 million hectares and the number of sugar processing factories fell from 189 to 107 (HLG 2019). Beet producers were compensated for 64% of the price decline through additions to their Single Farm Payments. Additional restructuring aid of EUR 5.4 billion was provided to beet growers and processors, funded by a levy on quota sugar,

---

[32] With the Appellate Body in *EC - Export Subsidies on Sugar* also declining to complete a legal analysis on the alternate argument, the relationship between export subsidies as defined by Art. 9.1(c) and Illustrative List item (d) or SCM Art. 1.1(a)(2) remains unresolved by the dairy and sugar disputes, specifically the extent to which Art. 9.1(c) and item (d) overlap and whether finding export subsidies under Art. 9.1(c) may support finding that the conditions in item (d) are met.

[33] Ackrill and Kay (2009) highlight the effectiveness of *EC - Export Subsidies on Sugar* in prompting reform compared to the ineffectiveness of disputes brought in 1978 and 1982 under the GATT and conclude that a "learning-by-dispute" process led to the Uruguay Round addressing multiple weaknesses in the GATT rules. Ackrill and Kay (2011) see the WTO ruling as only one of several pressures for the sugar reform. McMahon (2006), Elbehri et al. (2008), Gotor (2009), and Aquino Bonomo (2019), among others, also assess *EC - Export Subsidies on Sugar* in relation to EU sugar policies and trade.

while ACP producers received little compensation. Domestic sugar prices generally fell in parallel with the lower intervention prices and the EU eliminated production quotas in 2017. The most efficient EU sugar processors expanded production and domestic prices came to track world prices. Thus, the EU sugar market was transformed from one of the most highly regulated markets in agriculture to one largely liberalized and integrated into the world market.[34] High import tariffs remain in place, with imports under preferential agreements around 1.3 million tonnes, primarily from Economic Partnership Agreement (EPA, formerly ACP) and EBA countries but also under TRQs for Central American countries, South Africa and others. Ethanol production absorbs about 7% of EU sugar production.

7.5 Disputes and the Disciplines on Domestic Support

This chapter has reviewed the circumstances, rulings and implications for domestic support measures of the respondents in *China – Agricultural Producers, India – Sugar and Sugarcane, US – Upland Cotton* and *EC – Export Subsidies on Sugar*. Additionally, the disputes concerning *Korea – Various Measures on Beef* and *Canada – Dairy* provide important rulings in their own right that were drawn upon in the four disputes reviewed. Several points emerge from the disputes involving domestic support measures and support amounts.

The Agriculture Agreement and the SCM Agreement place domestic support measures in favor of agricultural producers under different but overlapping sets of legal obligations. A challenge of a member's compliance with its domestic support obligations under the Agriculture Agreement requires no evidence of adverse effects, injury or serious prejudice. Yet, a finding of violation normally leads, by way of being considered to have nullified or impaired the benefits accruing to another member, to the presumption that it has an adverse impact. A challenge regarding actionable subsidies under the SCM Agreement must affirmatively establish adverse effects. The arguments presented in domestic

---

[34] In contrast, Canada retained its milk price support and production quota measures while resolving the *Canada – Dairy* dispute by eliminating its low-price category of milk for export processing and modifying its dairy import TRQs to meet the Dispute Settlement Body rulings and recommendations. With the support regime remaining in place, new issues concerning pricing and exports of certain milk products as well as TRQ market access arose in negotiating and from 2020 implementing the United States-Mexico-Canada Agreement (USMCA).

support disputes under the two agreements are therefore different. Under the Agriculture Agreement, a finding of violation can create leverage for change in the respondent's support measures to reduce some domestic support, as seen in *China – Agricultural Producers*. If the complainant considers, possibly based on further proceedings regarding compliance, that the respondent continues to violate its obligations, it may seek authorization to suspend concessions. At that stage the difference between the Agriculture and SCM Agreements in terms of demonstrating adverse effects of domestic support measures narrows. If the case proceeds to arbitration, the level of suspension needs to be equivalent to the level of nullification or impairment, and countermeasures under the SCM Agreement need to be commensurate with the adverse effects. In less precise terms, the governing question in arbitration is determining the size of any retaliation for the violation of obligations under either agreement, which is related to the economic harm it caused. While no dispute over domestic support under the Agriculture Agreement has gone to that stage, the arbitrator determined countermeasures based on adverse effects under the SCM Agreement in *US – Upland Cotton*.

Export subsidies can be challenged under either agreement using similar but distinct arguments. Export subsidies were found to violate obligations under both the Agriculture and SCM Agreements in *India – Sugar and Sugarcane* (under appeal) and *US – Upland Cotton*. Export subsidies resulting from a domestic support regime have been challenged under the Agriculture and SCM Agreements in *EC – Export Subsidies on Sugar* and *Canada – Dairy*, but rulings were made only under the Agriculture Agreement.

The reviewed disputes, initiated by eight complainants, were directed toward the four members with the largest agricultural production and among the five with the most domestic support. The potential effects on world markets of any policy change resulting from the dispute could therefore be large, and the commercial interest in the outcome was likely important. Each of the reviewed disputes arose in relatively egregious circumstances where the challenged support measures at the time involved substantial policy interventions in markets. In *China – Agricultural Producers* and *India – Sugar and Sugarcane* economic price support had sharply increased prior to the initiation of the dispute. In *US – Upland Cotton* price-contingent payments had reached unprecedented levels compared to value of production and the US share of the world cotton market had increased. In *EC – Export Subsidies on Sugar*, the EU was a major exporter despite internal sugar prices far above world levels.

While this was a long-standing distortion, challenged in earlier GATT disputes, the Agriculture Agreement and DSU gave members a different avenue for challenge.

Relatively few disputes have been pursued over agricultural domestic support. A member's claim of compliance with its obligations in a notification, or not calculating support under a measure, does not preclude it being the respondent in a dispute, as seen respectively in *China – Agricultural Producers* and *India – Sugar and Sugarcane*. So far, only *US – Upland Cotton* has been pursued about adverse effects of domestic support policies under the SCM Agreement. This suggests that it is easier to characterize agricultural markets as broadly experiencing distortions due to high levels of support or to show support in excess of a limit than it is to demonstrate under legal scrutiny that a member's particular measures are market-distorting to the extent that they cause adverse effects in another member's domestic market or on its export opportunities.

Each of the reviewed disputes clarified the interpretation of the rules of the Agriculture or SCM Agreement. *China – Agricultural Producers* confirmed the earlier finding in *Korea – Various Measures on Beef* that governments could for measurement of MPS explicitly limit eligible production to less than total production. It also clarified the years on which an accession member could properly base its reference prices for MPS. In *India – Sugar and Sugarcane* (under appeal), the panel found that MPS does not have to involve government purchases and provided a ruling in which MPS measured under the Agriculture Agreement far exceeded economic price support. *US – Upland Cotton* established that price-contingent payments contributed to price suppression even if made on a base of past output, while payments fixed at a given level each year based on past output did not. This mirrored academic assessments of at most minor production effects of fixed payments, although findings in subsequent subsidy disputes indicate that even minor additional effects might be included in an adverse effects determination if their contribution is non-trivial. *EC – Export Subsidies on Sugar* built on *Canada – Dairy* and determined that a domestic price support regime could cross-subsidize exports and cause a violation of export subsidy commitments.

Decisions in these disputes adopted by the Dispute Settlement Body contributed to some modifications of the respondents' domestic support policies. Not surprisingly, the extent of reform was determined in the context of each member's broader political economy of agricultural support. The decisions in *EC – Export Subsidies on Sugar* were significant in ending EU subsidized sugar exports, which could be accommodated in the context of CAP reform. China signaled during the dispute proceedings that its support prices were out of line with world prices, eliminated support prices for corn and reduced support prices for wheat and rice. A period of policy revamping in the United States following the rulings in *US – Upland Cotton* eventually resulted in retention of domestic support measures similar to those that were challenged but, as market conditions had changed, the effects of those policies were of less concern. The panel findings in *India – Sugar and Sugarcane* imply that achieving compliance would require substantial modification of the sugarcane price support program. India appealed the panel decision and the political economy of India regarding agricultural price support did not at time of the panel ruling seem conducive to reforms that would bring India into compliance with its sugar AMS obligations as determined by the panel.

A final observation concerns measurement of MPS. Contrasting the policy circumstances of China and India underscores the different complexities in relying on the Agriculture Agreement to constrain price support. China, with positive economic support for wheat and rice faces only modest constraints on its price support programs under the rulings in *China – Agricultural Producers*. In contrast, under the panel findings in *India – Sugar and Sugarcane*, price support measured under the Agriculture Agreement is both far larger than India's limit of 10% of value of production and far exceeds India's economic price support. Likewise, for wheat, rice, cotton and pulses in India, counter-notifications calculated large positive MPSs under the Agreement despite mostly negative economic price support. Comparison with alternative measurements demonstrates the influence on the counter-notified MPS of the fixity of the reference price combined with support prices being raised in the presence of inflation.

Overall, the potential lack of economic meaning of MPS measured under the rules of the Agriculture Agreement often precludes sensical consequences to abiding by the Agreement's limits when AMSs include that price support. This underscores the need to update the rules through negotiations, such as making the measurement of price support more economically relevant. One such alternative measurement – LRP MPS – is based on a price gap between an AAP and a moving average of lagged border prices and with total production as eligible production. For wheat in China and India during 2008–18, the LRP MPS tracks economic MPS more closely than the MPS calculated under the Agriculture Agreement.

8

Addressing Twenty-First-Century Policy Priorities

As agricultural policy priorities evolve, governments shift support in favor of agricultural producers among the categories of domestic support or change their total amount of support. The rules in the 1994 Agreement on Agriculture may accommodate or hinder policy efforts to address the evolving concerns. This chapter reviews several priorities in agriculture that have gained profile in recent years and discusses the classification of and constraints on associated support within the rules of the Agriculture Agreement while also raising points relating to the SCM Agreement. The selected policy priorities are productivity growth, biosecurity in agriculture, water management, safeguarding and enhancing biodiversity and mitigation of climate change. Addressing climate change may become the predominant priority where, along with the interest in reducing the emission of greenhouse gases (GHGs), the potential for withdrawing carbon from the atmosphere and storing it in farmland soil attracts policy attention.

The selection of a small number of evolving priorities among many draws on recurring themes in international discussions over recent years. An overarching concern is the triple challenge for food systems of ensuring food security and nutrition, supporting the livelihoods of producers and doing so in environmentally sustainable ways. Superimposed over these challenges is the need for food systems to become resilient to adversity, which the Covid-19 pandemic from 2020 onwards made poignant. Some of the United Nations Sustainable Development Goals of 2015 reflect the evolving policy priorities in agriculture. Food security (encompassing availability, access, utilization and stability) is distinct from self-sufficiency and is a prominent part of the zero hunger goal, under which one target is to correct and prevent trade restrictions and distortions in world agricultural markets. This target is in focus throughout this book, as it overlaps with the objective of the Agriculture Agreement and those being pursued in the continued negotiations on domestic support.

Policy priorities of heightening salience are often environmental in the sense of linking to the physical, biological or climatic conditions for agricultural production but also have implications for the tackling of overarching concerns. The discussion of the selected priorities in relation to the rules on domestic support in favor of agricultural producers may facilitate drawing inferences applicable also to a wider set of priorities.

8.1   Trade Distortions in the Context of Evolving Priorities

The recognition of evolving policy priorities may prompt a reconsideration of the balance between addressing them and addressing trade distortions while also strengthening the trading system as it adapts to the changing world. In a prescient analysis, Josling (2015) considers in broad terms the balance among priorities such as avoiding trade distortions while supporting farm incomes and providing public goods, which would include mitigation of climate change. In 2021, three United Nations organizations jointly issued a call for repurposing agricultural support to transform food systems (FAO, UNDP and UNEP 2021). The report considers that much of the large amount of agricultural producer support estimated for the world relies on measures that distort both production and trade and are harmful for nature, climate, nutrition, health and equity. These consequences would motivate a repurposing by reducing the most distorting and environmentally or socially harmful support and redirecting resources toward provision of public goods and services for agriculture. While reducing the most distorting support is a focus of continued negotiations on the Agriculture Agreement, priorities with reference to an environmentally or socially beneficial repurposing of harmful subsidies receive less attention.

The Agriculture Agreement's rules on domestic support in favor of agricultural producers allow green box support to be exempted from AMSs and it is thus not subject to limit. To qualify for the green box exemption, the measure providing the support must meet the fundamental requirement of having "no, or at most minimal, trade-distorting effects or effects on production" (para. 1, Annex 2) and accordingly conform to basic and policy-specific criteria and conditions.[1] The basic criteria of Annex 2 require support under the measure to be provided

---

[1]   This chapter assumes that consistency with the fundamental requirement and with the criteria and conditions are freestanding obligations. While this is a common interpretation, it has not been clarified in dispute adjudication (see Chapter 2).

through a publicly funded government program not involving transfers from consumers and not having the effect of providing price support (paras. 1(a) and (b)). Policy-specific criteria and conditions are set in 12 additional paragraphs. The green box *General services* (para. 2, Annex 2) distinguishes expenditures that provide services to agriculture or the rural community from direct payments to producers or processors (paras. 5–13, Annex 2).

Trade-distorting effects of domestic support are most easily understood as resulting from effects on production. At the time of negotiating the text of Annex 2 in the early 1990s, increases in production beyond the levels that would have been observed in the absence of the support were the policy-induced effects of concern. The role if any that green box exempted measures may play in inducing more than minimal increases in production was later examined in, for example, Meléndez-Ortiz et al. (2009) and as discussed in Chapters 3 and 7.

Policy measures can also have production-reducing effects. An example would be a requirement that the producer bear the cost that the production imposes on others, that is, the producer must internalize production externalities, leading to less production. Levies on the use of fertilizer and pesticides to reduce water pollution are one case of inducing some internalization of an externality by means of negative policy support. If a government payment offsets the producer's cost of internalization, the externality cost is effectively not internalized by the producer. However, the conditions the producer needs to meet in order to receive the payment may achieve the internalizing effect and also reduce production. For example, payments may be conditional on the producer not cultivating a parcel of land to maintain certain biodiversity valued by the public.

Whether a negative effect on production that is more than minimal would disqualify a measure from the green box exemption has not been a principal concern in implementing the Agriculture Agreement, but the use of production-reducing measures to address evolving priorities may elevate this question. Relatively less concern with production-reducing effects of green box measures reflects that internalizing or reducing externalities by means of policy need not be a distortion in economic terms, as well as the mercantilist consideration that such effects do not lessen, and may increase, market opportunities for other members' agricultural producers. Introducing a policy intervention to internalize or reduce an externality could, in combination with the existing support policies, also result in less distortion of production and trade.

The SCM Agreement differs from the disciplines in the Agriculture Agreement by prohibiting export and domestic content subsidies, disciplining subsidies that cause adverse effects and, in some circumstances, permitting members to take countermeasures. The priorities examined in this chapter are in many instances likely to lead to policy measures that constrain or reduce a member's production. This would make it difficult for another member to show adverse effects as identified in the SCM Agreement, that is, injury, nullification or impairment or serious prejudice. However, the potential for increased production enters the discussion in some cases. Imposing domestic content requirements on subsidies that pursue the priorities considered would violate the SCM Agreement.

8.2 Five Salient Priorities

8.2.1 Productivity Growth

Productivity growth in agriculture is a long-standing policy objective, which has taken on greater urgency because of the need to enhance sustainability by producing more with the same or fewer inputs and because productivity growth can contribute when addressing other priorities of increased profile. Much support in favor of agricultural producers is delivered through policy measures not designed specifically to increase productivity, but the support may in addition to having other effects, and when sustained over time, hasten producers' development and adoption of techniques that increase yield or reduce inputs, that is, they may accelerate productivity growth. While the motivation for limiting AMS or other Art. 6 support is its effect of directly distorting agricultural production and trade, any concomitant indirect improvement in productivity is not seen as a problem but as an element of economic growth. Support payments exempted from limit on green box grounds may have less distorting effect while also accelerating productivity growth. The use of specific subsidies causing adverse effects to the interests of other members, which could relate to prices, production or trade, is subject to the rules of the SCM Agreement.

Government expenditures aimed purposefully at continued or accelerated productivity growth relate particularly to general services of research, training services, extension and advisory services and marketing services as specified in the green box paras. 2(a), (c), (d) and (f). Expenditures on research and services that advance productivity growth tend to lower producers' costs and increase production over time. However, the effects on production and trade of such expenditures in the short run with given production technology and resources are minimal, in line with the green box fundamental requirement. This helps to explain the lack of controversy about exempting from AMSs those expenditures designed to raise productivity as long as they meet the specific but generally phrased para. 2 conditions. Productivity growth over time can improve both the food availability and food access dimensions of food security.

Green box para. 2(a) clarifies that it applies to general research as well as research in connection with environmental programs and research programs relating to particular products, both of which could include research to strengthen the knowledge base for policy decision making. The broad applicability allows exemption from limit of expenditures on research directly accelerating productivity growth as well as research needed to address any priorities where productivity growth matters. Producing more with the same or less inputs means emitting less GHGs per unit of output, which can be crucial in climate change mitigation. Research, training services, extension and advisory services and marketing services can also help producers adapt to climate change.

8.2.2 Biosecurity in Agriculture

Vigilance against the spread of pests and diseases among crops and livestock has long been a priority for governments, referred to here as biosecurity. The 1987 confirmation of the presence of bovine spongiform encephalopathy (BSE) in the UK, commonly known as mad cow disease, made such vigilance a greater government priority as the Uruguay Round negotiations were getting underway. Concerns about human, animal or plant life or health resulted in the negotiations generating the Agreement on the Application of Sanitary and Phytosanitary Measures (SPS Agreement) and the Agreement on Technical Barriers to Trade (TBT Agreement). Numerous such concerns have later attracted policy attention. For example, the broad issue of antimicrobial resistance resulting from the use of antibiotics as a growth promoter in livestock production, particularly its implications for human health protection but also for the treatment of livestock disease, has come to the fore as a concern. A different concern raised under biosecurity headings relates to any of the various ways to manipulate genetic material.[2]

---

[2] The SPS and TBT Agreements and the plant and animal biosecurity and human health and safety issues they address are beyond the scope of this book. Josling et al. (2004)

Expenditures on pest and disease control, such as early warning systems, quarantine and eradication, and on inspection services, including inspection for health and safety, can be exempted from AMSs under paras. 2(b) and (e) of Annex 2. Every member could have an interest in all members spending more on some forms of pest and disease control in order to reduce the risk of transmission to others. The requirement that expenditures on general services cannot include direct payments to producers or processors may make the control measures less effective in a case of quarantine or eradication, since producers who are not paid compensation or, in their view, are paid too little may have an incentive not to report the pest or disease in question.

To facilitate countermeasures, a government may seek to encourage producers to follow appropriate risk management practices and report as early as possible the presence of a pest or disease. Making direct payments to producers large enough to compensate for the destruction of a crop or the culling of animals may have this effect. Designing such payments to conform with green box para. 7 or para. 12 might be possible, relating, respectively, to *Government financial participation in income insurance and income safety-net programmes* and *Payments under environmental programmes.* Payments for control of pests and diseases could be designed in particular to meet the criteria under green box para. 8 concerning relief from natural disasters, whether made directly or through government financial participation in crop insurance schemes. Alternatively, payments could be accounted for as Art. 6 support.

Para. 8 requires the government's formal recognition of a disease outbreak or pest infestation as a necessary condition for payment eligibility. Moreover, payment eligibility requires the production loss to be larger than 30% of a moving average of past production. While this narrows the scope for exempting biosecurity-related payments under para. 8, destroying a producer's crop or culling a whole herd would meet the loss criterion. Paras. 8(b), (c) and (d) constrain the amount of payment in several ways relating to the kind of loss suffered, the replacement cost and prevention of further loss. These conditions reduce the risk of disaster relief programs becoming vehicles for support of production or producer incomes that overly compensate for losses, but they also disincentivize pest or disease control efforts.

provide an early appraisal and Karttunen (2020) a historical evaluation of these agreements. Annual reports from the SPS and TBT committees summarize the issues members have raised, among which a number have led to adjudicated disputes.

The Doha Round draft modalities tabled but not agreed in 2008 expanded in several ways the circumstances in which a payment could be exemptible under para. 8 in the case of controlling or preventing certain pests, diseases, disease-carrying organisms or disease-causing organisms (WTO 2008a). The payment would be exemptible when related to the destruction of animals or crops and this even if the loss was less than 30% of an average. Members' interest in making the Agriculture Agreement accommodate certain expenditures involving biosecurity in agricultural production had thus strengthened and has not since waned. As negotiations proceed, members may be in a position to make the conditions in para. 8 of the green box more like those formulated in the 2008 draft modalities. While the Covid-19 pandemic from 2020 increased the awareness globally of possible links between animal and human health, this did at least not in the first few years translate into related major policy initiatives concerning biosecurity in agriculture.

8.2.3   Water Management

While the shaping of appropriate policies regarding water in agriculture has long been a priority for governments in dry regions of the world, it has also gained priority elsewhere. The importance of water as a production input combines with concerns about the food availability dimension of food security and agriculture's adaptation to climate change to raise the profile of water management policies. They operate in many different ways, such as a government regulating the institutions that manage the allocation of water among users, supporting capital investment in dams and canals, or subsidizing producers' on-farm use of water. While issues concerning water and agriculture mainly involve scarcity of water, concerns about flooding and the effects of agriculture on water quality are also prevalent.

Analysis of policy issues in water and agriculture tends to emphasize the need to develop appropriate institutions. Rosegrant (2019) underlines improving the governance of water resources through effective institutions, allocating water more efficiently through pricing, regulations and subsidy reform, improving productivity per unit of water through agricultural research, technology and extension, diversifying agriculture to reduce the demand for water and increasing the supply of water and the irrigated area through investment in infrastructure. Taking India as an example, Gulati et al. (2019) consider improved allocation and efficient use of water as essential for achieving farm policy objectives and outline possible enabling changes in institutional design and practice. Ringler et al. (2021) conclude that stronger institutions for water management and allocation are needed along with investment in technologies. The Water Global Practice (2022) stresses institutional strengthening in designs for climate-related irrigation and drainage project activities.

In the green box, para. 2 offers a variety of avenues to develop the appropriate institutions and direct general services expenditures toward improving the management of scarce water resources. Developing the institutions and practices for exchanging rights to use water may take the form of or be complemented by expenditures on research, training and advisory services and water market information. Some water-related expenditures, such as expenditures on soil conservation and resource management, drought management and flood control, and issuance of property titles, may be exempted from limit under the additional para. 2 item decided at the 2013 WTO ministerial conference (WTO 2013a).

Green box para. 2(g) allows exemption of expenditures on infrastructural services, including "electricity reticulation, roads and other means of transport, market and port facilities, water supply facilities, dams and drainage schemes, and infrastructural works associated with environmental programmes." Members exempt much of their water policy support for agricultural producers from limit as expenditures under this paragraph. Like productivity-enhancing research, these infrastructure investments may increase production over time. While the paragraph is clear about in all cases not exempting subsidies to inputs, operating costs or preferential user charges, as distinct from the provision or construction of capital works, it is not evident that members strictly apply this distinction. The exemption of a wide variety of water support expenditures as infrastructural services under para. 2(g) indicates that members see this paragraph as offering considerable flexibility.

Some subsidies that are not exemptible from AMSs on green box grounds can be exempted by developing countries except China and Kazakhstan under the Agriculture Agreement's Art. 6.2. Investment subsidies, such as subsidies for on-farm irrigation facilities, that are generally available as well as those input subsidies, such as irrigation subsidies or preferential user charges, that are generally available to low-income or resource-poor producers can be exempted. Developed countries must include such water-related subsidies in their AMSs. Water-related support that does not qualify for exemption under Annex 2 or Art. 6.2 would be accounted for as AMS support by developed and developing countries.

Subsidies that encourage the use of water in ways that may at one time have been desirable but are no longer justified or sustainable could be reduced or withdrawn, but progress in completing such initiatives has been slow. If compensation for the subsidy change was warranted, it could take the form of payments consistent with green box para. 5 or para. 6. This would preclude basing the current year's amount of payment on current production, prices or input use after a prior base period, but payments could be determined by production, income or inputs in a base period at the time the water subsidies were withdrawn. When scarce water needs to be distributed among users with different rights, an agricultural producer who holds water rights may commit not to use a given volume of that water in exchange for a government payment. Relating the amount of payment to water use in a past base period again might qualify it for para. 5 or para. 6 exemption. The payment might alternatively be made under an Art. 6 measure, possibly with a production-reducing effect.

As droughts and flooding are expected to become more frequent and more severe as a result of climate change, governments may seek new ways to reduce the harmful consequences for agricultural producers. Apart from general service expenditures, governments may design payments to address income or production losses to be consistent with para. 7 and para 8, as in the case of pursuing biosecurity in agriculture. Losses can be caused by not enough or too much water compared to the expectations on which producers based their short-term and long-term decisions. If the frequency or severity of water-related events increase in years to come, many producers' averages of past income or production would decline over time. This makes it more difficult to be eligible for payment and reduces the amount of payment under para. 7 and para. 8, which require an exemptible program to calculate a year's loss in relation to a past average. Pressure could build for negotiations to loosen the criteria for eligibility and amount of payment, in which case it would be important to retain the fundamental requirement in terms of at most minimal effects on trade or production.

General services expenditures and direct payments with regard to water management, even if qualifying for green box exemption under the Agriculture Agreement, are for cases of specific subsidies subject to the provisions of the SCM Agreement on actionable subsidies. For example, a subsidy for constructing a dam or for pumping water in agriculture might result in larger agricultural production causing adverse effects to the interests of another member, requiring the removal of the adverse effects or withdrawal of the subsidy. No such challenge has been advanced.

8.2.4   Safeguarding and Enhancing Biodiversity

The green box paragraph headed *Payments under environmental programmes* (para. 12, Annex 2) details criteria and conditions particularly relevant to exemption of direct payments relating to the priorities of safeguarding and enhancing biodiversity and mitigation of climate change. Increasing priority on environmental stewardship in a broad sense is reflected in greater amounts of payments exempted under para. 12 in later years. To be exemptible, payments must be made under clearly defined environmental or conservation programs. Members' understanding of such programs when drafting para. 12 was informed by those they operated in base years for their domestic support commitments.[3] Environmental policy priorities have since evolved as evidenced by members' increased use of labels such as environmental sustainability, eco-schemes and ecosystem services to complement or replace the earlier environmental or conservation labels often relating to land or water.

One condition under para. 12 of the green box is that eligibility for payments must depend on fulfilling "specific conditions under the government programme, including conditions related to production methods or inputs." It is thus clear that if there are conditions related to production methods or inputs among the program conditions, eligibility for payment must depend on fulfilling them. It is unclear whether among the program conditions there must be specific conditions related to production methods or inputs. Clarity regarding this question could influence governments' design of payment programs intended to satisfy the eligibility conditions of para. 12. The inclusion of conditions with an environment or conservation dimension may contribute to the program being so characterized.

Para. 12 also sets the condition that the amount of payment must not exceed the extra costs or loss of income from complying with the program. This guards against making payments so large that they incentivize more than minimal changes in production with associated trade effects. A payment-induced move toward the environmental target can

---

[3] Exempted direct payments under environmental programs in 1986–88 of original members providing the most support in 2016–18 were as follows. United States: agricultural conservation programs, conservation operations, Great Plains conservation program, resource conservation and development; EU: protection of the environment, preservation of the countryside, control of soil erosion, extensification, aid for environmentally sensitive areas; India: soil conservation and watershed management in certain areas, fodder grassland and pasture development, desert development; and Japan: payments for conversion from rice production. China later exempted 1996–98 payments for afforestation, desert control and prevention, water resources protection, water and soil conservation.

nevertheless lead to larger production of some products. For example, shifting land use from arable crops to pasture with more biodiversity can increase ruminant livestock production.

The condition that the payment under para. 12 not exceed the extra costs or loss of income from complying with the program also raises questions about the effectiveness of the payment as an incentive for producers to achieve the environmental outcome and in what situations it constitutes support in favor of agricultural producers in the sense used in the Agriculture Agreement. A measure in favor of agricultural producers may mean that it makes them better off than other producers or it makes them better off than if the measure did not exist. The proper characterization of the measure would depend on the alternatives in relation to which it is assessed.

A growing need for stronger policy action to safeguard and enhance biodiversity undergirds the evolution of policy priorities under para. 12. For example, while none of the 20 goals of the United Nations Strategic Plan for Biodiversity 2011–2020 were achieved, the adoption in 2021 of the Kunming Declaration by the UN Biodiversity Conference added impetus to mainstreaming biodiversity in policy making (CBD 2021).[4] The many definitions of biodiversity generally relate to the number or diversity of species in a given area and encompass organisms of many kinds. Agriculture depends on biodiversity for crop and animal genetic diversity, pest control, pollination and healthy soils, while agricultural activities affect biodiversity by, for example, depleting soils, eliminating habitat for wild species and reducing diversity of flora and fauna (Blandford 2019, DeClerck et al. 2021). Members' agricultural policies vary in how explicitly they recognize biodiversity.[5]

Payments under para. 12 regarding biodiversity are often based on land as a factor of production, that is, the area used or could potentially be used for agricultural production and which the agricultural producer

---

[4] In the 2021 Kunming Declaration, named for the city in China where it was agreed, governments committed to develop, adopt and implement an effective post-2020 global biodiversity framework that would put biodiversity on a path to recovery by 2030 at the latest.

[5] One of the nine objectives of the EU's CAP for 2023–27 is to contribute to the protection of biodiversity, enhance ecosystem services and preserve habitats and landscapes. The UK's Local Nature Recovery program plans from 2024 to pay farmers and other land managers for reversing the decline in biodiversity. Many initiatives identified under the conservation title of the US farm bill running through fiscal year 2023 relate to some definitions of biodiversity.

controls. A biodiversity payment on part or all of that land may be practice-based with conditions related to production methods or input use, including constraints that rule out producing any agricultural product for many years. Definitional issues may arise with respect to identifying the payment recipient as an agricultural producer because of production on other land than the land to which the biodiversity payment relates.[6] A biodiversity payment may, for greater effectiveness, be based on an area where agricultural production is not feasible but which an agricultural producer controls, giving rise to similar definitional issues.

Payments for the achievement of a given outcome defined in terms of biodiversity are increasingly complementing payments to producers for using certain production or land use practices. Called, for example, value-based, results-based or outcome-based, such payments remunerate the producer for delivering a measured level of biodiversity on a given area of land. Progress has been made in developing methods for measuring biodiversity, attaching a value to it and designing payment schemes.[7] Program conditions related to production methods or input use may be minimal or absent.

The government's assessed value of the biodiversity outcome compared to the status quo may be higher than the producer's extra costs or loss of income, creating an incentive for the producer to achieve the outcome. However, such a payment is precluded from exemption by the para. 12 requirement that the amount be no larger than the extra costs or loss of income involved in program compliance. It may be possible to design annual payments exceeding costs or lost income under a practice-based biodiversity measure to be exempt under para. 10 on *Structural adjustment assistance provided through resource retirement programmes*. Consistency with para. 5 or para. 6 concerning income support would be difficult to reach with a practice-based measure if the land area committed to biodiversity continues to be used as a factor of production and conditions are set on other input use or production practices.

---

[6] In cases where no agricultural production takes place, it even might be questioned whether it is a measure providing support to agricultural producers. Some payment programs refer to, for example, beneficiaries, operators or farms, which may differ from producers.

[7] Chaplin et al. (2019) and Henderson and Lankoski (2019), *inter alia*, discuss measurement and valuation. Wuepper and Huber (2022) show an example where outcome-based payments were more effective than action-based payments. Sumrada et al. (2022) found that the majority of farmers in a choice experiment would prefer an outcome-based over a practice-based payment scheme.

Para. 5 or para. 6 consistency would more easily be met by an outcome-based biodiversity program where no conditions were set on current or future production or input use. Meeting the biodiversity outcome could be stipulated as a condition for payment eligibility in addition to meeting the criteria and conditions in para. 5 or para. 6, which include that the land area on which payments are made not be based on or related to production after a base period.

Payments that do not qualify for green box exemption in any of these or other ways would be accounted for as AMS or other Art. 6 support. This might raise considerations in classifying the payments as product-specific or non-product-specific. If the payment is considered only as a calibrated remuneration for delivering a measured biodiversity outcome, which is not a basic agricultural product, the payment would not be product-specific. The payment might be part of the non-product-specific AMS as support in favor of agricultural producers in general. Taking into account the structure, design and operation of the payment program would help to account for the support correctly.

Altogether, environmental programs are evolving with the changing policy priorities. The rules of the Agriculture Agreement, formulated in the Uruguay Round negotiations of 1986–94, allow the exemption of certain payments under environmental programs from AMS support. These rules could benefit from clarification and updating in light of evolving priorities and programs, including the design of outcome-based biodiversity payments.

8.2.5 Mitigation of Climate Change

The need to strengthen the global response to the threats posed by climate change is building. While policy measures in favor of agricultural producers involving adaptation to or mitigation of climate change were not prominent at the time the Agriculture Agreement was negotiated, they have since gained attention. The United Nations 2015 Paris Agreement on climate change sets legally binding international treaty commitments. Policy discussions and associated economic and legal research increasingly relate to climate change. The call for repurposing agricultural subsidies saw climate change as an emergency (FAO, UNDP and UNEP 2021).

Agricultural producers adapting to climate change effects derive private benefits from doing so, in contrast to the social or public benefits generated by mitigation of climate change. Annex 2 of the Agriculture

Agreement offers many avenues for exempting from AMSs expenditures on general services for the sector and direct payments to producers that facilitate adapting to changing circumstances, including those linked to climate. However, support intended to facilitate adaptation can postpone producers' adaptive decisions or even lead to maladaptation in the sense of their adaptation worsening the impact of climate change on society (McCarl et al. 2016, Hassapoyannes and Blandford 2019). Measures supporting producers' adaptation to climate change may be production and trade distorting and, if included in AMSs, the support would be subject to limit. Häberli (2021) notes the incongruence of AMS support and sustainability and climate change goals.

Reducing Agricultural GHG Emissions

Agricultural policies to achieve mitigation of climate change respond to the role of crop and livestock production as the largest contributor to emissions of methane and nitrous oxide and to agriculture inducing the second-largest contribution to emissions of carbon dioxide. Emissions of these GHGs may result from using land in agriculture, keeping livestock or converting land from other uses into agriculture by, for example, deforestation. Mitigation policies to reduce emissions in agriculture can subsidize producers' cost of the reduction or tax GHG emissions, with regulation of quantities of GHGs emitted also a policy option. Many green box provisions of the Agriculture Agreement are relevant to the design of emission-reducing mitigation policies.

Government expenditures under the heading of *General services* can be designed as programs to reduce GHG emissions. Exemptible expenditures include, for example, research, advice and training for producers to reduce the emission of methane by ruminants and to manage land to reduce the emission of nitrous oxide. Expenditures on laboratories to measure and analyze carbon flows and stocks are other examples.

Subsidies for the reduction of GHG emissions in agriculture often link to producers' adoption of practices associated with reduced emissions, such as minimum tillage, restoration of degraded soils and retirement of carbon-rich soils from agricultural production (Hassapoyannes and Blandford 2019). The reason for this indirect way of reducing emissions with the help of subsidies is the difficulty in targeting the subsidy and calibrating its size to achieve a specific emissions outcome. The difficulty suggests a need for research to enable more directly tying payments to producers' actual achievement in terms of emission reduction rather than to land use or production practices more or less strongly associated with these outcomes.[8] This parallels the growing interest in outcome-based payments pertaining to biodiversity but is even more complex.

Payments to mitigate climate change may, as with securing and enhancing biodiversity, be designed most directly to conform with the criteria under green box para. 10 and para. 12. Removing land from production to meet the conditions of para. 10 would remove a source of GHG emissions. Under para. 12, eligibility for payment must be determined as part of an environmental or conservation program. A payment for climate change mitigation thus needs to be understood as part of such a program. Since mitigation of climate change was likely not contemplated when the criterion was formulated, a definitional question might arise whether the term environmental includes climate change. As climate change has effects on the physical surroundings of human activity, that is, the environment in a dictionary definition, environmental programs could encompass mitigation of climate change and its effects.[9]

Para. 12 also requires eligibility for payment to depend on fulfilling specific conditions under the program, which in the case of a payment for practice-based mitigation measures could be a requirement not to use certain production methods or inputs. The condition that the amount of payment not exceed the extra costs or loss of income in complying with the program precludes rewarding the recipient for taking the mitigating action. The effect of the program in mitigating climate change may thus suffer, similarly to measures addressing biosecurity and biodiversity, compared to the effect if the action was rewarded beyond only offsetting the costs or loss of income. Eligibility of a mitigation program for para. 5 or para. 6 exemption faces issues similar to programs related to sustaining or enhancing biodiversity.

---

[8] A producer's continuation of a practice that emits less GHGs than the producer's earlier practice does not reduce emissions: the reduction took place when switching to the low emission practice. An ongoing payment that subsidizes the continuation of the producer's low emission practice may enable the producer not to revert to the earlier practice and increase emissions but it does not induce a further reduction of emissions. It is unclear how governments address issues like these when considering policies to mitigate climate change. Similarly, it is unclear how governments target and calibrate payments to induce a producer to make a change, as distinct from subsidizing a change that the producer would have made anyway – the question of additionality (Glauber 2018a, Pannell and Claassen 2020).

[9] The Preamble of the Marrakesh Agreement Establishing the World Trade Organization mentions protecting and preserving the environment, which appears to support this interpretation.

Reducing the emission of GHGs by taxing it may help to mitigate climate change without providing positive support in favor of agricultural producers. Taxing the emissions of GHGs of agricultural producers less than the same emissions of other producers could be a form of support in favor of agricultural producers. Support measured as government revenue forgone would seem difficult to exempt on green box grounds since current production generates the current emissions that benefit from the lower tax. Alternatively, taxing agricultural producers' GHG emissions at higher rates than emissions by others would generate negative support, which, if in an AMS, would offset part or all of any positive support and make the AMS smaller or nil. If mitigating climate change were the overriding priority, a case might be made for letting any negative AMS calculated as a result of a tax on GHG emissions offset positive AMSs in the CTAMS. The indirect taxing of emission of GHGs through a cap-and-trade scheme could be accounted for in terms of support in favor of producers in similar ways as direct taxing. The intended reduction in emission of GHGs might in either case be achieved by producer decisions that would reduce production, although to an extent not directly proportional to the emissions reduction.

Withdrawing and Storing Carbon

Withdrawing carbon dioxide from the atmosphere and storing carbon as part of organic matter in farmland soil, which together are activities with a potential to mitigate climate change, have emerged to garner keen policy attention. Often called carbon farming, some consider it a new revenue stream for agricultural producers. A business outside of agriculture that, due to a regulatory cap or corporate objective, seeks to offset its GHG emissions buys a credit for a reduction in atmospheric carbon dioxide estimated to be achieved by an agricultural producer. The agricultural producer takes action projected to increase the quantity of carbon withdrawn from the atmosphere and which must be stored for a long time as carbon compounds in farmland soil. An intermediary business usually facilitates the transaction. The effects of such transactions and the complexity of accurately measuring the carbon credit have been analyzed by, for example, Thamo and Pannell (2016) and Henderson et al. (2022).

The keywords measurement, reporting and verification are often used with reference to issues in withdrawing carbon dioxide and storing carbon in soil. They include, for example, whether the producer's action is additional to what the producer otherwise would have done, the limits on the capacity of soils to store increasing quantities of carbon, the correct measurement of change in carbon stock at field or farm scale (as distinct from model-based inferences at regional scale) and the price paid to the agricultural producer. Transactions can involve assuring storage not only for decades but for hundreds of years, which requires protocols to ensure continuity and longevity of storage, including proper accounting for costs and revenues.

As mitigation of climate change becomes more urgent, governments may seek ways to foster carbon withdrawal and storage beyond market-based initiatives through support measures in favor of agricultural producers. Some measures involving withdrawal and storage of carbon could have the effect of reducing production similar to measures to safeguard or enhance biodiversity or reduce GHG emissions. A change in production practice may reduce the crop yield per area and the quantity produced. However, more carbon contents in soil can over time increase yields, production and the value of land.

Government expenditures on general services can, in parallel with those designed to reduce emissions, be oriented toward managing land to increase the quantity of atmospheric carbon withdrawn and retained in soil. This can be accompanied by research expenditures on, for example, easing the difficulties encountered in the area of monitoring, reporting and verification. Payments related to the use of certain practices could be designed to meet the conditions in green box para. 10 or para. 12, as for biodiversity and emission mitigating measures. Relating the amounts of ongoing payments over many years to an area of land employed in current production or to the production practices used on that land would preclude consistency with para. 5 or para. 6. Payments not compliant with the green box would be accounted for as Art. 6 support, perhaps as input subsidies.

A government program to pay for the additional carbon withdrawn and stored in soil for a long time would face similar issues as business-driven transactions, such as the difficulties in linking payment amounts to measured quantities of carbon and their lengths of storage time and values. Further research will advance the methods for these measurements and establish baselines from which to remunerate increases in withdrawal and storage. This would enable the design of outcome-based measures that more directly and in a calibrated way pay a producer for the delivery of a measured effect that contributes to mitigation of climate change. Measures based on carbon storage outcomes, as opposed to production practices imperfectly correlated to those outcomes, might be consistent with payments under green box para. 5 or para. 6. Similar to outcome-based biodiversity measures, this could give incentives beyond cost or income-loss recovery for producers to participate.

The new revenue stream would accrue to agricultural producers who produce and sell not only quantities of basic agricultural products but also the additional quantities of carbon withdrawn and stored for an agreed number of years. While policy measures to deliver such payments may be designed to fit within the rules on domestic support, a case might be made that, for greater certainty or for more effective policy, those rules would need to be clarified or modified.

Balance between Production Neutrality and Mitigation of Climate Change

Difficulties in accommodating payments for mitigation of climate change under para. 12 of the green box could generate interest in clarifying or relaxing the conditions of that paragraph. For example, the mention of environmental or conservation programs could be expanded to mention also programs for climate change mitigation to enhance certainty of interpretation.

If programs for mitigation of climate change were on some basis found not to be environmental or conservation programs under para. 12, introducing additional provisions in Annex 2 specifically to allow exemption of direct payments under mitigation programs might be considered. Within Annex 2 such provisions would operate in conjunction with the fundamental requirement regarding no, or at most minimal, trade-distorting effects or effects on production and the basic criteria that the support be provided through a publicly funded government program and not have the effect of providing price support to producers. The provisions could be tailored to accommodate particular features of payment programs in response to the increasing urgency of mitigation of climate change. This could include larger-than-cost payments, with adequate guardrails, to obtain quicker or larger results or payment features that account for any required continuity and longevity of the mitigating actions.

In developing appropriate rules for measures relating to mitigation of climate change, one important consideration would be the balance between achieving certain mitigating effects and addressing distortions of trade or effects on production in agriculture. The Annex 2 fundamental requirement may need balancing against pressure to exempt mitigation measures of a size and a kind that do not meet this requirement. The applicability of the fundamental requirement with regard to mitigation measures that are effective but also have the effect of reducing production may need to be clarified.

An exemption from limit on support might be considered outside Annex 2 for measures meeting particular criteria even if they have more than minimal effects on trade or production. The development of appropriate criteria would benefit from thorough analysis of potential program designs considering their effectiveness in addressing an evolving priority, such as mitigation of climate change, and the trade off against accepting more than minimal trade or production effects. The blue box (Art. 6.5) exemption is an example of but not a model for such provisions.

8.3   Contemporary Policy Priorities and Green Box Compatibility

Productivity growth, biosecurity, water management, safeguarding and enhancing biodiversity and mitigation of climate change are among the policy concerns in agriculture of heightened salience to which governments assign increasing priority. Addressing evolving policy priorities may shift the types or raise the amounts of domestic support. Policy measures conforming with the requirements, criteria and conditions of the green box (Annex 2) of the Agriculture Agreement allow support addressing policy priorities of increased profile to be exempted from the limits on AMS support although conceptual and definitional issues arise. The potential green box accommodation of the measures reviewed for the selected high-profile priorities extends in similar ways to domestic support measures in pursuit of other evolving policy priorities in agriculture. Greater clarity might be sought regarding the accommodation of measures with the effect of reducing production within the Annex 2 requirement of at most minimal trade-distorting effects or effects on production. While the subsidy provisions of the SCM Agreement apply, the generally neutral or reducing effect on production and exports under many policy measures addressing these priorities would make the causation of adverse effects unlikely.

As mitigation of climate change may become an overriding priority, related policy measures may increase in number and variety. Making such measures consistent with the green box would be consistent with the objective and purpose of the Agriculture Agreement. Questions may arise whether the Annex 2 policy-specific criteria and conditions are too restrictive in how they relate eligibility for payment and amount of payment to production methods, inputs or certain costs or losses. If compatibility with these criteria and conditions were considered too constraining, interest could develop in crafting additional provisions in the green box relating to climate change mitigation. Advances in design of outcome-based measures, as distinct from practice-based measures, also may allow income support payments to producers larger than costs or income losses associated with those measures. Exemptions from AMS limits of support relating to mitigation of climate change might also be considered. However, in expanding green box eligibility or allowing AMS support in excess of limits, the balance between addressing the priority on mitigating climate change and pursuing the objective of substantially reducing trade-distorting support and protection would need careful consideration. Reducing the losses in the overall economy that result from distortions in agriculture and freeing up resources for the most effective ways to mitigate climate change could be part of such consideration.

9

Lessons from the Experience

This book reviews the rules concerning domestic support of the Agreement on Agriculture and evaluates the space they generate that governments of different WTO members can use for different types of policies and amounts of support. Domestic support remains a high-profile issue in implementing the Agreement and for ongoing negotiations. Several WTO disputes have adjudicated domestic support issues. Domestic support policies operate in a complex and dynamic environment of multidimensional policy influences within and beyond agriculture. While the book mostly has a tight focus, it also examines the place of members' domestic support obligations in this broader context.

After presenting the domestic support rules of the Agriculture Agreement and those of the SCM Agreement that apply subject to the Agriculture Agreement, the book reviews economic analysis regarding key types of support. It presents an overview of the major changes over time in members' domestic support in different categories as reported in their notifications to the WTO Committee on Agriculture for the years 1995 to 2016–18, complemented by selected observations for subsequent years. Exchanges within the Committee on Agriculture through 2021 over the notified information and other questions about members' support are summarized. The options members consider in the continuing but piecemeal negotiations about domestic support are examined. The measurement of MPS is evaluated in the context of *Korea – Various Measures on Beef*, *China – Agricultural Producers*, notifications and counter-notifications of India's support and *India – Sugar and Sugarcane*. Constraints on domestic support adjudicated in *US – Upland Cotton*, *EC – Export Subsidies on Sugar* and *Canada – Dairy* are also reviewed. Finally, the book explores the capacity of the domestic support rules of the Agreement on Agriculture to accommodate policy priorities concerning productivity growth, biosecurity in agriculture, water management, safeguarding and enhancing biodiversity and mitigation of climate change that have gained prominence since the Agreement was finalized in 1994.

This concluding chapter draws upon and integrates across the descriptive material and analysis presented. The purpose is to use the nearly 30 years of experience to identify how the domestic support provisions of the Agreement might be improved to strengthen its contribution to the objective of establishing a fair and market-oriented agricultural trading system. The Agriculture Agreement was formulated as the first step in negotiations to discipline both border measures and agricultural domestic support within the framework of the WTO, to establish strengthened and more operationally effective GATT rules and disciplines and to achieve substantial progressive reductions in support and protection. Only little has been accomplished over the years in taking the second step toward attaining these goals.

This chapter assesses aspects of the Agreement that have proven problematic and those that have proven less problematic than might have been expected. It draws on descriptions and assessments that concern and cut across the eight questions identified for analysis in the first chapter. What emerges is that many issues remain to be addressed in the area of domestic support if the Agriculture Agreement, reinforced through members' compliance with other WTO obligations, is to contribute to curbing excessive distorting domestic support. Reductions in trade-distorting support need to be achieved on a systematic, rules-based and multilateral basis, while leaving room for contributions to climate change mitigation and achievement of other welfare-enhancing non-trade objectives.

9.1   Overview Considerations

Several general observations merit reassertion and emphasis. First, the Agriculture Agreement is a multilateral undertaking. Domestic support disciplines are rarely if ever observed in plurilateral or regional trade agreements. While a participant's border policies can be targeted to benefit other participants in such an agreement, this is not possible with domestic support policies. The benefits of domestic support disciplines in a plurilateral or regional agreement would accrue not only to the participants but also to others who have not taken on the same obligations. This makes the Agriculture Agreement unique as the venue for domestic support disciplines.

Second, while the Agriculture Agreement is designed to limit some of the trade-distorting support and protection that adversely affect other members, each member is nonetheless the primary stakeholder affected by its own policies. The rules and commitments under the Agreement, which both govern and accommodate members' choice of domestic support measures and the amounts of support they provide, have served to move these choices in certain directions, but they are far short of a blueprint for efficient and non-distorting policy design. The Agreement will have to continue to discipline in a mutually effective manner a diverse set of support measures since the measures different members use have not coalesced. Members watch other members' compliance with their domestic support obligations, as the ongoing monitoring, negotiations and disputes demonstrate.

Third, the negotiations to revise the Agriculture Agreement take place in the shadow of complex broad challenges and calls for reform of the WTO in its implementation, negotiation and dispute settlement functions. Some of the developments underlying these broad challenges are evident when reviewing agricultural domestic support – the emergence of China and India as the members notifying the most Art. 6 support, for instance – but the broad challenges cannot be resolved in negotiations about a single sector. The larger context includes the challenge of again composing the Appellate Body such that a robust dispute settlement process is functional and the question of what role any distinction between developing and developed country members will play in the continued negotiations and the eventual result. These and other dimensions of the trade governance context make it uncertain when, or even whether, a substantive and systematic renegotiation of the Agriculture Agreement including its domestic support provisions might conclude. It is also uncertain whether incremental progress can be made on the issues that have remained under discussion on domestic support rules and commitments, the consequences of developing-country acquisition at administered prices of public stocks for food security purposes and cotton support. Reaching an outcome on any of these issues will depend not only on what changes may be agreed in the domestic support provisions but also in other provisions of the Agriculture Agreement and in wider negotiations in the WTO.

Beyond these contextual points, the major change since 1995 in the composition of all support should be recognized. Support in terms of the different categories defined by the Agriculture Agreement has shifted significantly in the direction the Agreement was intended to induce. Trade-distorting Art. 6 support has fallen nominally and as a percentage of the world total value of production in agriculture. This has occurred despite the amount of some such support not being subject to limit and allowances for other such support having grown under the Agreement's *de minimis* provisions. Conversely, green box support, amounts of which are not limited, has risen both nominally and as a percentage of global agricultural value of production.

Decisions in the several WTO disputes involving domestic support measures have contributed to the shift in the composition of support. These disputes were each brought in circumstances of substantial market interventions and the outcomes reinforced the boundaries on levels of certain support under members' obligations. Findings of excessive MPS in *China – Agricultural Producers* and *India – Sugar and Sugarcane* (under appeal) have clarified the calculations under the Agriculture Agreement and created some leverage to constrain domestic support by lowering administered prices. Findings of significant price suppression and serious prejudice to the interests of Brazil under the SCM Agreement in *US – Upland Cotton* led to a period of US policy revamping. Findings that a domestic support regime was a cause of excessive export subsidies in *EC – Export Subsidies on Sugar* contributed to substantial reform of the sugar regime consistent with other CAP reforms in the EU. Together with the increase in the share of green box support these rulings might lead a casual observer to conclude that the problem of excessive trade-distorting support that the Agriculture Agreement addresses largely has been solved.

A closer observation finds much that remains to be addressed. An observer of the discussions on domestic support within the WTO in later years may see both hopeful signs of progress and areas where differences among members' preferred processes or contents of the discussions seem less conducive to progress. Members' penchant for using terminology that deviates both from the Agreement and that used by other members makes it more difficult for others to embrace constructive ideas about complex rules and relationships and also for anyone to estimate the consequences for the policies of individual members. Putting these difficulties aside, other concerns come to the fore.

9.2   Problematic Dimensions of the Agriculture Agreement

The Agriculture Agreement was a major innovation by creating disciplines on domestic support. The starting point was fitted to the diversity of types and levels of support members provided at the time of the Uruguay Round negotiations. Agreeing on the rules and commitments involved concessions and political compromises. Major problematic aspects of the

Agreement and those less so were to be anticipated and some of them have been the focus of members' monitoring, continued engagement in negotiations and dispute adjudication.

Understanding this context yield insights about the areas where change is needed to strengthen the role of the Agriculture Agreement and a negotiated successor in ensuring substantial progressive reductions in agricultural support and protection while helping to achieve salient non-trade objectives. The insights allow identification of issues where trade-offs or improvements to strengthen the rules and commitments might be found. The analysis, at its core, seeks to further limit the room governments have for trade-distorting domestic support and provide the policy space for socially beneficial agricultural support by ensuring that the Agreement's rules for classifying support measures and measuring support align more closely with the impacts of support in economic terms.

9.2.1   Concentration of Support

Among the 136 members with an applicable WTO schedule, only a small number are responsible for both the vast bulk of domestic support and the overwhelming majority of Art. 6 support – that is, the sum of AMS support (whether *de minimis* AMSs or larger), Art. 6.2 support and blue box support. This concentration of support highlights that renegotiation of the Agreement would involve intense discussion among a small group of members with large stakes in the outcome but diverse support policies. Negotiating limits to apply uniformly among those members who have recently provided the largest amounts of Art. 6 support would run counter to special and differential treatment for China, India and possibly several other relatively large-support developing country members. It would align with some members' call for a structural reform under which more advanced and larger developing country members forgo some dimensions of such treatment and take on greater responsibility.

The amounts of Art. 6 support of most members in later years have been small compared to the support of the five or ten members with the largest amounts. Relatively little additional effect on the amount of support in the world would therefore be achieved by applying the same limitations for all other members as for the selected members. However, beyond the selected members, the support of some members is large relative to their agricultural value of production. Moreover, the tendency to let members' past support in different categories guide the development of new rules can have unforeseen consequences. Using only information from the past may say little about the future. The fact that many members continually lag in circulating information about recent years through notifications to the Committee on Agriculture exacerbates the problem of designing new rules.

9.2.2   Bound Total AMS

The BTAMS commitments based on amounts of certain support in 1986–88 (or later for some accession members) gave members with the largest amounts at that time the space to maintain support for individual products and non-product-specific support above the *de minimis* level. This created a problematic but unchanging bifurcation of members. Members with a positive BTAMS have more flexibility, especially in supporting certain products, than members with no or a nil BTAMS. The amounts of support counting against a BTAMS were well below this limit during 2016–18 among the members with the most such support. Realigning BTAMS based on the observed lower amount of support in later years would require a negotiated concession from members having the BTAMS flexibility. It would reduce the scope of the problem in empirical terms but not eliminate the problematic structural bifurcation unless BTAMS of all members were brought to nil. The ongoing negotiations have seen less ambitious suggestions to reduce the advantage of a positive BTAMS by reducing BTAMS without eliminating it, while also capping product-specific AMSs, and proposals to effectively eliminate BTAMS for developed country members. Developments such as the marked increases in CTAMS of the United States in 2018–20, in contrast to a longer-term decline in the EU, the United States and Japan, make negotiating tighter BTAMSs more difficult.

9.2.3   De Minimis *Allowances*

The *de minimis* AMS allowance is the *de minimis* percentage times the current value of production of a product or the agriculture sector. When implementation of the Agriculture Agreement began, members with no or a nil BTAMS generally had low levels of support but some have subsequently increased their support. Since the *de minimis* allowances grow with agricultural values of production, they provide room for larger AMSs over time, which is a potentially problematic expansion whether the allowances are limits or thresholds.

The sum of just 10 major members' *de minimis* allowances could approach USD 1,000 billion in 2030. The growing room for *de minimis* AMSs makes the fixed BTAMSs (summing to about USD 171 billion for all members) relatively less important over time, although a positive BTAMS still affords a member flexibility in supporting some products at higher than *de minimis* levels.

The *de minimis* allowance encapsulates the notion that the distortion associated with a relatively small AMS as a percentage of value of production is of less concern than higher levels of trade-distorting support. As value of production increases, the allowance increases and the nominal AMS can increase within it even while remaining constant as a percentage of production value. This constancy would be expected not to change the distorting effect of the support, but if applied to a larger quantity of production the effect on trade could increase. The AMS could also be increased in nominal and percentage terms within its original or a larger *de minimis* allowance. This larger AMS, although remaining a *de minimis* AMS, would distort more, again particularly if the underlying larger value of production results from a larger quantity of production.

The accommodation of increasing nominal AMSs within growing *de minimis* allowances could be curbed by reducing the *de minimis* percentages. Alternatively, the *de minimis* allowance could be set as a fixed nominal amount based on a given percentage and the value of production in a base period. The value of this fixed allowance relative to an increasing value of production would decline over time. However, rules involving fixed nominal values can have unexpected consequences, as experienced with FERPs in the calculation of MPS. The fixing of limits in nominal or in inflation-adjusted terms affects the strictness of the discipline differently. While similar issues arise with BTAMS, most members with positive BTAMS have kept CTAMSs well below this limit even with any inflation that has occurred over three decades.

An additional problematic aspect of the *de minimis* allowances arises because each member supports only certain products within its agriculture sector. As a member increases the number of products supported, while keeping support for each product within its *de minimis* limit or threshold, the member's summed AMS support can increase. While again tempered by the relatively low level of support for each product, the larger amounts of summed support might fuel a concern to be addressed in a renegotiated Agreement.

9.2.4   Product-Specific versus Non-Product-Specific Support

The Agriculture Agreement's definition of an AMS makes a binary distinction between support in favor of the producers of a basic agricultural product and support in favor of agricultural producers in general. Some members report AMSs not only for a number of individual products but also for a group of some of the same products. The values of production of those individual products are thus counted twice and generate double *de minimis* allowances. The practice effectively increases the room for AMS support within *de minimis* allowances. Such double-counting has not been a critical issue in the past, but it might be exploited on a greater scale in a situation where declining limits on product-specific AMSs were to apply.

A parallel issue is the interpretation of what constitutes non-product-specific AMS support, which may be important not only in a situation of declining limits on product-specific AMSs. One reading might require the support to be in favor of all producers, another in favor of producers of a group of products, such as certain crops. In either case, the total agricultural value of production is used to determine the non-product-specific *de minimis* allowance. A member could be advantaged by labeling more of its AMS support as non-product-specific and thus make its product-specific allowances less constraining. This could allow essentially product-specific support for the producers of each of several individual products in excess of each product's *de minimis* allowance to be accommodated within the non-product-specific *de minimis* allowance. A related issue arose in the case of classification by the United States of certain price-contingent cotton payments as non-product-specific AMS support because planting flexibility allowed crops other than cotton to be grown on the base acres. In *US – Upland Cotton*, it was nevertheless found that these payments, when made on acres planted to cotton, contributed to significant price suppression in the world cotton market.

9.2.5   Market Price Support

Measuring MPS under the Agriculture Agreement has proven problematic. The MPS measurement as adjudicated in *China – Agricultural Producers* imposed only modest constraint on the economic price support for wheat and rice. The MPS measurement as calculated in counter-notifications for wheat, rice, cotton and pulses in India, and determined by the panel in *India – Sugar and Sugarcane* (under appeal), is much larger than the economic price support. Disparities like these make the Agreement MPS measurement a prime candidate for renegotiation.

The MPS as calculated under the Agriculture Agreement has two underlying problems. The use of a very out-of-date reference price to determine the price gap that enters the calculation makes the gap in many cases generate a large amount of MPS even if there is only little or no support in economic terms. Also, allowing eligible production to be defined by legislated caps on purchases distances the Agreement's MPS from an economic measurement, in this case allowing less support to be calculated than if total production were used.

The MPS measured under the Agriculture Agreement therefore often misrepresents the actual amount of support that might distort trade. Economic effects in the form of production and trade distortions do not derive from the MPS so measured but from the MPS measured through economic methods. Designing new AMS limits based on the amount of MPS members have measured under the Agreement would not address the real source of distortions, that is, economic support. It would invite members to design policies to comply with certain limits without necessarily constraining their distorting support. China took steps to comply with the Agreement's limits by reducing MPSs for wheat and rice measured as adjudicated in dispute settlement. However, the caps on eligible production that China introduced in its support legislation allowed the reductions of price support in economic terms to be modest.

The counter-notifications about India's MPSs claim that India's use of administered prices makes those measurements greatly exceed India's limits. Yet, as India's administered prices have often been below international prices, a successful challenge on MPS would have accomplished little in terms of reducing distortions. The situation for sugarcane in India is different with support mostly positive in economic terms. In this case, a finding of excessive MPS under the Agriculture Agreement could help to constrain economic price support. But with the MPS assessed by the panel in *India – Sugar and Sugarcane* far exceeding the economic MPS for sugarcane in the years under dispute, questions are raised about the usefulness of the measurement under the Agreement.

If new rules for domestic support are to be effective, they need to be designed on the basis of economic realities, not merely on the often misleading indications generated by the Agreement's measurements. The 2013 ministerial decision and subsequent decision by the General Council conditionally preclude a challenge of an excessive AMS resulting from acquisition of stocks at administered prices for food security purposes in developing countries. While this reduces the likelihood of members, including India, being challenged regarding compliance with their obligations, it does not resolve the problematic disparity between the Agreement MPS and economic support.

Measuring MPS in a more economically meaningful way in the Agriculture Agreement could dissipate some of the tension surrounding acquisition at administered prices of public food stocks by more closely aligning the measured support with the economic support provided. Economic MPS is often less than MPS measured under the current Agreement. Although members have given a large profile to the stocks acquisition issue any economic analysis has played a minor role in the discussions. There is a dearth of analysis of the difference between acquiring stocks at market prices and acquiring at administered prices. Since much of the discussions seems to assume that the only way to accumulate public stocks is to purchase at administered prices, economic analysis of the advantages and drawbacks of a stockholding scheme of purchasing at market prices and at administered prices could also be useful for finding a permanent solution.

9.2.6   Article 6.2

The Art. 6.2 exemption from limit of certain investment and input subsidies in developing countries was at the time a significant concession to those members. India has exempted vastly larger amounts of support than other members under this provision since 1995. India's exemption of increasingly large amounts under Art. 6.2 created a gap between India's Art. 6 support and one measurement of support on which limits were under negotiation early in the Doha Round, namely all Art. 6 support except Art. 6.2 support. Momentum toward reaching a Doha Round agreement weakened, in part because of this exception. Even if moderately used by many developing country members so far, Art. 6.2 remains a potentially problematic avenue for the exemption of large amounts of trade-distorting support from limits. Placing constraints on the Art. 6.2 exemption would narrow this possibility. Constraints proportionately related to levels of past use would accord the largest space for this category of distorting support to India.

9.2.7   Blue Box

The decision by the EU and the United States to define and include the blue box exemption in the Agriculture Agreement was a crucial step in concluding the Uruguay Round. The exemption was then a stepping-stone in the subsequent EU policy transition from mostly Art. 6 support to mostly green box support, while the United States used it for only one year. Both the EU and the United States have thus moved away from relying on the blue box exemption. The exemption has therefore not proven as problematic as it might have been if large payments had continued to be exempted under it. The requirements that blue box measures be production-limiting and that payments be made on a fixed base likely make blue box payments less distorting in economic terms than price support or input subsidies.

Compliance with the blue box requirements merits monitoring in the context of China having begun using the blue box exemption in 2016 and its potential use by other members. Compliance monitoring would be more effective if it was clearer what meaning attaches in Art 6.5 to production-limiting programs. Including blue box payments under a cap on, for example, all Art. 6 support might further incentivize members to use the green box exemption so that blue box payments continue to be low and used by only a few members. If an inclusive cap on Art. 6 support was set high enough to accommodate a member's past blue box payments, the few past users would obtain relatively more space for distorting forms of support than other members.

9.2.8   Green Box

Green box exemptions have grown since the inception of the Agriculture Agreement. Growth in green box direct payments, such as *Direct payments to producers* and *Decoupled income support* (para. 5 and para. 6, Annex 2), has been substantial, including large payments in the EU, the United States (for a time) and later China and India. Direct payments to provide income support exempted on the green box grounds of not being related to prices, production or input use after a prior base period are not particularly problematic in terms of achieving the objective of the Agreement. Economic research indicates that in most circumstances income support payments in the green box are less trade or production distorting than Art. 6 support. The amounts of direct payments exempted from limit under the green box thus give less reason for concern than is sometimes expressed. Monitoring of compliance with the green box criteria remains important.

Many policy priorities in agriculture are different in later years from when the Agriculture Agreement was negotiated, and measures that provide domestic support in favor of agricultural producers increasingly address these evolving priorities. Green box general services expenditures have merit because public goods are provided that improve market performance, enhance long-term productivity growth, address other policy priorities that have gained profile and have implications for the tackling of overarching concerns. These are positive outcomes in terms of efficient resource use and sustainably meeting future world food demand.

The application of the Agreement's domestic support provisions to measures in priority areas of productivity growth, biosecurity in agriculture, water management, safeguarding and enhancing biodiversity, mitigation of climate change and others needs further deliberation. In addition to general services, direct payments to producers under the green box can address salient priorities of increased profile. Clarity is lacking whether a more than minimal negative effect on production that results from addressing a production externality would disqualify a measure from green box exemption. The amounts of payment under measures fitting within several green box paragraphs are subject to conditions related to producers' increased costs or losses, which constrains offering incentives for participation. Clarification is also needed in particular to increase certainty of interpretation for designing properly exemptible measures for climate change mitigation. There could be a need to negotiate particular provisions for measures that mitigate climate change while meeting the fundamental green box requirement of at most minimal trade-distorting effects or effects on production or for exempt measures outside the green box that have more than minimal production effects.

9.3   Addressing the Problematic Dimensions

Taking the above observations into account, discussion can turn to changes needed to strengthen the Agriculture Agreement in line with its objective and intent. While not raised by members, one question to ask is whether the Agriculture Agreement after 30 years has served its purpose and should be realigned – in the sense of melding its three pillars into other agreements that are not specific to agriculture – rather than being retained or renegotiated. Concluding not, options to address the problematic aspects of the domestic support rules and commitments of the Agriculture Agreement are outlined in four areas: balancing and reducing the amount of Art. 6 support, improving the measurement of MPS within Art. 6, managing domestic support in the post-Covid-19 era and enhancing policy space to address sustainability and mitigation of climate change.

9.3.1 Retaining the Agriculture Agreement

When the Agreement was negotiated, agriculture had largely been left outside of GATT disciplines. Among developed countries, there were high levels of border protection, domestic price support, payments to producers and export subsidization, while among developing countries there was generally little support or even discrimination against agriculture. Bringing some disciplines to this chaotic policy and global market situation was a high priority of many governments and was seen to require negotiations unique to agriculture.

The situation is quite different in recent years. Tariffication of various non-tariff measures that had been prevalent in agriculture was accomplished. Tariffs remain higher in agriculture than other sectors, and TRQs and provisions for special safeguards under the Agriculture Agreement are sector-specific, but tariff and related market access negotiations might be feasible under a common process covering manufactured and agricultural goods. Affected interest groups and other stakeholders, and negotiating responsibilities and capacity among government ministries, would continue to focus on different sectors and products, but the need for a separate agreement for agriculture is less apparent than it was.

Likewise, there has been fundamental change in commitments on export subsidies. The Uruguay Round negotiations achieved commitments to limit and modestly reduce export subsidies, even as use of such subsidies was declining. By 2015, members decided to eliminate export subsidies for agricultural products, albeit over extended timelines, and to discipline export financing support and food aid. With export subsidies prohibited for non-agricultural goods and prohibited or eliminated for agricultural goods, the SCM Agreement might be adequate to discipline their use. The export subsidies identified in Art. 9 of the Agriculture Agreement could be integrated with those in the SCM Annex I Illustrative List, with any repetition eliminated and any needed agricultural wording included. Arguments in disputes already draw on the SCM Art. 1 definition of a subsidy and the Illustrative List to claim that certain measures involving agricultural products are export subsidies. With export subsidies prohibited or eliminated in agriculture, members face obligations with equal effects for agricultural and other products.

These considerations leave domestic support as the pillar of the Agriculture Agreement that remains unique. If the Agreement were not retained two issues arise: would this reduce policy transparency and would it weaken the discipline on certain trade-distorting agricultural support or the guidance given by the Agreement toward less distorting measures and support?

Suppose, for example, that the SCM Agreement were the primary basis for disciplining domestic support in favor of agricultural producers.[1] Although the lack of up-to-date notifications sometimes undermines the ability of the Committee on Agriculture to carry out its review mandate, it has proven a forum for exchange and discussion of members' obligations, support measures and calculations of support as notified and yet to be notified. Discussions not only alert members to distorting policies of other members but also inform about the feasibility and pragmatic dimensions of implementing less distorting support measures. Notification requirements of the SCM Agreement would need retailoring to generate the kind of agricultural policy information used in the Committee on Agriculture's review process. With the SCM Committee as the forum for all discussion of agricultural support, time and participant focus would be more constrained. This would be inimical to rather than supportive of greater transparency about agricultural support among WTO members.

While policy monitoring by the OECD and other institutions and networks offers transparency through alternative systematic databases and analysis, those efforts typically do not link well to WTO members' legal obligations. Transparency across economic and legal considerations would be improved if WTO members were to more explicitly develop notifications from public data bases that use economically meaningful classifications and measurement. However, the distance between the Agriculture Agreement's rules and those of economic measurements needs to be narrowed for such efforts to become feasible, which speaks for continued reliance on and enhancement of the transparency generated in the Committee on Agriculture's review of progress in the implementation of members' commitments.

If the limits on AMS support, and the potential for making other trade-distorting support subject to similar limits, were not retained then the measures offering such support would primarily be disciplined by members' obligations under the SCM Agreement. With some differentiation between developed and developing countries, subsidies as defined

---

[1] The symmetric question would be whether the provisions and experience of implementing the Agriculture Agreement offer lessons for enhancing disciplines on non-agricultural subsidies. Such an assessment is beyond the scope of this book.

in SCM Art. 1, which include price support, should not cause adverse effects to the interests of other members. Adverse effects essentially involve injury to another member's industry, nullification or impairment of benefits accruing to other members under GATT 1994 or serious prejudice to another member's interests.[2] Only in the single dispute, *US – Upland Cotton*, has domestic support in agriculture been challenged on this basis. Thus, years of experience demonstrate that despite widespread prevalence it is difficult to establish under legal scrutiny that a member's particular domestic support measure is market-distorting in the sense of causing adverse effects in another member's domestic market or on its export opportunities.

Trade-distorting domestic budgetary subsidies in agriculture thus continue to flow in the hundreds of billions of USD annually, with MPS under administered prices adding to the support subject to Agriculture Agreement rules and commitments. The relative impacts on trade opportunities and producer incomes of budgetary support are estimated to be increasing compared to border protection. Although members' notified AMS support is usually well below applicable limits, this is not always so. Members thus need to keep their WTO obligations under consideration as they implement support measures. This suggests that without Agriculture Agreement limits on AMS support there would likely be more, not less, trade-distorting support. However, reducing trade-distorting support requires more effective limits than under the Agreement's rules and commitments, which includes aligning the reach and size of the limits with the economic impacts of the support.

9.3.2   Balancing and Reducing Article 6 Support

The long-term objective of renegotiating the Agriculture Agreement should be to achieve more consistency of the rules among different groups of members and lower levels of Art. 6 support measured with more correspondence to its economic effects. Some members prioritize reducing or eliminating BTAMS, that is, eventually making it impossible

---

[2] Without the limits on AMS support of the Agriculture Agreement, support in whatever amount would not in and of itself result in nullification or impairment of benefits accruing to another member. Nationally determined CVD measures also potentially discipline domestic support and might proliferate, with a corresponding increase in tariff protection. Only a fraction of these measures implemented during 1995–2020 were challenged at the WTO.

for any AMS of any member to exceed its *de minimis* level. Reducing or eliminating BTAMS is one important element of leveling the future playing field but cannot by itself do as much to improve market orientation as it would in combination with ensuring that all forms of distorting support are subject to limit and, eventually, cutting back on all members' *de minimis* allowances.

Under the objective of reducing the amount of Art. 6 support provided globally, one way forward would be to focus on those members that provide the largest amounts of support. Eliminating over time the entitlements to large or unlimited amounts of support other than green box support of a small number of members would go a long way toward reducing the large amounts of Art. 6 support these members could otherwise provide in the future.

Product-specific support has been reported to be regularly cited by members as the most distorting form of support in agricultural trade, likely referring to product-specific AMSs. The analytical basis for this selection of the most distorting form of support is not clear. Economic analysis demonstrates that product-specific MPS, appropriately measured, is part of the potentially most distorting support. But analysis also shows that on a per currency-unit basis subsidies for the unconstrained use of variable inputs distort as much as or more than price support. Some input support has escaped limits through the Art. 6.2 exemption. Constraining only product-specific AMSs as one of the most distorting forms of support would therefore reduce the effectiveness of future rules in reducing trade-distorting support.

Comprehensive reductions of Art. 6 support could take the form of eliminating the entitlements to AMS support above *de minimis* limits (i.e., eliminating the BTAMS) and eliminating the exemption of Art. 6.2 support and blue box support not only from CTAMS but also from individual AMSs. This would result in only green box support being exempt from limit. A member's *de minimis* limits would apply not only to AMS support as presently defined but to the sum of all categories of Art. 6 support. To achieve this outcome, concessions by members with positive BTAMS under the Agriculture Agreement would be matched by concessions from members with entitlement to Art. 6.2 exemptions and a leveling of the *de minimis* percentages between developed and developing country members. The first concessions would have been unachievable from the starting point of AMS support levels at the time of the Uruguay Round but is more plausible from the lower levels of support during later years, with the larger CTAMS of the United States in some of those years a complicating but possibly transitory factor. The second concessions are likely out of reach as long as some members retain the advantage of a positive BTAMS. The joint outcome would recognize the realities of the distribution of Art. 6 support, where the largest amounts are seen in both developed and developing country members, not just developed country members.

Making the rules and commitments for the large-support members less incongruous leaves open the question of what obligations would apply to other members. Since the amount of Art. 6 support of most members in recent years has been small compared to the support of a few members, all other members could, for example, be exempted from the elimination of entitlements to BTAMS or the Art. 6.2 and blue box exemptions. If it was seen as crucial to eliminate or reduce Art. 6 support beyond *de minimis* levels for all members, the rules could be implemented over a longer period or be designed to apply differently to different groups of members.

Eliminating BTAMS and including Art. 6.2 support and blue box support in the AMS calculations of five or ten selected members would result in their Art. 6 support being bounded by their *de minimis* limits. This would allow the specific and more ambitious outcome with regard to cotton to take the form of a lower *de minimis* percentage for the limit on Art. 6 cotton support than the *de minimis* percentages for other Art. 6 support.

More openness among members to envisage alternative future scenarios for the support of the major agricultural producers could be a first step in the process of finding rules and commitments that are more effective in countering distortions. This transparency would need to be combined with strengthened monitoring of compliance and the institutionalization of a process to review and update the disciplines as the world changes.

9.3.3 Improving the Measurement of Market Price Support

Because the MPS measured under the Agriculture Agreement is problematic, this book proposes an alternative MPS measurement. It retains the administered price in the measured price gap but replaces the FERP with a moving average of lagged border prices. Using such reference prices would in many cases reduce or eliminate positive price gaps. When also counting all production as eligible production, the resulting LRP MPS would often differ less from the economic MPS than does the

Agreement MPS, as illustrated for wheat in China and India during 2008–18. Use of a lagged moving average of world prices as the basis for the reference price for MPS would improve the rules for all members.

The LRP MPS measurement enables the government to use an administered price to benchmark producer prices in the domestic market within the space that is available from the separately negotiated border protection. The administered price often sets a floor for domestic market prices, which some members see as an essential policy option. The LRP MPS also allows for circumstances in which the market price exceeds the administered price. This accommodates the effects on domestic prices of tariffs or other border or behind-the-border policy measures without making these effects subject to the domestic support discipline, a flexibility that is important to some members. The use in the LRP MPS of a moving average of lagged border prices to calculate the reference price is not ideal compared to using the current border price. However, it allows the reference price in many situations to be closer to the current border price than using a FERP based on increasingly distant past years.

Improved measurement of MPS would bring the effects of AMS limits closer to what they would be if applied to an AMS including the economic MPS. The use of a moving average reference price in MPS calculations was discussed in the Uruguay Round negotiations as was the idea of a FERP being fixed only for five years. Neither idea received substantial consideration in subsequent negotiations although the issue garnered somewhat more attention in the draft decision on agriculture prepared for, but not adopted at, the 12th ministerial conference in 2022. The experience gained over time of implementing price support policies and applying the rules of the Agreement suggests replacing the FERP with a moving average of lagged border prices warrants additional consideration.

In particular, adopting an LRP MPS that tracks economic MPS could on its own underpin a permanent solution to the public stockholding impasse, not just be a secondary consideration while permanently insulating MPS arising from acquisition of stocks at administered prices from dispute challenge or limit. Economic MPS is often less than MPS measured under the Agreement, especially for developing countries. If they did not face the need to keep the artificially high measurement of MPS within limits, many developing countries could be more accepting of limits continuing to apply to producer price support resulting from stocks acquisition for food security programs. Proponents of retaining the limits should also be reassured – any objections to limits on a measurement of

MPS that comes closer to the measurement of economic support, which is what distorts markets, would be less well founded than objections to limits on the artificial Agreement MPS. Lessening the contention concerning the measurement of MPS more generally under the Agriculture Agreement would allow members to turn more attention in the Committee on Agriculture and in negotiations to other areas where their efforts could enhance the global regime of domestic support policies.

9.3.4 Managing Domestic Support in the Post–Covid-19 Era

A broad set of challenges arose from the Covid-19 global pandemic starting in early 2020. Many of the issues this book addresses become even more germane in the pandemic's aftermath. As agricultural and food production and distribution were disrupted, support to farmers and food processors rose as part of some countries' policy responses to the pandemic and its economic effects. The increase in domestic support payments in the United States was notable in this context. Initial increases in 2018–19 offset losses associated with retaliation against US tariff policy decisions, not the pandemic, highlighting the interrelationship of border protection and domestic support. Subsequent pandemic-related US support for agriculture pushed its CTAMS to a record USD 18.2 billion in 2019 and large amounts of such support were also provided in 2020. These levels of support will weaken the interest of the United States in tighter support limits under the Agriculture Agreement. Many other members also included support in favor of agricultural producers within their Covid-19 relief measures, whether as AMS support or in other categories.

A large increase in members' Art. 6 support in response to the extraordinary event of the pandemic could contribute to a reversal of the global downward movement of trade-distorting support observed from 1995 through the late 2010s. Large Covid-19-related Art. 6 support will be less problematic if it proves temporary over no more than a few years than if it raises members' support amounts on a continuous basis. The issue of some members repeatedly raising support in response to unanticipated adverse domestic or global developments while others do not remains a systemic imbalance.

Governments need to manage situations such as those arising from the Covid-19 pandemic while continuing to strengthen the multilateral obligations on domestic support. Pragmatism going forward will be needed, along with keeping a focus on long-term goals and the role of the WTO. Strong international institutions and cooperation will be needed to help counter tendencies to forgo rather than safeguard the benefits of economic integration. Reinvigorated engagement through the WTO may prevail but cannot be taken for granted. Forward-looking initiatives will need to include revisiting the rules and commitments in agriculture, including those for domestic support.

9.3.5   Sustainability and Mitigation of Climate Change

Members have over the years increasingly chosen to pursue evolving policy priorities by means of support through measures they exempt under the green box of the Agriculture Agreement. Stronger emphasis on some long-standing priorities and clearer recognition of newer ones help to set directions for domestic support policy in agriculture. Engaging internationally, members pursue or have entered into a number of commitments on policy action that relate to agriculture and food. The United Nations Sustainable Development Goals of 2015 are a case in point, joined by other processes addressing the triple challenge concerning food security, livelihoods and environmental sustainability. Formulating and achieving policy objectives with regard to mitigation of climate change have become high priorities. While the policy response to the evolving priorities could involve allocating larger amounts of support in favor of agricultural producers, it has also been expressed as a need to repurpose the support, that is, using current amounts of support for other objectives in agriculture.

The rules of the Agriculture Agreement offer many options to accommodate policy efforts to address salient priorities, but there are also constraints and some definitional ambiguities concerning the use of such measures. At a deep level, a clearer Annex 2 fundamental requirement may need to be articulated to make explicit that measures that provide public goods or that reflect internalizing or reducing externalities by means of policy qualify for exemption from AMS support limits. Such a requirement would supplant the stipulation that green box measures have at most minimal trade-distorting effects or effects on production. Ambiguity would thus be removed as to whether certain measures meet the fundamental requirement of the green box. The resulting clarity would apply to general service measures providing public goods that enhance production over time, such as investments in agricultural research or irrigation infrastructure and direct payment measures that reduce production more than minimally, such as certain programs to safeguard or enhance biodiversity or mitigate climate change. While considerations like these have not been principal concerns in the implementation of the Agriculture Agreement, evolving priorities concerning sustainability and mitigation of climate change have elevated them. Addressing these considerations would require guardrails within the policy-specific criteria and conditions to continue ensuring that the measures do not cross a line and create trade-distorting incentives or effects on production not related to their non-trade objectives.

In absence of such a basic rewording, a number of issues arise. Focusing on mitigation of climate change, which may become the predominant priority, a climate change measure must be understood as part of an environmental or conservation program in order to qualify for exemption under the green box *Payments under environmental programmes* (para. 12, Annex 2). Clarity is needed on the scope of this exemption. If programs for mitigating climate change were on some basis found not to be environmental or conservation programs under para. 12, introducing additional provisions in Annex 2 could be considered. A second ambiguity concerns whether a measure must include specific conditions related to production methods or inputs. As outcome-based environmental programs become more prominent, with program conditions related to production methods or input use minimal or absent, this ambiguity will need to be addressed.

The assessed value of a climate change mitigation outcome compared to the status quo may be higher than the producer's extra costs or loss of income, creating an incentive for the producer to achieve the outcome. However, such a payment is precluded from exemption by the para. 12 requirement that the amount be no larger than the extra costs or loss of income involved in program compliance. Reconsideration of this provision may be warranted in relation to some priorities, particularly when a measure is likely to reduce production and there are global non-trade concerns as in the case of climate change.

Green box *Decoupled income support* and similar direct payments have been instrumental in some members' movement away from trade-distorting support. These categories of payments can likewise facilitate certain sustainability measures. For example, payments meeting the criteria and conditions of these paragraphs could be offered to producers who relinquish subsidized rights to water use, providing an income-support incentive for program participation determined by a base period at which the rights were relinquished. Consistency with para. 5 or para. 6

related to income support would be difficult to reach with practice-based measures to mitigate climate change if the land area committed to that objective continues to be used as a factor of production and conditions are set on other input use or production practices. Para. 5 or para. 6 consistency would more easily be met by an outcome-based mitigation program where no conditions were set on current or future production or input use. Advances in technologies for outcome-based measures would allow an income support incentive for program participation, circumventing the payment restriction to costs or lost income in para. 12.

Payments to producers addressing evolving policy priorities do not need to be green-box compliant, although compliance would be preferable. As many members have notified an absence of AMS support or support below applicable limits, they can pursue evolving priorities to some extent by using AMS support. At some point, a priority may take on such urgency that it is best addressed by Art. 6 measures, possibly in amounts exceeding applicable limits on AMS support. The characteristics of such measures are not easy to envisage but could lead to renegotiating the Art. 6 provisions.

9.4   Challenges and Promise Ahead

This book evaluates domestic support in favor of agricultural producers and presents evidence and analysis to evaluate how it has been disciplined under the rules and commitments of the Agreement on Agriculture complemented by the SCM Agreement as applicable. Drawing on this evaluation, the book examines the challenges in disciplining domestic support going forward under the Agriculture Agreement and what new WTO obligations might be needed for the future. Addressing salient non-trade priorities is found compatible with strengthened rules to reduce trade and production distortions. Less distorted trade, governed by systematic and multilaterally agreed rules, would bring global benefits. Dissensions have prevented the negotiations on agriculture from establishing the rules and commitments to further reduce trade-distorting support and protection that would allow attaining those benefits. The faltering of the Doha Round has not meant a continuation of the status quo. Rather, a crisis of commitment engulfs the multilateral trade system under a changing global policy landscape. Perhaps a new sense of purpose will motivate new appreciation of the value members derive from the global trade system with the WTO as its central institution. That could require substantial change in the WTO but also reaffirm its relevance. Agricultural negotiations will have to be part of any endeavor to revitalize members' engagement. This necessity motivates making an assessment of the experience concerning domestic support in agriculture under the WTO over nearly three decades and looking forward at prospects for the future.

REFERENCES

Abbott, P., B. Johnston, D. Blandford et al. 1988. Bringing agriculture into the GATT: Assessing the benefits of trade liberalization. Commissioned Paper No. 2. International Agricultural Trade Research Consortium.

Abler, D., and D. Blandford. 2005. Decoupling – Policy implications. Working Party on Agricultural Policies and Markets, Committee for Agriculture. AGR/CA/APM(2005)22/FINAL. Organisation for Economic Co-operation and Development.

Ackrill, R., and A. Kay. 2011. Multiple streams in EU policy-making: The case of the 2005 sugar reform. *Journal of European Public Policy* 18(1): 72–89.

2009. Historical learning in the design of WTO rules: The EC sugar case. *The World Economy* 32(5): 754–771.

AgIncentives. 2021. International Organizations Consortium for Measuring the Policy Environment for Agriculture. www.ag-incentives.org.

Agreement on Agriculture. 15 April 1994. LT/UR/A-1A/2. https://docs.wto.org.

Agreement on Subsidies and Countervailing Measures. 15 April 1994. LT/UR/A-1A/9. https://docs.wto.org.

Aguiar, A., M. Chepeliev, E. Corong, R. McDougall and D. van der Mensbrugghe. 2019. The GTAP data base: Version 10. *Journal of Global Economic Analysis* 4(1): 1–27.

Ahn, D., and D. Orden. 2021. China – Domestic Support for Agricultural Producers: One policy, multiple parameters imply modest discipline. *World Trade Review* 20(4): 389–404.

Anderson, K. (ed.). 2009. *Distortions to Agricultural Incentives: A Global Perspective 1955–2007*. London: Palgrave Macmillan; Washington, DC: World Bank.

Anderson, K., and E. Valenzuela. 2021. What impact are subsidies and trade barriers abroad having on Australasian and Brazilian agriculture? *Australian Journal of Agricultural and Resource Economics* 65(2): 265–290.

Aquino Bonomo, C. S. 2019. Reshaping international trade with the WTO Dispute Settlement: The sugar case (DS 265/266/283). In *The WTO Dispute Settlement Mechanism: A Developing Country Perspective*, ed. A. Amaral Júnior, L. M. Oliveira Sá Pires, and C. L. Carneiro. Cham: Springer Nature Switzerland AG, pp. 289–303.

Banga, R. 2014. Impact of green box subsidies on agricultural productivity, production and international trade. Background Paper No. RVC-11. United Nations Conference on Trade and Development, Geneva.

Bartels, L. 2016. The relationship between the WTO Agreement on Agriculture and the SCM Agreement: An analysis of hierarchy rules in the WTO legal system. *Journal of World Trade* 50(1): 7–20.

Barton, J. H., J. L. Goldstein, T. E. Josling and R. H. Steinberg. 2006. *The Evolution of the Trade Regime*. Princeton: Princeton University Press.

Birner, R., S. Gupta and N. Sharma. 2011. *The Political Economy of Agricultural Policy Reform in India: Fertilizers and Electricity for Irrigation*. Washington, DC: International Food Policy Research Institute.

Blandford, D. 2019. Policy challenges in the management of natural resources. In *Global Challenges for Future Food and Agricultural Policies*, ed. D. Blandford and K. Hassapoyannes. Singapore: World Scientific, pp. 125–151.

Blandford, D., and T. Josling. 2007. Should the green box be modified? IPC Discussion Paper. International Food & Agricultural Trade Policy Council, Washington, DC.

Bown, C., and M. Kolb. 2020. Trump's trade war timeline: An up-to-date guide. Trade and Investment Policy Watch. Peterson Institute for International Economics, Washington, DC.

Brink, L. 2021. An ensemble of potential changes in the WTO rules on domestic support in agriculture: Comparing support space and measured support. Slide presentation. International Agricultural Trade Research Consortium, Annual Meeting, December 12–14.

2020. Measuring price support under WTO domestic support rules: How much advantage from being an Article XII member? Slide presentation. International Agricultural Trade Research Consortium, Annual Meeting, December 15.

2019. Product-specific, non-product-specific or in between: Practices and consequences under the WTO Agreement on Agriculture. Slide presentation. Annual Meeting, International Agricultural Trade Research Consortium, December 8–10.

2018a. Farm support, domestic policies and the WTO rules: The world is changing. In *Volume III: International Trade Rules for Food and Agricultural Products, Handbook of International Food and Agricultural Policies*, ed. K. Meilke and T. Josling. Singapore: World Scientific, pp. 243–275.

2018b. Two indicators, little in common, same name: Market Price Support. CAP Reform. www.capreform.eu/.

2015a. Policy space in agriculture under the WTO rules on domestic support. Working Paper #15-01. International Agricultural Trade Research Consortium.

2015b. Investment and input subsidies: A growing category of farm support exempted from WTO limits. Slide presentation. Annual meeting, International Agricultural Trade Research Consortium, December 13–15.

2011. The WTO disciplines on domestic support. In *WTO Disciplines on Agricultural Support*, ed. D. Orden, D.Blandford, and T. Josling. Cambridge: Cambridge University Press, pp. 23–58.

2006. WTO constraints on U.S. and EU domestic support in agriculture: The October 2005 proposals. *The Estey Centre Journal of International Law and Trade Policy* 7(1): 96–115.

Brink, L., and D. Orden. 2020. Taking stock and looking forward on domestic support under the WTO Agreement on Agriculture. Commissioned Paper 23. International Agricultural Trade Research Consortium.

Bureau, J.-C. 2017. Does the WTO discipline really constrain the design of CAP payments? CAP Reform. www.capreform.eu/.

Cahill, C., and S. Tangermann (coordinators). 2021. New pathways for progress in multilateral trade negotiations in agriculture. With L. Brink, S. Fan, J. Glauber, A. González, T. Groser, A. Gulati, J. Hewitt, A. Hoda, A. Matthews, and G. Valles Galmés. Pathways Group.

Cahill, S. 1997. Calculating the rate of decoupling for crops under CAP/Oilseeds reform. *Journal of Agricultural Economics* 48(3): 349–378.

Chambers, R., and D. Voica. 2016. "Decoupled" farm program payments are really decoupled: The theory. *American Journal of Agricultural Economics* 99(3): 773–782.

Chaplin, S., V. Robinson, A. LePage et al. 2019. Pilot results-based payment approaches for agri-environment schemes in arable and upland grassland systems in England. Final Report to the European Commission. Natural England and Yorkshire Dales National Park Authority.

Chen, B., N. Villoria and T. Xia. 2020. Import protection in China's grain markets: An empirical assessment. *Agricultural Economics* 51(2): 191–206.

CBD (Convention on Biological Diversity). 2021. Kunming Declaration. CBD/COP/15/5/Add.1. Secretariat of the Convention on Biological Diversity, Montreal.

Coppens, D. 2014. *WTO Disciplines on Subsidies and Countervailing Measures: Balancing Policy Space and Legal Constraints.* Cambridge: Cambridge University Press.

Coppess, J. 2018. *The Fault Lines of Farm Policy: A Legislative and Political History of the Farm Bill.* Lincoln: The University of Nebraska Press.

Daugbjerg. C., and A. Swinbank. 2009. *Ideas, Institutions and Trade: The WTO and the Curious Role of EU Farm Policy in Trade Liberalization.* Oxford: Oxford University Press.

Davey, W., and A. Sapir. 2010. United States – Subsidies on Upland Cotton Recourse to Article 21.5 by Brazil, WT/DS267/AB/RW (2 June 2008). *World Trade Review* 9(1): 181–199.

DeClerck, F. A. J., I. Koziell, A. Sidhu et al. 2021. Biodiversity and agriculture: Rapid evidence review. Colombo, Sri Lanka: International Water Management

Institute (IWMI) and CGIAR Research Program on Water, Land and Ecosystems (WLE).

de Gorter, H. 2009. The distributional structure of U.S. green box subsidies. In *Agricultural Subsidies in the WTO Green Box: Ensuring Coherence with Sustainable Development Goals*, ed. R. Meléndez-Ortiz, C. Bellmann and J. Hepburn. Cambridge: Cambridge University Press.

de Gorter, H., D. R. Just and J. D. Kropp. 2008. Cross-subsidization due to inframarginal support in agriculture: A general theory and empirical evidence. *American Journal of Agricultural Economics* 90(1): 42–54.

Dewbre, J., J. Antón and W. Thompson. 2001. The transfer efficiency and trade effects of direct payments. *American Journal of Agricultural Economics* 83(5): 1204–1214.

DFAT (Department of Foreign Affairs and Trade). 2021. India – Measures Concerning Sugar and Sugarcane (DS580). Australia's Integrated Executive Summary. 20 May.

Díaz-Bonilla, E. 2017. Food security stocks and the WTO legal framework. In *Agriculture, Development, and the Global Trading System: 2000–2015*, ed. A. Bouët and D. Laborde Debucquet. Washington, DC: International Food Policy Research Institute, pp. 285–324.

Effland, A. 2011. Classifying and measuring agricultural support: Identifying differences between the WTO and OECD systems. Economic Information Bulletin Number 74. Economic Research Service, US Department of Agriculture.

Elbehri, A., J. Umstaetter and D. Kelch. 2008. The EU sugar policy regime and implications of reform. Economic Research Report Number 59. Economic Research Service, US Department of Agriculture.

FAO, UNDP and UNEP. 2021. A multi-billion-dollar opportunity: Repurposing agricultural support to transform food systems. Rome: Food and Agriculture Organization of the United Nations, United Nations Development Programme and United Nations Environment Programme.

FAO (Food and Agriculture Organization of the United Nations). 2021. Value of agricultural production. FAOSTAT.

1975. Agricultural protection and stabilization policies: A framework of measurement in the context of agricultural adjustment. Conference. C 75/LIM/2.

1973. Agricultural protection: Domestic policy and international trade. Conference. C 73/LIM/9.

Ford, J. R. D. 2021. Domestic support in the WTO agriculture negotiations: Outcomes for MC12: Decreasing trade distorting domestic support to increase food security. CUTS International, Geneva.

Gale, F. 2021. Potential wheat demand in China: Applicants for import quota. Economic Research Report Number 295. Economic Research Service, US Department of Agriculture.

Galtier, F. 2017. Looking for a permanent solution on public stockholding programmes at the WTO: Getting the right metrics on the support provided. Think Piece. The E15 Initiative: Strengthening the Global Trade and Investment System for Sustainable Development. International Centre for Trade and Sustainable Development and World Economic Forum, Geneva.

　2015. Identifying, estimating and correcting the biases in WTO rules on public stocks. A proposal for the post-Bali food security agenda. Working Paper MOISA 2015-5. UMR Marchés, organisations, institutions et stratégies d'acteurs. CIRAD, Montpellier, France.

García Vargas, A. 2021. Promoting transparency on agricultural policies at the WTO: Lessons from Latin America and the Caribbean. In *The Road to the WTO Twelfth Ministerial Conference: A Latin American and Caribbean Perspective*, ed. V. Piñeiro, A. Campos and M. Piñeiro. San José, Costa Rica: Interamerican Institute for Cooperation on Agriculture and International Food Policy Research Institute, pp. 97–120.

General Agreement on Tariffs and Trade 1994. 15 April 1994. LT/UR/A-1A/1/ GATT/1. https://docs.wto.org

GATT (General Agreement on Tariffs and Trade). 1988a. The Trade Distortion Equivalent (TDE): An aggregate indicator of adverse trade effects of measures of support and protection for agriculture. MTN.GNG/NG5/W/46.

GATT. 1988b. Short-term measures (other than immediate measures) in the framework of the measures proposed by the European Communities. MTN.GNG/ NG5/W/62.

　1987. United States Proposal for Negotiations on Agriculture. MTN.GNG/NG5/ W/14.

　1958. *Trends in International Trade – Report by a Panel of Experts.* Sales No. GATT/ 1958-3. Geneva: The Contracting Parties to the General Agreement on Tariffs and Trade.

Glauber, J. W. 2018a. Domestic support measures in the context of adaptation / mitigation to climate change. Background Paper for The State of Agricultural Commodity Markets 2018. Food and Agriculture Organization of the United Nations, Rome.

　2018b. Unraveling reforms? Cotton in the 2018 farm bill and beyond. In *Agricultural Policy in Disarray*, ed. V. H. Smith, J. W. Glauber and B. K. Goodwin. Washington, DC: American Enterprise Institute.

Glauber, J., and S. Lester. 2021. China – Tariff Rate Quotas for Certain Agricultural Products: Against the grain: Can the WTO open Chinese markets? A contaminated experiment. *World Trade Review* 20(4):1–16.

Glauber, J., and T. Sinha. 2021. Procuring food stocks under World Trade Organization farm subsidy rules: Finding a permanent solution. IISD Report. International Institute for Sustainable Development, Winnipeg.

Glauber, J., D. Laborde and V. Piñeiro. 2021. New disciplines for domestic support. In *The Road to the WTO Twelfth Ministerial Conference: A Latin American and Caribbean Perspective*, ed. V. Piñeiro, A. Campos and M. Piñeiro. San José, Costa Rica: Interamerican Institute for Cooperation on Agriculture and International Food Policy Research Institute, pp. 29–42.

Glauber, J. W., J. Hepburn, D. Laborde and S. Murphy. 2020. What national farm policy trends could mean for efforts to update WTO rules on domestic support. IISD Report. International Institute for Sustainable Development, Winnipeg.

Gohin, A., and J.-C. Bureau. 2006. Modelling the EU sugar supply to assess sectoral policy reforms. *European Review of Agricultural Economics* 33(2): 223–247.

Goodwin, B., and A. Mishra. 2006. Are "decoupled" farm program payments really decoupled? An empirical evaluation. *American Journal of Agricultural Economics* 88(1): 73–89.

Gotor, E. 2009. The reform of the EU sugar trade preferences toward developing countries in light of the Economic Partnership Agreements. *The Estey Centre Journal of International Law and Trade Policy* 10(2): 15–29.

Grant, J. H., C. Xie and K. A. Boys. 2022. Firms, agricultural imports and tariff-rate quotas: An assessment of China's wheat, corn and rice imports using firm-level data. Commissioned Paper 28. International Agricultural Trade Research Consortium.

Grossman, G. M., and A. O. Sykes. 2011. 'Optimal' retaliation in the WTO – a commentary on the Upland Cotton arbitration. *World Trade Review* 10(1): 133–164.

Gulati, A., and S. Narayanan. 2003. *The Subsidy Syndrome in Indian Agriculture*. New Delhi: Oxford University Press.

Gulati, A., D. Kapur and M. Bouton. 2019. Reforming Indian agriculture. CASI Working Paper. Center for the Advanced Study of India (CASI) and Indian Council for Research on International Economic Relations (ICRIER), New Delhi.

Häberli, C. 2021. Sustainable agriculture and trade. In *Trade and Environmental Law. Volume XI, Elgar Encyclopedia of Environmental Law*, ed. P. Delimatsis and L. Reins. Cheltenham; Northampton: Edward Elgar, pp. 692–703.

Hassapoyannes, K., and D. Blandford. 2019. Agriculture and climate change: National and international policy response. In *Global Challenges for Future Food and Agricultural Policies*, ed. D. Blandford and K. Hassapoyannes. Singapore: World Scientific, pp. 217–248.

Hasund, K., and M. Johansson. 2016. Paying for environmental results is WTO compliant. *EuroChoices* 15(3): 33–38.

Hedley, D. D. 2017. Governance in Canadian agriculture. *Canadian Journal of Agricultural Economics* 65(4): 523–541.

Henderson, B., J. Lankoski, E. Flynn, A. Sykes, F. Payen and M. MacLeod. 2022. Soil carbon sequestration by agriculture: Policy options. OECD Food, Agriculture and Fisheries Papers, No. 174. Paris: OECD.

Henderson, B., and J. Lankoski. 2019. Evaluating the environmental impact of agricultural policies. OECD Food, Agriculture and Fisheries Papers, No. 130. Paris: OECD.

Hendricks, N., and D. Sumner. 2014. The effects of policy expectations on crop supply, with an application to base updating. *American Journal of Agricultural Economics* 96(3): 903–923.

HLG (High Level Group). 2019. Report of the High-Level Group on Sugar. Agriculture and Rural Development, European Commission, Brussels.

Hoda, A. 2017. Public stockholdings issue in the WTO – The way forward for India. ICRIER Policy Series No. 17. Indian Council for Research on International Economic Relations, New Delhi.

Hoda, A., and A. Gulati. 2013. India's agricultural trade policy and sustainable development. Issue Paper No. 49, ICTSD Programme on Agricultural Trade and Sustainable Development. International Centre for Trade and Sustainable Development, Geneva.

Hoekman, B., and R. Howse. 2008. EC – Sugar. *World Trade Review* 7(1): 149–178.

Hoekman, B. M., and M. M. Kostecki. 2009. *The Political Economy of the World Trading System: The WTO and Beyond.* Oxford: Oxford University Press.

Huang, H. 2013. Agricultural domestic support. In *Global Trade, Assistance, and Production: The GTAP 8 Data Base*, ed. B. N. G. Walmsley, A. Aguiar and R. McDougall. West Lafayette, IN: Center for Global Trade Analysis, Purdue University, chapter 10.A:1–3.

Hufbauer, G. C. 2021. Will industrial and agricultural subsidies ever be reformed? Policy Brief 21-5. Peterson Institute for International Economics, Washington, DC.

ICTSD (International Centre for Trade and Sustainable Development). 2016. Public stockholding for food security purposes: Options for a permanent solution. Issue Paper. International Centre for Trade and Sustainable Development, Geneva.

IMF (International Monetary Fund). 2021. Exchange Rates, Domestic Currency per U.S. Dollar, Period Average, Rate. International Financial Statistics.

Irwin, D. 2017. *Clashing over Commerce: A History of U.S. Trade Policy.* Chicago: University of Chicago Press.

Jackson, L. A., F. Maggi, R. Piermartini and S. Rubínová. 2020. The value of the Committee on Agriculture: Mapping Q&As to trade flows. Staff Working Paper ERSD-2020-15. Economic Research and Statistics Division, World Trade Organization, Geneva.

Janow, M. E., and R. W. Staiger. 2004. Canada – Measures Affecting the Importation of Dairy Products and the Exportation of Milk. *World Trade Review* 3(2): 277–315.

Josling, T. 2015. Rethinking the rules for agricultural subsidies. Think Piece. The E15 Initiative: Strengthening the Global Trade and Investment System for Sustainable Development. International Centre for Trade and Sustainable Development and World Economic Forum, Geneva.

Josling, T., and K. Mittenzwei. 2013. Transparency and timeliness: The monitoring of agricultural policies in the WTO using OECD data. *World Trade Review* 12(3): 533–547.

Josling, T., D. Roberts and D. Orden. 2004. *Food Regulation and Trade: Toward a Safe and Open Global System*. Washington, DC: Institute for International Economics.

Josling, T. E., S. Tangermann and T. K. Warley. 1996. *Agriculture in the GATT*. New York: St. Martin's Press.

Karttunen, M. B. 2020. *Transparency in the WTO SPS and TBT Agreements: The Real Jewel in the Crown*. Cambridge: Cambridge University Press.

Knudsen. A.-C. L. 2009. *Farmers on Welfare: The Making of Europe's Common Agricultural Policy*. Ithaca: Cornell University Press.

Konandreas, P. 2020. WTO negotiations on agriculture: An out-of-the boxes approach to reform trade-distorting domestic support. CUTS International, Geneva.

Konandreas, P., and G. Mermigkas. 2014. WTO domestic support disciplines: Options for alleviating constraints to stockholding in developing countries in the follow-up to Bali. FAO Commodity and Trade Policy Research Working Paper No. 45. Food and Agriculture Organization of the United Nations, Rome.

Kwa, A., and P. Lunenborg. 2019. Notification and transparency issues in the WTO and the US November 2018 communication. Research Paper 92. South Centre, Geneva.

Lau, C., S. Schropp and D. A. Sumner. 2015. The 2014 US farm bill and its effects on the world market for cotton. Issue Report No. 58. International Centre for Trade and Sustainable Development, Geneva.

Marrakesh Agreement Establishing the World Trade Organization. 15 April 1994. LT/UR/A/2. https://docs.wto.org.

Martin, W., and A. Mattoo (eds.). 2011. *Unfinished Business? The WTO's Doha Agenda*. Washington, DC: World Bank and Centre for Economic Policy Research.

Martini, R. 2011. Long term trends in agricultural policy impacts. OECD Food, Agriculture and Fisheries Papers No. 45. Paris: OECD.

Matthews, A. 2015. Food security, developing countries and multilateral trade rules. Background Paper for The State of Agricultural Commodity Markets 2015–16. Food and Agriculture Organization of the United Nations, Rome.

2014. Food security and WTO domestic support disciplines post-Bali. Issue Paper 53. ICTSD Programme on Agricultural Trade and Sustainable Development., International Centre for Trade and Sustainable Development, Geneva.

Matthews, A., L. Salvatici and M. Scoppola. 2017. Trade impacts of agricultural support in the EU. Commissioned Paper 19. International Agricultural Trade Research Consortium.

Mazza de Andrade, L., and L. F. Flores Schmidt. 2019. The cotton case: Litigation, retaliation, negotiation. In *The WTO Dispute Settlement Mechanism: A Developing Country Perspective*, ed. A. Amaral Júnior, L. M. Oliveira Sá Pires and C. L. Carneiro. Cham: Springer Nature Switzerland AG, pp. 269–287.

McCarl, B. A., A. W. Thayer and J. P. H. Jones. 2016. The challenge of climate change adaptation for agriculture: An economically oriented review. *Journal of Agricultural and Applied Economics* 48(4): 321–344.

McMahon, J. A. 2006. *The WTO Agreement on Agriculture: A Commentary.* Oxford: Oxford University Press.

Meléndez-Ortiz, R., C. Bellmann and J. Hepburn (eds.). 2009. *Agricultural Subsidies in the WTO Green Box: Ensuring Coherence with Sustainable Development Goals.* Cambridge: Cambridge University Press.

Mercier, S. A., and S. Halbrook. 2020. *Agricultural Policy of the United States: Historic Foundations and 21st Century Issues.* Cham: Palgrave Macmillan.

Montemayor, R. 2014. Public stockholding for food security purposes: Scenarios and options for a permanent solution. Issue Paper No. 51. ICTSD Programme on Agricultural Trade and Sustainable Development. International Centre for Trade and Sustainable Development, Geneva.

Moro, D., and P. Sckokai. 2013. The impact of decoupled payments on farm choices: Conceptual and methodological challenges. *Food Policy* 41: 28–38.

Moyer, H. W., and T. E. Josling. 2002. *Agricultural Policy Reform: Politics and Process in the EU and US in the 1990s.* Aldershot: Ashgate.

Musselli, I. 2016. Farm support and trade rules: Toward a new paradigm under the 2030 Agenda. Policy Issues in International Trade and Commodities Research Study Series No. 74. United Nations Conference on Trade and Development, Geneva.

NDRC (National Development and Reform Commission). 2020. Notice on announcement of 2020 minimum purchase prices for rice. 2 February. (unofficial translation).

2019. Notice on improvement of policies related to minimum price purchases of wheat. 12 October. (unofficial translation).

Nedumpara, J. J., S. Janardhan and A. Bhattacharya. 2022. Agriculture subsidies: Unravelling the linkages between the amber box and the blue box support. *World Trade Review* 21(2): 207–223.

O'Donoghue, E., and J. Whitaker. 2010. Do Direct Payments distort producers' decisions? An examination of the Farm Security and Rural Investment Act of 2002. *Applied Economic Perspectives and Policy* 32(1): 170–193.

OECD (Organization for Economic Cooperation and Development). 2021a. *Agricultural Policy Monitoring and Evaluation 2021: Addressing the Challenges Facing Food Systems*. Paris: OECD.

2021b. Agricultural policy monitoring and evaluation. Country data. www.oecd .org/agriculture/topics/.

2021c. Agriculture Statistics. Reference tables. OECDiLibrary. www.oecd-ilibrary.org.

2018. *The Economic Effects of Public Stockholding Policies for Rice in Asia*. Paris: OECD.

2001. *Market Effects of Crop Support Measures*. Paris: OECD.

1987. *National Policies and Agricultural Trade*. Paris: OECD.

Orden, D. 2021. Multilateral rules for food and agricultural trade. In *Current Issues in Global Agricultural and Trade Policy: Essays in Honour of Timothy E. Josling*, ed. D. Blandford and S. Tangermann. London: World Scientific, pp. 135–158.

Orden, D., D. Blandford and T. Josling (eds.). 2011. *WTO Disciplines on Agricultural Support: Seeking a Fair Basis for Trade*. Cambridge: Cambridge University Press.

Orden, D., R. Paarlberg and T. Roe. 1999. *Policy Reform in American Agriculture: Analysis and Prognosis*. Chicago: University of Chicago Press.

Pannell, D., and R. Claassen. 2020. The roles of adoption and behavior change in agricultural policy. *Applied Economic Perspectives and Policy* 42(1): 31–41.

Permanent Mission of India to the WTO. 2018. India's market price support to sugarcane: Counter notification by Australia. Statement by India in the WTO Committee on Agriculture meeting held on 26–27 November 2018. www.pmindiaun.gov.in/pages/MTU0MA.

Ringler, C., N. Perez and H. Xie. 2021. The role of water in supporting food security: Where we are and where we need to go. In *Agricultural Development: New Perspectives in a Changing World*, ed. K. Otsuka and S. Fan. Washington, DC: International Food Policy Research Institute, pp. 661–680.

Roningen, V., and P. Dixit. 1989. Economic implications of agricultural policy reforms in industrialized market economies. Staff Report No. AGES 89-36. Economic Research Service, US Department of Agriculture.

Rosegrant, M. W. 2019. From scarcity to security: Managing water for a nutritious food future. The Chicago Council on Global Affairs, Chicago.

Rude, J. 2008. Production effects of the European Union's Single Farm Payment. *Canadian Journal of Agricultural Economics* 56(4): 457–471.

2001. Under the green box: WTO and farm subsidies. *Journal of World Trade* 35(5): 1015–1033.

Sapir, A, and J. P. Trachtman. 2008. Subsidization, price suppression, and expertise: Causation and precision in Upland Cotton. *World Trade Review* 7(1): 183–209.

Schnepf, R. 2021. EU agricultural domestic support: Overview and comparison with the United States. CRS Report R46811. Congressional Research Service, Washington, DC.

2020. US farm support: Outlook for compliance with WTO commitments, 2018 to 2020. CRS Report R46577. Congressional Research Service, Washington, DC.

2018. Seed cotton as a farm program crop: In brief. CRS Report R45143. Congressional Research Service, Washington, DC.

Sharma, S. K., A. Das, S. Neogi, T. Lahiri and P. Mathur. 2021. Agricultural domestic support negotiations at the 12th WTO Ministerial conference: Diluting the development agenda. Working Paper CWS/WP/200/65. Centre for WTO Studies, Indian Institute of Foreign Trade, New Delhi.

Staff of IMF, OECD, World Bank and WTO. 2022. Subsidies, trade and international cooperation. International Monetary Fund, Washington, DC.

Steenblik, R., and C. Tsai. 2009. The environmental impact of green box subsidies: Exploring the linkages. In *Agricultural Subsidies in the WTO Green Box – Ensuring Coherence with Sustainable Development Goals*, ed. R. Meléndez-Ortiz, C. Bellmann and J. Hepburn. Cambridge: Cambridge University Press, pp. 427–467.

Steinberg, R. H., and T. E. Josling. 2003. When the peace clause ends: The vulnerability of EC and US agricultural subsidies to WTO legal challenge. *Journal of International Economic Law* 6(2): 396–417.

Sumner, D. A. 2021. A half century of US agricultural policy and trade. In *Current Issues in Global Agricultural and Trade Policy: Essays in Honour of Timothy E. Josling*, ed. D. Blandford and S. Tangermann. London: World Scientific, pp. 87–110.

Sumrada, T., A. Japelj, M. Verbič and E. Erjavec. 2022. Farmers' preferences for result-based schemes for grassland conservation in Slovenia. *Journal for Nature Conservation* 66: 126143.

Swinbank, A. 2021. Europe's Common Agricultural Policy. In *Current Issues in Global Agricultural and Trade Policy: Essays in Honour of Timothy E. Josling*, ed. D. Blandford and S. Tangermann. London: World Scientific, pp. 63–86.

2009. The reform of the EU's Common Agricultural Policy. In *Agricultural Subsidies in the WTO Green Box: Ensuring Coherence with Sustainable Development Goals*, ed. R. Meléndez-Ortiz, C. Bellmann and J. Hepburn. Cambridge: Cambridge University Press, pp. 70–85.

Swinbank, A., and R. Tranter. 2005. Decoupling EU farm support: Does the new Single Payment Scheme fit within the green box? *The Estey Centre Journal of International Law and Trade Policy* 6(1): 47–61.

Thamo, T. and D. J. Pannell. 2016. Challenges in developing effective policy for soil carbon sequestration: Perspectives on additionality, leakage, and permanence. *Climate Policy* 16(8): 973–992.

Tong, L., C. Pham and M. Ulubaşoğlu. 2019. The effects of farm subsidies on farm exports in the United States. *American Journal of Agricultural Economics* 101(4): 1277–1304.

Understanding on Rules and Procedures Governing the Settlement of Disputes. 15 April 1994. LT/UR/A-2/DS/U/1. https://docs.wto.org.

USDA (United States Department of Agriculture). 1987. Government intervention in agriculture: Measurement, evaluation and implications for trade negotiations. Foreign Agricultural Economic Report No. 229. Economic Research Service, US Department of Agriculture.

USTR (United States Trade Representative). 2020. Economic and trade agreement between the government of the United States of America and the government of the People's Republic of China. Washington, DC.

Wagener, A., and J. Zenker. 2021. Decoupled but not neutral: The effects of counter-cyclical cash transfers on investment and incomes in rural Thailand. *American Journal of Agricultural Economics* 103(5): 1637–1660.

Water Global Practice. 2022. Irrigation & Drainage (I&D). Learning Note. The World Bank Group, Washington, DC.

Wuepper, D., and R. Huber. 2022. Comparing effectiveness and return on investment of action- and results-based agri-environmental payments in Switzerland. *American Journal of Agricultural Economics* 104(5): 1585–1604.

WTO (World Trade Organization) documents with a document symbol are available at WTO Documents Online https://docs.wto.org.

2022a. Procedures to enhance transparency and strengthen notification requirements under WTO agreements. Communication from Albania; Argentina; Australia; Brazil; Canada; Chile; Colombia; Costa Rica; the European Union; Iceland; Israel; Japan; Republic of Korea; Liechtenstein; Mexico; Republic of Moldova; Montenegro; New Zealand; North Macedonia; Norway; Paraguay; Peru; the Philippines; Singapore; Switzerland; the Separate Customs Territory of Taiwan, Penghu, Kinmen and Matsu; Thailand; United Kingdom; the United States and Uruguay. General Council, Council for Trade in Goods. JOB/GC/204/Rev.11. 14 July.

2022b. Ministerial decision on World Food Programme food purchases exemption from export prohibitions or restrictions. WT/MIN(22)/29; WT/L/1140. 22 June.

2022c. Ministerial declaration on the emergency response to food insecurity. WT/MIN(22)/28; WT/L/1139. 22 June.

2022d. Sanitary and phytosanitary declaration for the twelfth WTO Ministerial conference: Responding to modern SPS challenges. Ministerial Declaration. WT/MIN(22)/27; WT/L/1138. 22 June.

2022e. Draft Ministerial decision on agriculture. WT/MIN(22)/W/19. 10 June.

2022f. Public stockholding for food security purposes. Proposal by the African Group, the ACP, and G33. JOB/AG/229. 31 May.

2021a. Agriculture Information Management System (Ag-IMS). https://agims.wto.org/.

2021b. India – Measures Concerning Sugar and Sugarcane. Reports of the Panels. WT/DS579R; WT/DS580R; WT/DS581R. 14 December.

2021c. Report by the Chairperson, H.E. Ms Gloria Abraham Peralta, to the Trade Negotiations Committee. Committee on Agriculture in Special Session. TN/AG/50. 23 November.

2021d. Director-general's consultative framework mechanism on cotton. Evolving table – 32nd version. Sub-Committee on Cotton. WT/CFMC/6/Rev.31. 27 October.

2021e. Cotton. Background paper by the Secretariat. Committee on Agriculture, Special Session, Sub-Committee on Cotton. TN/AG/GEN/34/Rev.15; TN/AG/SCC/GEN/13/Rev.15. 22 October.

2021f. Update to Canada's analytical tool on domestic support. Submission by Canada. Committee on Agriculture, Special Session. JOB/AG/219. 23 September.

2021g. Agriculture negotiations at the WTO. Communication by the co-sponsors of the sectoral initiative on cotton. TN/AG/GEN/52; TN/AG/SCC/GEN/23. 8 September.

2021h. Proposal for a Ministerial decision on transparency improvements in agriculture. Communication from Canada, the European Union, Japan and the United States. Committee on Agriculture, Special Session. JOB/AG/213. 26 July.

2021i. Public food stockholding for developing country members. Communication from the African Group. JOB/AG/204. 12 July.

2021j. Compliance with notification obligations. Note by the Secretariat. G/AG/GEN/86/Rev.42. 4 June.

2021k. Transparency issues in domestic support notifications. Submission by Canada. Committee on Agriculture, Special Session. JOB/AG/197. 18 May.

2020. Notification of select domestic support variables in the WTO. Submission by the United States. Committee on Agriculture, Special Session. JOB/AG/181. 19 February.

2019a. Higher and higher – Growth in domestic support entitlements since 2001. Submission from Australia and New Zealand. Committee on Agriculture, Special Session. JOB/AG/171. 22 November.

2019b. China – Tariff Rate Quotas for Certain Agricultural Products. Report of the Panel. WT/DS517/R. 18 April.

2019c. China – Domestic Support for Agricultural Producers. Report of the Panel. WT/DS511/R. 28 February.

2019d. Certain measures of India providing market price support to pulses, including chickpeas, pigeon peas, black matpe, mung beans and lentils. Communication from Australia, Canada and the United States of America Pursuant to Article 18.7 of the Agreement on Agriculture. Committee on Agriculture. G/AG/W/193 (and correction). 12 February (and 5 March 2019).

2018a. Notification. China's notifications of domestic support for 2011 to 2016. Committee on Agriculture. G/AG/N/CHN/42–48 (various dates).

2018b. India's measures to provide market price support for sugarcane. Communication from Australia Pursuant to Article 18.7 of the Agreement on Agriculture. Committee on Agriculture. G/AG/W/189. 16 November.

2018c. Certain measures of India providing market price support to cotton. Communication from the United States of America Pursuant to Article 18.7 of the Agreement on Agriculture. Committee on Agriculture. G/AG/W/188. 9 November.

2018d. Revisiting G/AG/2 – Time for review after twenty-three years. Submission by Norway, Committee on Agriculture. G/AG/W/185. 17 September.

2018e. Certain measures of India providing market price support to rice and wheat. Communication from the United States of America Pursuant to Article 18.7 of the Agreement on Agriculture. Committee on Agriculture. G/AG/W/174. 9 May.

2016a. China – Tariff Rate Quotas for Certain Agricultural Products. Request for Consultations by the United States. WT/DS517/1; G/L/1171. 15 December.

2016b. China – Domestic Support for Agricultural Producers. Request for Consultations by the United States. WT/DS511/1; G/AG/GEN/135; G/L/1150. 20 September.

2015a. Export competition. Ministerial Decision of 19 December 2015. Ministerial Conference: Tenth Session. WT/MIN(15)/45; WT/L/980. 21 December.

2015b. Public stockholding for food security purposes. Ministerial Decision of 19 December 2015. Ministerial Conference: Tenth Session. WT/MIN(15)/46; WT/L/979. 21 December.

2014. United States – Subsidies on Upland Cotton: Notification of a mutually agreed solution. WT/DS267/46. 23 October.

2013a. General services. Ministerial Decision of 7 December 2013. Ministerial Conference: Ninth Session. WT/MIN(13)/37; WT/L/912. 11 December.

2013b. Public stockholding for food security purposes. Ministerial Decision of 7 December 2013. Ministerial Conference: Ninth Session. WT/MIN(13)/38; WT/L/913. 11 December.

2013c. G-33 non paper. Committee on Agriculture, Special Session. JOB/AG/25. 3 October.

2012. United States – Measures Affecting Trade in Large Civil Aircraft (Second Complaint). Report by the Appellate Body. WT/DS353/AB/R. 12 March.

2009. United States – Subsidies on Upland Cotton. Recourse to Arbitration by the United States under Article 22.6 of the DSU and Article 4.11 of the *SCM Agreement*. Decision by the Arbitrator. WT/DS267/ARB/1. 31 August.

2008a. Revised draft modalities for agriculture. Committee on Agriculture, Special Session. TN/AG/W/4/Rev.4. 6 December.

2008b. United States – Subsidies on Upland Cotton. Recourse to Article 21.5 of the DSU by Brazil. Report of the Appellate Body. WT/DS267/AB/RW. 2 June.

2007. United States – Subsidies on Upland Cotton. Recourse to Article 21.5 of the DSU by Brazil. Report of the Panel. WT/DS267/RW. 18 December.

2005a. European Communities – Export Subsidies on Sugar. Award of the Arbitrator. WT/DS265/33; WT/DS266/33; WT/DS283/14. 28 October.

2005b. European Communities – Export Subsidies on Sugar. Report of the Appellate Body. WT/DS265/AB/R; WT/DS266/AB/R; WT/DS283/AB/R. 28 April.

2005c DS267 AB Report. United States – Subsidies on Upland Cotton. Report of the Appellate Body. WT/DS267/AB/R. 3 March.

2004a. European Communities – Export Subsidies on Sugar. Complaint by Australia. Report of the Panel. WT/DS265/R. Identical separate panel reports for DS266 (Brazil) and DS283 (Thailand). 15 October.

2004b. United States – Subsidies on Upland Cotton. Report of the Panel. WT/DS267/R. 8 September.

2003. European Communities – Export Subsidies on Sugar. Request for Consultations by Thailand. WT/DS283/1. 14 March.

2002a. Canada – Measures Affecting the Importation of Milk and the Exportation of Dairy Products (Second Recourse to Article 21.5). Report of the Appellate Body. WT/DS103/AB/RW2; WT/DS113/AB/RW2. 20 December.

2002b. United States – Subsidies on Upland Cotton. Request for Consultations by Brazil. WT/DS267/1. 3 October.

2002c. European Communities – Export Subsidies on Sugar. Request for Consultations by Australia. WT/DS265/1. 27 September.

2002d. European Communities – Export Subsidies on Sugar. Request for Consultations by Brazil. WT/DS266/1. 27 September.

2002e. Canada – Measures Affecting the Importation of Milk and the Exportation of Dairy Products (Second Recourse to Article 21.5). Report of the Panel. WT/DS103/RW2; WT/DS113/RW2. 26 June.

2001a. Canada – Measures Affecting the Importation of Milk and the Exportation of Dairy Products. Recourse to Article 21.5 of the DSU by New Zealand and the United States. Report of the Appellate Body. WT/DS103/AB/RW; WT/DS113/AB/RW. 3 December.

2001b. Ministerial Declaration Adopted on 14 November 2001. Ministerial Conference: Fourth Session. WT/MIN(01)/DEC/1. 20 November.

2001c. Canada – Measures Affecting the Importation of Milk and the Exportation of Dairy Products. Recourse to Article 21.5 of the DSU by New Zealand and the United States. Report of the Panel. WT/DS103/RW; WT/DS113/RW. 11 July.

2000a. Korea – Measures Affecting Imports of Fresh, Chilled and Frozen Beef. Report of the Appellate Body. WT/DS161/AB/R; WT/DS169/AB/R. 11 December.

2000b. Korea – Measures Affecting Imports of Fresh, Chilled and Frozen Beef. Report of the Panel. WT/DS161/R; WT/DS169/R. 31 July.

1999a. Canada – Measures Affecting the Importation of Milk and the Exportation of Dairy Products. Report of the Appellate Body. WT/DS103/AB/R; WT/DS113/AB/R. 13 October.

1999b. Canada – Measures Affecting the Importation of Milk and the Exportation of Dairy Products. Report of the Panel. WT/DS103/R; WT/DS113/R. 17 May.

1999c. Korea – Measures Affecting Imports of Fresh, Chilled and Frozen Beef. Request for Consultations by Australia. WT/DS169/1; G/L/307; G/AG/GEN/37; G/LIC/D/29. 19 April.

1999d. Korea – Measures Affecting Imports of Fresh, Chilled and Frozen Beef. Request for Consultations by the United States. WT/DS161/1; G/L/292; G/AG/GEN/32; G/LIC/D/28. 4 February.

1995a. Notification requirements and formats. Committee on Agriculture. G/AG/2. 30 June.

1995b. Organization of work and working procedures of the Committee on Agriculture adopted by the Committee at its meeting on 28 March 1995. G/AG/1. 30 March.

INDEX